Empowering the Earth

Book

Alex Begg was born in 1968. While studying Politics at Leeds University, he became involved in campaigns for development, corporate responsibility and the environment. Soon after, he founded Cornerstone Housing Co-operative and Cornerstone Resource Centre in Leeds, and through them became involved in Radical Routes, the network of radical co-operatives.

His protest activities led to him forming an Earth First! group in Leeds, and taking part in actions against tropical deforestation, third world debt, opencast mining and nuclear weapons. He has protested against roads from Blackburn to East London by way of Winchester.

At the same time, he became increasingly involved in the Green Party, and in 1994 was elected to the National Executive as the Local Party Support Co-ordinator. In 1997, he was elected to the Executive again, this time as Campaigns Co-ordinator.

He has written articles for magazines including *Resurgence* and *Green Line*, and a series of booklets for the Green Party.

In 1997 he founded a workers' co-operative called UpStart, which provides training and services for the social economy, particularly for enterprises using ecological technology or with political objectives. He has a partner and two children, and lives in Somerset.

Empowering the Earth

Strategies for Social Change

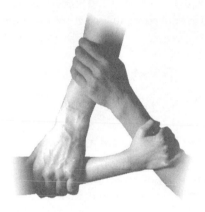

ALEX BEGG

GREEN BOOKS

First published in November 2000
by Green Books Ltd
Foxhole, Dartington
Totnes, Devon TQ9 6EB

For further information, visit the book's website at
www.greenbooks.co.uk/empower

Typeset at Green Books

Design by Rick Lawrence

Printed by Biddles Ltd, Guildford, Surrey

A catalogue record for this book is
available from The British Library

ISBN 1 870098 92 7

Contents

Contents (continued)

Acknowledgements

My thanks to Ian Wingrove, without whom this book would never have been conceived, let alone written.

A note to the reader

Throughout this book, I frequently refer to the 'Green movement'. I am aware that many, if not most, of the people who fit this description do not identify themselves as 'Greens', and that many who do are not in fact particularly interested in empowerment. Although it is a poor shorthand, I have used it firstly because I believe the Green movement has the best chance of any social movement of fulfilling this role, and secondly because of my own personal attachment to the label. I hope this will not unduly interfere with your reading.

Dedicated to my family:
Sarah, Jack, and one more with no name yet.

Introduction

It was in September 1990 in the Civic Centre in Wolverhampton, amidst tears, shouting, pleading and guile, that I realized I wanted to start researching the issue of power. The hall was full, and a febrile, urgent atmosphere gripped everyone present. From the podium on the stage, two session chairs held to the rules of order as dozens of amendments (whittled down from the hundred odd that had been submitted), on the most divisive motion the Green Party had ever discussed in its first 20 years, were debated. Friendships were lost, desperate alliances formed, and tactics of procedure, emotion, reason and money employed in the frantic need to prevail.

To someone outside the organization, this might perhaps be arcane, or academic. I did not have the luxury of objectivity. I was as involved as anyone, standing most of the time, applauding frantically, or gritting my teeth and shaking my head grimly. I spoke on the motion itself, two minutes of rapid, urgent speech with reason, sarcasm, spite and remonstration in equal part. My heart pounded, sweat flowed, my face was pale. Others were no less intense. By the end, delegates wept openly and embraced, or gazed with frank hatred at one another.

The debate was a demonstration of power—counting votes, winning the unconverted, obstructing and counterattacking—but it was also a debate about the nature of power. The motion was known as 'Green 2000' and was a proposal on how the Green Party could and should gain power, in order to implement its policies (which were, in the main, shared by all present). One side—the proposers—believed that power was gained through the conventional tactics of political parties, such as manifestos and public statements, which led to election victories, which led to policies being passed. The others (myself included) saw this as simplistic, and believed that support could be built from the bottom up, campaigning for policies inside and outside institutions, and putting them into practice through direct action.

Beyond this, the debate ran deeper still—about what kind of power, if any, we wanted. Some of us saw power itself as the enemy, and refused all co-operation or support for its use. Others supported some forms of power, or some uses of power, but not others. Others saw power as neutral; simply a way to get things done, regardless of what those things were.

In short, we were an otherwise united movement, with agreement on most of the features of the society that we wanted to establish, but utterly riven on the issue of power. What is more, our division (and confusion) on this issue was paralysing us as an organization, because our beliefs about power led us to certain beliefs on strategy, and those beliefs led us to take one form of action rather than another. The disagreement was simply over what to do next. Having had a certain amount of success in a recent election, expectations were heightened. As we could see our increased membership falling away at dizzying speed, the sense of imminent peril was also intense. These two powerful emotions brought the unresolved issue to the fore.

The issue of power was not explicitly addressed in the motion, yet its manifestations certainly were. Leadership was a word that crystallized the division; participation was set against it as an opposite. Decentralization summed up the countercultural ethos many of us espoused; realism, or professionalism, were totems of the opposite side.

An intelligent and open debate on power was taking place, as a sideline, and here it seemed the differences were less pronounced. There were a lot of distinctive ideas on power, shared on both sides. But the possibility of an agreement was far away.

I knew that the wounds opened here would not be easily healed—in fact, they can be heard recurring in the Green Party today, some nine years later. Today, there is evidence of compromise on both sides, with participation and local autonomy practised at the same time as executive powers and delegated leadership. Perhaps the extremes of both viewpoints have proved wrongheaded. Power is not a legally defined object to be formally taken up and directed at will. Power is a subtle effect of social interconnections that repeats and reinforces its effects as it circulates. The practice of power in modern industrial society is more than just unsuitable for a Green Party. It is the heart of the crisis that the Green Party and other social change organizations were established to challenge.

Power is seen in many different places by different observers, and everyone who says 'Here! I've found it here!' has only part of the story. In order to understand it perfectly we would have to understand ourselves perfectly, and I don't believe that will ever happen. My goal in this book is to illuminate as many of its bases as I can, and more importantly, to show the connections between them and the essentially systemic nature of power.

We do not just happen to see power in one place rather than another, but to some extent we choose to. By exposing ourselves to a wide variety of experiences, rather than remaining within a limited range, we may open our minds further. My opportunities to work in communities and bureaucracies, in direct action protests and in electoral contests, in co-operatives of all shapes and sizes and in legislatures in the UK and US, have all helped greatly.

But no experience will inform us, if our minds are closed to its meaning. Power is more than something we use, or even something that uses us. It makes us, shapes us and defines us; our personalities are the stuff of power. If I raise something as an issue of power which you find it hard to accept as such, then I would ask you to look carefully at the source of your resistance.

Power is frightening, to put it bluntly. If it doesn't scare you, then you probably haven't understood it. It invites denial and inner resistance, and is challenging in the most basic way. We don't want to acknowledge things that chip away at our identity, that take away the freedom or the aspirations we thought were ours. I have had to confront possibilities that I would much rather not allow, and I would ask readers to be ready to slay some demons of their own.

Whether you share my background in the Green movement or not, you will find something in here that you don't just disagree with but actually don't *want* to agree with. When you stumble over that feeling of resistance, or denial, it is rarely wise to pass by. This is where you find a truth about your study, and indeed about yourself.

The study of power should be frightening, and it should break down some of the walls we raise around our egos. But its study does liberate; those walls needed bringing down. Rather than hide behind intellectual defences and justifications, we can open ourselves to a somewhat reduced sense of self—and perhaps a heightened sense of community. It is sometimes said that power is an 'essentially contested concept': I think that is because you cannot speak of it without attacking people where it hurts them most.

Part One

Power

Chapter 1

In the Presence of Power

Definitions of power are famously diverse, and each seems to have a part of the truth. I explain what I am trying to do in this book, and begin by choosing an unusually broad definition. This is to open up our awareness of power so that we can see it even in distant or everyday relationships. It may seem as though this is a pessimistic view, leaving no escape from control, but there is another side to that; we all have access to power and we are all capable of making a difference. Language is a good illustration of the subtleties of power, as we see how the choice of words can determine the outcome or conclusion of a conversation. This difference between different discourses suggests that we become more powerful when we exercise a moral choice in things that are typically taken for granted—although it may not appear to reward our interests. There are discourses that value and protect life more than others—it is our responsibility to choose them rather than discourses of dominance or violence.

What is Power?
- The production of intended effects (Russell)[1]
- A has power over B to the extent that he can get B to do something that B would not otherwise do (Dahl)[2]
- A's ability to do something against B's interests (Lukes)[3]
- Present means to achieve future good (Hobbes)[4]
- A has power over B if B does something because of B's awareness of A's desires, intentions, abilities, etc. (Nagel, later withdrawn)[5]
- A power relation is an actual or potential causal relation between an actor's preferences regarding an outcome, and the outcome itself (Nagel)
- Power is a capacity to overcome part or all of the resistance, to introduce changes in the face of opposition (Etzioni)[6]
- The capacity to carry through one's will in a social relation against resistance, irrespective of the sources of that capacity (Weber)[7]
- G has power over H with respect to the values K if G participates in the making of decisions affecting the K-policies of H (Lasswell and Kaplan)[8]
- A relation creating the possibility of restricting action alternatives of others (Valkenburgh)[9]
- Power is the capacity of actors (persons, groups or institutions) to fix or to

change (completely or partly) a set of action or choice alternatives for other actors. Influence is the capacity of actors to determine partly the actions or choices of other actors within the set of action alternatives available to those actors (Mokken and Stokman)[10]

- The power of A over B is mediated by A's control over the events that interest B; the power of A over B admits of degrees; a positive amount of power of A over B is compatible with a positive amount of power of B over A (Coleman, quoted by Elster)[11]
- Where there's fear, there's power (traditional, quoted by Starhawk)[12]
- Power occurs when A affects B in a way which intrudes on the formative practice of B or contrary to B's autonomous formation of interests (West)[13]
- There is a power relation when an individual or a group of individuals can ensure that another or others do or not do something, want or do not want something, believe or do not believe something, irrespective of the latter's interests (Carter)[14]
- A way in which certain actions may structure the field of other possible actions (Foucault)[15]
- Power is energy over time (any physics textbook)
- Power, the ability to affect change, works from the bottom up more reliably and organically than from the top down. It is not power over, but power with; this is what systems scientists call 'synergy' (Macy)[16]
- Ability to do or act, a faculty or active property, delegated authority (Oxford Pocket Dictionary)

Obviously these people are not all describing the same thing. We use the word 'power' freely as though everyone will know what we mean, and yet when intelligent people attempt to define it they come up with wildly varying results. We are all so deeply immersed in power that it is hard to see the wood for the trees.

But we have to try to understand better. At the start of the 21st century, humanity is facing a time of global crisis. Trends of resource use, pollution, climate change and per capita nutrition all say the same thing: without fundamental change, disaster can only be delayed, and not averted. There is no shortage of information, and even public awareness, about these problems. Those trying to develop solutions are increasingly frustrated when their proposals are received with: "You're probably right, but it just can't be done." We have a problem with power: we can see what needs to happen, but as a society we seem unable to put it into practice. For this reason there is more urgency in studying power than ever before.

In each chapter of this book I will attempt three things. I will try to establish a method for finding meaning in power, I will use this to establish guidelines for social change, and I will illustrate this with reference to the practical examples of social change around us.

In this chapter, I will begin by defining power, or rather explain why I refuse to define power too closely. Then I will try to sift through the different grades of power, from the coarse level of coercion, through the co-operation of exchange to the subtleties of deception—and self-deception. I conclude that if power is everywhere, no one can truly claim to be powerless. The illustrations used throughout this chapter examine language—the medium that our interaction and even our thought must go through.

Problems of Definition

My first question is simply: what is power? Where do we look for it? How do we recognize it? What I have provided above is a far from complete survey of the answers that others have provided to this question, and it rapidly becomes clear that no consensus is emerging. In fact, the divergence goes far beyond normal levels of disagreement—the various writers are pulling powerfully in utterly different directions. For many if not most of them, the issue is not one of how the word may be clarified, but how it can be used. They all have agendas—implicit or explicit, conscious or unconscious—and they use their analytic scalpels to cut out the things that threaten them. Some of the authors above are pluralists, others are élitists; there are communists and anarchists, radicals and conservatives. There are scientists, and there are witches.

The reason for definition is to exclude, and the contest over definition reveals the bias of the writers. One survey of over thirty studies of power in over fifty communities showed that the power structures uncovered corresponded closely to the methods used to identify them. Pluralists found a diversity of power centres; élitists found ascending pyramidal hierarchies, leftists found the rule of the bourgeoisie and conservatives a legitimate order. You find only what you're looking for.

All the different academic definitions are carefully calculated to resolve the debates that have raged over the nature of power. Is it a potential capacity, or does it have to be an actual deployment? Is there a counterfactual (an imaginary outcome had no power been present), or if not, how can power be identified? Is it the same as influence, or different? Does the subject of power have to be aware of it? Does an exercise of power have to realize the intentions of the power holder, or might it be unintentional? Simply because these questions are asked by academics does not make them obscure or irrelevant. Political theory cannot, of itself, change the world. But in a finely balanced situation, it can make the difference. Without it our actions may be futile, even counterproductive. Let's start by asking whether power is the source of our freedoms—or the limit on our freedoms.

Valkenburgh says that power is "a relation creating the possibility of restricting action alternatives of others". For him, any effect that increases action alternatives, or creates them, is not power. I don't go along with this, because my experience of power is of finding a new potentiality that did not exist before—not because someone else had restricted it but because there was some connection, realization or position that I did not have before. It doesn't seem to me that until someone exercises power, we are capable of anything. At a protest against nuclear weapons at Barrow-in-Furness, I saw nonviolent civil disobedience in action, and it inspired me: I became aware of the possibility of personally standing up to the military establishment. Without my being subject to any fewer restraints, I experienced a sense of 'empowerment'.

Hobbes speaks of the 'means to achieve good', and Macy of 'power with'. I feel that both go too far in the other direction, by ignoring that controlling, restricting potential of power. Much of the power that I have been concerned with is to prevent evil rather than to achieve good, whether by taking direct action in roads protests, or by gathering petitions against radioactive waste. It is surely power if I can prevent things from happening, and defend my interests. Maybe Hobbes would think I am being somewhat pedantic; but I believe the point is worth making that power is both positive and negative, both from above and from below.

Secondly, I am not willing to restrict myself to intentional effects. The global crises that the Green movement is trying to tackle have at their root millions of tiny decisions about consumption, all poorly informed and carelessly made. No one intends to destroy the life-support mechanisms of our planet— and yet such a process is taking place. If we cannot identify some power behind the massive endeavour that is the making and the unmaking of our world, then power is a meaningless term. Although power often involves intention, it is equally clear that at other times—perhaps most of the time—it is wholly accidental. It is true that looking at intentions would make it easier to identify holders of power; but that assumes that they will always be honest about their intentions. Furthermore, we have to assume that there is some connection between their having an intention and their having carried it out successfully. As we shall see in the next chapter, someone holding different intentions in the same situation with the same capabilities might have been much less effective. Overall, then, intention is not such a useful guide to power. This eliminates Russell, Lukes, Etzioni, Weber—intention has been a key feature of much recent academic study. This is not to say I take no further interest in any of their ideas, but it does mean I am looking further afield.

The power that I want to speak about may begin in the intentions and visible actions of people, but it goes deeper. It covers the effects resulting— however distantly—from their desires, impulses, beliefs and assumptions as well. It emerges from the history of all previous powers and their consequences. It is a broad scope, but not impossible to work with.

WORDS OF POWER

"The safest way [to avoid rebellions among slaves being transported] is to trade with different nations, on either side of the river, and having some of every sort on board, there will be no more likelihood of their succeeding than of finishing the tower of Babel."—William Smith, 1744[17]

Too often, our language passes us by. Concentrating on what we are trying to communicate, or the goals we are trying to achieve, we forget that we are working through a medium. Our listener will not respond if he or she doesn't use the same language, or if we use the language in the wrong way. Language amounts to a game whose rules we must follow, or face disqualification.

Political theories relating to language fall into three broad categories.[18] If politics is defined as the way people interact with bureaucracy and government, and impose their will through dialogue, we can see how mastery of language could be crucial. In this view, language is a power resource. Two people of equal physical strength, financial resources and social status might succeed to very different degrees in imposing their will if one had an extensive vocabulary, a confident manner, and the ability to construct phrases appropriate to the situation, and the other didn't. Although this might be an unexpected source of power, it is a very conventional type; one person imposes their will on another.

However, there is not just one language, but many; and even when we have a language in common, there are systematic inequalities in our access to the language we need. A second view is that language can be seen as an attribute that differentiates one group from another, and which reflects the power relations between them. At its simplest level, this involves studying the way in which an 'official' or formal language (say, legal English) is based on the language of the dominant group in society, and a regional dialect typical of a disempowered group carries no such formal power. This correlation between powerful people and powerful language is often seen as coincidental, but often the 'official' language is only established as such after a prolonged struggle. Use of a native language has been banned in many countries by invaders trying to subdue the populace. .

But this is surely not just a reflection of conflict, but an actual attempt to weaken resistance. The native language gives identity, community and pride in difference. Maybe even making someone use a different language will co-opt them into the social structures and values of the invader and normalize them. By making the Welsh speak English, they will be more firmly fixed into roles in the English society, they will have to express their aspirations in the terms of the English, and they will receive only the values and priorities that exist in English society.

This is the third view: that when we use a language, we are limited by what it is capable of expressing—the accumulated heritage of power from all the generations who built it up. There are subjects that cannot be talked about, or can only be talked about in certain ways. Sometimes the effect of this is to prevent us saying what we want to say, or limit its effectiveness; more subtly, it can make us feel differently about our experiences and condition our desires. For instance, the English 'policeman' comes from the Latin word 'politia' meaning administration, and carries a resonance of impersonal, legitimate authority. The native Australian language Kalkadoon (now sadly extinct) has the word 'kanimainjit' instead. This comes from the root 'kanimai', meaning to tie up, and carries a very different feeling. Someone discussing policemen in Kalkadoon cannot help conveying this repressive feeling; and if you consider that we think in a language as well as speaking in it, then you realize that 'objective thinking' is impossible. Even our feelings are conditioned—beyond physical pangs like hunger or pain. If we don't have any words for it, did it really happen to us? Even if—without any words to describe it—we are sure that it did, can we meaningfully communicate our experience to anyone else?

It is the case that often where words appear to have power, it is in fact people who have power, and words that reflect it. However, language is not simply a reflector of our society but to some extent a determinant of its direction. Only when we step outside the symbols, rituals and words of our environment, and look for their equivalents in cultures that live in radically different ways to ours, do we get a glimpse behind the façade (see also the discussion of perceiving processes in the next chapter). How much of our life's performance is a kind of karaoke—constructing our performance out of someone else's?

From the Overt to the Concealed

There are many layers, or strata, to power. On the surface, the most obvious and blunt; below it is progressively more subtle, to the point where we are less than clear whether it is power at all. As we peel the layers off, our awareness of power deepens. Who is most powerful? Perhaps it is rarely so clear—power at one level may conceal powerlessness at another.

The most obvious is that of brute force. When someone uses sheer physical force, or the threat of it, to achieve their ends, we have little difficulty in saying that they are using power. In a contest, it is easy to say that one is more or less powerful than another; it may not determine the outcome, but will certainly shift the balance of probability. So the exercise of force is clearly an exercise of power as well, regardless of whether or not it is actual or potential, in accordance with the subject's interests and intentions or not, in accordance with the power holder's interests or not. Where threats and violence are used to achieve ends, the thrill of power and the emptiness of powerlessness will both be experienced.

Beyond this surface layer, the story becomes more complex. Economic power is based on an exchange. At every stage in the process something is given in return—though not necessarily of equal value. There is power in any trade, and in all the other transactions that it may trigger. Economic power becomes increasingly coercive as the imbalance in the relationship becomes more and more pronounced. When your resources are most limited, your negotiating position becomes weaker. In any negotiation, your main protection against losing out is your BATANA (best alternative to a negotiated settlement[19]). If you cannot withhold from negotiations, you may be obliged to settle for a worse deal than would be fair.

Galbraith calls this type of power 'compensatory'[20]; it is the carrot to the stick of force. He argues that whereas threats can only be either empty or destructive, economic power has the potential to be productive. Somewhere along the chain of exchange, someone has to add value; that is how we meet our needs. It should be easy to see why it is more productive than threat-power: forcing someone to do something requires continued sustained efforts, and involves continuously overcoming resistance. An exchange can result in just as many benefits for the dominant side as the use of force. All over the world, there is no shortage of examples of employment that are tantamount to slave labour. In fact, the distinction between threat power and exchange power is not as clear as we might think. After all, exchange is based on property, and property is meaningless without exclusion. Ultimately, this exclusion from other people's property is based on force.

Some 'exchange theorists' have been tempted to regard all power as different kinds of exchange.[21] Power is undoubtedly communicative, and something must be exchanged in any communication.[22] But to assume that power is only about a two-way exchange, we would have to assume that no one ever exercises power over another for some reason connected with a third person. This implies a very simplistic view of society. In fact no exchange can be understood outside its social context. When an exchange of commodities takes place, there is a certain amount of labour value in those goods. However, this does not correspond to the real value of the labour put in, but to the abstract labour value associated with that type of product. Context, or environment, cannot be omitted.

Going deeper still, we find that many of our actions—perhaps even most—are not motivated by threats, nor by compensation, but by belief, obligation, love and all the other signs of our interdependence. Galbraith calls this 'conditioned power', and Boulding (who uses a similar schema) describes it as 'integrative'.[23] It covers the power of authority, leadership, affection, solidarity and respect. It is the engine of human activity, from religion to nationalism.

Is this really power? Certainly, it is important in our understanding of human society. But it could be argued that if there is no force, no exchange, then it is simply an uncontested expression which may be persuasive, but doesn't make anyone do anything. Although these big themes and big ideas might be used to dress up exercises of power, at the heart of the matter is the real negotiation or contest which is independent of the particular slogans or rituals around it.

Stephen Lukes has made a persuasive case that power exists here in his 'three dimensions of power'—another way of breaking down the big idea of power into different levels of operation. His definition above is that power consists of A making B do something against B's own interests. The 'first dimension' is when a conflict takes place, and A overcomes B's resistance. This is the overt display of power in an institutional setting or on a battlefield, where power is unquestionably present. The second dimension is more subtle. Here, the social practices have been rigged by A in such a way that the conflict is side-stepped, or avoided. B is denied even the opportunity to defend his or her interests, and loses by default. Rules, customs or economic relationships have been used in such a way as to deny an open contest. The third dimension goes further: A succeeds in convincing B that B's interests are different to what they really are. A has secured B's co-operation or approval for his or her own exploitation.

It is not hard to prove that this really takes place. The entire modern industry of advertising is founded on it. It could be argued that many soldiers, fighting to preserve a government for patriotic reasons without realizing that it is corrupt and exploitative, are fooled in this way.

Lukes is surely right that the ability to join people together in common enterprise is power. However, I have two problems with his schema. Firstly, I would reiterate that power can be a positive, creative force as well as negative. Those movements that have had the strongest shared culture have proved the hardest to overcome. Those based simply on mercenary interests, deceit or bullying by their leaders, have rapidly fallen apart.

My second objection is that power may in fact run deeper still. At the risk of hijacking Lukes' schema, I would like to suggest the possibility of a fourth dimension of power. As an example, let us consider the success of economic liberalism as a political force. For many years, politics has been characterized by a contest between the left and right. The left try to represent the views of the workers, the right the interests of the employers. However, in 1979 Margaret Thatcher came to power after an election in which she explicitly argued that the right alone had the answer for unemployment, and won over a substantial part of the traditional left vote. In fact, unemployment rose dramatically—a clear-cut example of the third dimension of power at work, perhaps, with people being fooled about their real interests. But the nature of the debate had changed, and was more and more about how the employers had to be rewarded for providing jobs, and workers forced to be more flexible and hence more attractive to overseas investors who would provide jobs. Today, this line of argument is being put forward not only by Conservatives but by Tony Blair's Labour Party, and it is the most popular government in history. It is broadly accepted even among those who are experiencing job insecurity and underfunded public services.

Are these people just being fooled into voting for their own oppression?

THE LIVING WORD

Language is a good example of our day-to-day complicity with power, but it can also be a metaphor for the general behaviour of power. The pattern that under-lies our casual interactions with other people is sometimes called a discourse. When we suggest choosing or modifying language in order to make our power work in a different way, we are in effect trying to change the discourse that we are a part of; we have to go beyond the words to consider all the little, everyday things that make up our culture and our lifestyle.

Some discourses are sustainable. Consciously or unconsciously, they regu-late our relationships with other humans, other species and the non-living envi-ronment. Stepping outside this discourse is difficult, because you risk an inability to communicate with other people, and you have no institutions or structures to support what you want to do. Foucault described his theories about power as fic-tions, not because he thought they bore no relation to reality but because the social forms that would prove his theories did not exist. For that reason you might say that it is in our interests to follow the established discourse.

Though the unspoken rules of our society do limit some actions and enforce others, they may not be totally arbitrary. The Tukano Indians of Columbia have a number of myths about other animals, describing how they have been punished for sins such as gluttony, improvidence and aggressiveness. The terri-ble punishments that are said to have been exacted on them serve as a warning that if humans exceed these boundaries they too will be punished by the gods. This belief may or may not be right or wrong; the point surely is that it has worked, that it has helped to maintain Tukano society as stable and secure.[24]

It is commonplace to speak of 'ancient wisdom', and yet we are only just starting to realize the extent of indigenous peoples' knowledge, and how it has regulated interaction with the land. The discourses of modern, industrial society are similar in the way that they work, but are very different in their effects. There have not been generations of trial and error to establish how technologies can be used sustainably. It is not even a part of our culture to believe that we will suffer if we harm the land. We cannot simply adopt an ancient belief system; it would be at odds with our lifestyle and environment. Instead, we need to adapt or change our existing discourse to guide society along a more viable path.

This sense of a path, or discourse, that leads us along the tightrope of social stability is reflected in a number of languages. The ancient Greeks referred to Themis, meaning laws established not by a legislature but by tradi-tion and experience.[25] The Chinese concept of the Tao (the basis of the Taoist spiritual system) has a similar sense of a timeless rhythm, or current in the uni-verse, which must be sensed and followed. There is no attempt to describe or detail the Tao; Lao Tse says, "The Tao that can be named is not the true Tao."[26]

In Ancient Egypt, Maat referred to the general order of society as established by creation, and in Vedic India R'ta referred to a pattern throughout the natural world that was the basis for moral law. Asha (in Persia) and Dharma (in Buddhist India) served similar functions.[27]

There is no exact equivalent in modern English. What distinguishes these words from law, or rule, is the refusal to define or specify the way—it is rather to be sensed, inferred, or remembered. Equally, decree, law and guide all have an author, whereas these concepts are encoded in the pattern of the universe—even the gods are said to follow the R'ta. The nearest translation is the Way, or Path—but the English language fails us when it tries to describe this kind of sustainable, organic way of life.

Perhaps, but I suspect deeper forces are at work. The fact is that the left, in their efforts to create safer, better paid jobs, have experienced a number of embarrassing failures. The planned economies of the East have failed to provide the riches of the West. The high-spending Labour governments of the 70s were forced into humiliating settlements with international bankers. And the increasingly mobile international capital that was providing employment was now dictating the conditions that it required. What if unemployed people voting for Blair are in fact well aware of what their interests are? What if the employers have succeeded in organizing themselves in such a way as to make it in the interests of the workers to accept—even call for—falling standards of protection? As Foucault suggests, their actions structure the field of other possible actions.

My fourth dimension of power is this: it is where A can actually change B's real, objective interests by changing the social and economic relationships B lives within. It is slow moving, and on a vast scale—we may be altogether unaware it is happening. The turkeys that vote for Christmas are not simply misguided or ill informed, but have realized that the best use of their vote is to support a well organized and internationally competitive Christmas.

Inclusive Boundaries
Words may sometimes fail us, but they remain the best means we have to discuss power. So it is worth going back to definitions, to see what pointers we can pick up from them.

The dictionary definition is also distinct from those preceding it. Free from the concerns of specificity and accuracy, and needing more to be inclusive and wide-ranging, the dictionary covers every usage from 'the power of flight' to 'the power of the President'. The power of the acorn to become an oak is as much included as the power generated by the largest power station.

Understandably, the more academic descriptions are concerned to limit themselves to social power—power in organizations, or between competing forces. However, I believe that for me this would be a dead end. To study only one kind of faculty without reference to any other is only ever going to give an incomplete picture. Would we say of a group of people, that the deaf one was the weakest even if he were also the only one that could see? Institutional power is only one source of power, and the dictionary reminds us that institutional power in one direction might well be offset by different kinds of power in another. This issue of 'different kinds of power' is examined in Chapter 5.

Thirdly, I want to value the role not just of humans, but of other species; even that of seemingly inanimate objects like rivers and mountains. This may seem romantic; after all, other species are unlikely to value me, so my 'all species' ethic is in fact a very human foible. While this is true, reciprocity isn't necessary for ethics; not all humans return the value I place on them, and yet nonetheless I do not consider their lives any less precious. Human society would be diminished if there were no trees; both because we cannot survive in a climate unregulated by trees, and because trees are part of our idea of a beautiful environment. I start from the assumption that no species makes its destiny alone.

This is not just about being able to say (to paraphrase Dahl) 'My cat has power over me to the extent that he can get me to feed him when I otherwise wouldn't'. This may be power, but I'm trying to make a deeper point, that my power to act as I choose is in some way similar to the acorn's power to grow into an oak. The significance of this may become more apparent in Chapter 4 (where I discuss ecological power), and also in Chapter 7 (where I look at 'power-to' in more detail). Essentially, I'm saying that human society is only one of many species on the planet, and the interactions between species are as important, and as much about making things happen, as those within a species.

Another problem I have with many of these definitions is that they deal with a cause and an effect that are too neatly connected. For me, there is no 'smoking gun' clearly linking the power holder to the crime. For example, Nagel's second definition is 'an actual or potential causal relation between an actor's preferences regarding an outcome, and the outcome itself'. In other words, power is what makes the link between will and outcome. The problem is that the relation exists in an environment and a history which loads the dice, so to speak. The actor's power is not the only determinant of the outcome, and even if it were, the actor has had his or her preferences and capacities shaped by past events. What is more, the causal relation is not just with the immediate outcome, but with all the subsequent outcomes which, like a series of falling dominoes, unfold into the future.

If this seems to prevent a clear allocation of responsibility, I can only say that the problem is not one of being unable to show the connection, but of finding too many connections. However far we follow the chains of cause and effect back, there seems to be no end to them. Sooner or later, as we go back through history, everyone is implicated. If there is a conspiracy, we are all part of it. Responsibility is important—but as Ben Elton's *Popcorn* brilliantly illustrated, it cannot be contained or evaded. To act responsibly means more than justifying the immediate or visible effect of your actions, but rather taking account of all their possible repercussions.

Hobbes' definition is still of interest, because it is the only one with any moral content: present means to achieve future *good*. He explicitly describes power as a force we use to achieve what we believe is 'good'. I am not suggesting that only those uses of power that make the world a better place should be covered here, but I am saying that to treat the enquiry as an abstract exercise would be both callous and vapid. The goal of understanding power should be to help us make more effective use of our compassion.

There is much to be gained from many of these definitions, and the ideas behind them will return throughout the book. It is interesting, for example that Mokken and Stokman make a distinction between creating possibilities and choosing between them. Most discussions of institutional power are limited by the rules of the game being played. In fact, those who are really powerful are those who can change the rules and change the game—which often involves stepping outside the institution and deliberately refusing the power that one could have had within it. Consider the way that Gandhi inspired and enabled people in India to refuse co-operation with the British authorities. Undoubtedly, this meant that they suffered and lost access to the many benefits of co-operation. But the effect was to build an alternative leadership for India that ultimately eclipsed that of the British.

To illustrate this point another way, let's look at the list of people that *Time* magazine described as 'the ten most powerful'.[28] They include Bill Clinton, Bill Gates, Rupert Murdoch, Alan Greenspan (Chairman of the US Federal Reserve), Michael Eisner (CEO of Disney), Jack Smith (CEO of General Motors). You have heard of all these people—or, if you haven't heard of them by name, you've heard of their organization and you knew that someone was at the top of it. But are they really all that powerful? Bill Clinton ditched bales of policy in order to get the support of Congress. Greenspan's decisions were within a very limited range of options—a percentage point here or there on interest rates. Certainly, the impact of their actions were immense, but if Bill Gates resigned from Microsoft (and in fact he has recently handed over the day-to-day running of the company) business would continue pretty much as usual. They hold power, but that doesn't really mean that they have achieved anything—for themselves or anyone else.

Time goes on to give much more space to a list of the most influential people, ones who have really made a difference. They are people like Jim Clark, Sandra Day O'Connor, Carol Gilligan, Edward Witten. You've never heard of any of them? Well, Jim Clark made the World Wide Web into a widely used

DISCOURSE AND ACTION

"The thing is, in this kind of discussion group, well, you know, you can't think of anything to put, you can't think of how you really feel, but you say something anyway, you know what to put."[29]

Ever known this feeling? You know what words are expected of you, and are appropriate in a context. You may be sincere enough when you say them—not lying, or pretending—but nonetheless be fitting into an established role. In other words you fit yourself into a social 'script', feeling that you are saying the right thing even though you can't be certain that it is the real you. Of course, through reflection, self-criticism and experimentation, it is possible to find a more authentic, more certain opinion; and perhaps when what you are expected to say contradicts this, you won't go along with it—you will part company with the script. But more often than not, unless you feel you have a position of some authority in that setting, what will actually happen is you will be silenced. You will feel unable to speak out, because there is no place for your feelings in that context.

Consider these two statements:

"Donna, Donna round the flats, she's a real slag."
"I hate it when boys call us slags, when they're sleeping around more, it's all right for them."

You would expect that if the second speaker were to hear what the first speaker had said, she would immediately contradict her, and challenge her use of the word 'slag'. However, the two statements were in fact made by the same girl. The change that had taken place was not a radical change of opinion or personality (the second statement was made ten days before the first) but simply of context. They are taken from conversation at a youth group in an inner city area. The first statement was made when the mode of discussion was one of 'gossip' or 'slagging off'; on the second occasion, it was the same group, but in a discussion on a feminist agenda—a type of discourse which the girls were equally familiar with, but whose values were radically different. [30]

These different discourses have implications beyond the words that we use. There are opinions, values, moral statements, and normative ideas about what should be. No matter whether the person is capable of using completely contradictory language in a different context, it is still the case that they might have very passionate feelings, and arouse their own feelings of justified outrage, when they speak. It doesn't have to be a large group for this effect to be evident—this is not the same as 'mob rule'. If a certain way of talking is the only one which they have access to, or experience of, then it will be the one in which their individual thought and reflection takes place. A certain discourse, or way of speaking, can create the expectation of action. The words have access to have power over our actions.

The same researchers also worked with a group of upper-class public school girls, and found a very different set of discourses in operation. They had the traditional/formal dialogue, and yet were equally capable of switching into a liberal feminist discourse. However, they had no experience of discussion groups, where co-operation, self-disclosure and honesty were expected. Initially, the girls were silenced by not knowing the 'script'—they had difficulty coping. But this was temporary; the group leader was able to 'teach' them a new way of speaking, and hence of relating to one another. Learning a new discourse can enable us to organize in different ways, to set and achieve new goals, and to establish new forms of knowledge.

It would be easy to say that one way of speaking—the formal/bureaucratic style—is a more powerful language because it is the language of money, or politics. However, in the communities these girls come from, their goals are in fact more achievable through the informal discourses they use. It is access to a range of discourses that widens their potential for effectiveness; and it is access to a discourse that puts them in touch with more authentic feelings (sometimes described as a 'language of liberation') that might help them achieve more fulfilment.

Perhaps the real issue is the power to establish a discourse—the power of the group leader in the discussion group. This might be associated with more traditional sources of power—the judge in a court, the senior of two executives, the teacher in a class. But their power is to establish one of a limited range of discourses—their choice limited by their setting, a setting they had to conform with in order to reach that position. If we do succeed in establishing the discourse we want, do we really know what discourse led us to want to establish it? Is power a faculty we command, or is it the maze we find ourselves in?

medium of communication; O'Connor's rulings on the Supreme Court interpreted the law in radical and creative ways; Gilligan's books on psychology forced women's experiences on to the agenda, and Witten may just prove to have made the key scientific discoveries that will lead to a theory of, well, everything. I will use the word 'power' in this book to cover their achievements just as much as those of the Presidents of the USA.

What *Time* magazine does not cover is influence at a deeper level still. Jim Clark's company launched the internet; it required widespread computer technology as a launchpad. Witten made scientific discoveries, but only because of the particular direction and preferences of the research funding programme. These people have set agendas and given us new things to desire; but other people, even less well known, each adding a tiny piece to the structure, are even now building a platform from which the movers and shakers of the next century will hold forth.

Is There any Way Out?

By suggesting that power, the motive force behind events, is encoded so deeply in us, I imply that it is inescapable. We are creatures of power; the whole world is a product of these flows of energy. This offends against a popular under-standing of power as a dangerous, corrupting force, which is to be combated and contained. Should we give up resisting power? I am not a fatalist, arguing that we should embrace a necessary evil. Rather, I am suggesting that good and bad alike need power to exist—that it is at least as constructive and cre-ative as it is destructive and repressive. The nature of principled political action is rather choosing between different power options.

But what options are there? If we cannot talk without exercising power, if our thoughts are conditioned and guided by power, if our desires and our understanding of our experiences can all be influenced, if even our perception of the world comes through a filter of power, do we have any room left for inde-pendent action? Where is the firm ground from which we can see clearly? The certainty of religion and tradition have been steadily undermined by the aware-ness that other cultures have as good a grasp on reality as we have, as well as by a global culture of superficiality and materialism—a lowest common denominator. Science is an alternative source of truth, but is at pains to stress that its findings are only provisional. Technology has produced a series of mixed blessings—concern about war, environmental damage and a sense of helplessness before technology, offset the material gains. Attempts to develop a political view based on objective science have in fact produced dozens of competing sects, and some ill-fated experiments. Finally, 'new science' has abandoned any claim to certainty; it describes a world of flux and probability (see Chapter 8).

Some have suggested that this 'postmodern condition' leaves us in a moral vacuum. If all values are relative, and there is no certainty, we seem to have no basis on which to argue for one course of action over another—other than the individual's gut desires. Do right and wrong mean anything any more? Is any-thing really real?

Although I am postmodern in the sense that I do not believe that we can see the world objectively, I remain committed to making moral choices— about power as much as anything else. Just because we experience the world subjectively (that is, from a very personal point of view) and understand it imperfectly, does not mean that there is no reality out there. When we deal with other people, we try to work out their intentions and beliefs, in order to respond appropriately, even though we cannot know them perfectly. We have to learn a new way of dealing with the world. Instead of just trying to establish some exact, true measurement of reality, we must also learn to sense, or read its signs more intuitively.

There are two reasons for trying to do this. The first is to respond to the intuitive moral sense that (postmodern condition or no postmodern condition) continues to drive us. A philosophy lecturer may leave a class that has just agreed that no absolute truth can be established, see someone about to be run over by a truck and try to save them.

The second reason is a wider one. If we believed that there was no external reality, we might be tempted to act without regard for anyone but ourselves. As the old pagan saying has it, 'the evil that you send out returns threefold'. We can pretend that our individual desires are all that matter, but the social consequences of such a belief will endlessly frustrate our efforts to fulfil those desires.

Power's Hall of Mirrors

In finding the definition of power that I want, West, Foucault, Nagel, Mokken and Stokman and Macy have much to offer. I'm also interested in the similarities between the scientific definition of power, 'Power is energy over time', and Foucault's 'A way in which certain actions may structure the field of other possible actions'. After all, 'energy' is another way of saying 'possible action'. 'Energy over time' can mean a flow of current, an acceleration, or any other description of the rate at which energy is delivered—in other words, the structure of possible actions. The laws of thermodynamics state that energy can neither be created nor destroyed, only transformed—so any flow of energy will create the possibility of another flow of energy, until it has been perfectly dispersed through the universe. I don't think that Foucault was intentionally drawing on the laws of thermodynamics, and yet his concern to broaden the scope of the academic study of social power has led to a definition covering the same ground as that of science. Behind the different discourses, they are groping for the same truth.

However, at this stage the only definition that really covers what I want to talk about is the dictionary one: a faculty or active property—that which makes things as they are. I consider power to be the property that guides change, or that maintains, reproduces or changes the status quo.

There is a problem with analysing this sort of power. Before, we could measure the presence or absence of power by asking, "What would have happened otherwise?" We can construct a hypothetical scenario free from power, in which life carried on as usual (what the academics call a counterfactual). We can hold people accountable by asking if their use of power made the world a better place. If we say that all ties that make us social beings (indeed, that make us human) are sources of power, then there is no counterfactual, and we cannot see the moral wood for the power-relation trees.

Different theorists have ventured into this area in different ways. Steven Lukes' definition of power is 'A's ability to do something against B's interests'. For him, the counterfactual is that B's interests are unaffected. In his 'third dimension' of power, the advertising industry, clever demagogues or corrupt religious leaders are persuading B that his or her interests are different to what they really are. Even B doesn't really know what those interests are—but Lukes argues that we can objectively determine what they are, and whether they have been compromised by power.[31]

But in practice this assessment has proved hard to make, and defending those interests harder still. If it is clear enough that some of the people are being fooled some of the time, it is equally clear that no one can agree on who they are. 'Real interests' has been the justification for paternalist authority since the state first sought legitimacy. Misfits and dissenters have been incarcerated in mental institutions, 're-education camps', prisons and job training schemes 'for their own interests' all over the world. Is there anyone who does not have a vested interest in the definition of our real interest?

Alan Carter's answer to this is to return to a more straightforward definition of power as making someone 'do or not do something, want or not want something, irrespective of their 'real interests' (see above).[32] He has restored the counterfactual by insisting on the intention to control as a defining feature of power. Again, I believe that the 'tyranny of small decisions' shows that the sense of powerlessness and helplessness that many of us feel is precisely because of the unaccountable and unintentional face of social power. He relies too heavily on the free will of the individual unaffected by power. In reality, we have all been through a lifetime of interaction with family, friends, colleagues, functionaries, officials, long-dead authors, animals, our biological environment and our built environment, all of which have made us the people we are. If we had not had this background, surely we would be very different people today—doing different things, wanting different things.

David West has another approach, which is more helpful. He sees a human life in a similar way, as being a process of formation of personality, interests, and identity. We go through life trying to achieve a greater correspondence between our lived experience and what we might call our 'inner nature'. West calls this authenticity, and takes as the ideal example the experiences of gay men 'coming out' and recognizing their sexuality. In many cases this involves a great deal of hardship and suffering—seemingly against their real interests—but it allows them to feel more fulfilled and more true to themselves. West sees power as anything that interferes with this 'free formation'. This could be any phenomena from peer pressure and social expectations to guilt and shame.

As Carter points out, although real interests are not referred to, establishing the counterfactual means describing the authentic formation of someone's

THE DISCOURSE OF AFFINITY

On a cold, windy December night in a field near Frome, Somerset, I was sitting in a tarpaulin-covered dome with a dozen or so others. We were planning to stage a direct action at Whatley Quarry, a gigantic gravel pit supplying road builders and construction companies all over England. They planned a massive expansion which we believed would irreparably damage the local environment and the water table.

Throughout our discussion, I was shifting through a range of discourses. Part of our work was consciousness-raising—by discussing an effective, physical protest, we were discovering our power to influence events. The language of ecology—both in a scientific and an emotional sense—was an important part of this, fuelling and stabilizing our intentions. There was also a discourse of conflict resolution: we expected to encounter many people (policemen, truck drivers, quarry workers, security men) who would be opposed to our action, and we were rehearsing a discourse that would reduce tension and minimize the risk of violence. We also adopted techniques more often found in self-help groups, as we opened up and admitted our fears and our concerns. Arrest, criminal charges and violence were the main concerns, as well as ineffectualness, local hostility or contempt. Supporting each other, establishing the boundaries of what we were happy doing, and building courage required a sensitive and honest language.

At regular intervals, a pseudo-military discourse would develop as we arranged meeting points, timings, transport to the site and strategies and contingency plans. This was precise, dispassionate and focused, and helped us to prepare for decisive and co-ordinated action. The whole discussion was punctuated by irreverent, surrealistic bursts of humour which brought us closer and defused much of our tension and fear. Elsewhere around the campsites, a dozen or so other groups were engaged in similar discussion and choosing their particular goals. Each adopted its own name: some literal, some humorous.

The 'affinity' group takes its name from the units developed in the Spanish Civil War. An anarchistic impulse denied the more conventional military structure, leading to the development of small, autonomous groups that co-operated to achieve shared goals. The discipline of an army not being present, it was a different glue that held them together—'affinity'. Rather than a nation or a leader 'out there' for the army to follow, there was instead a sharing of visions and beliefs and a bond of trust that could only develop in a smaller, more personal team.

The next large-scale application of the affinity group model was at the Clamshell protests against nuclear power in the United States; but the idea of consciousness-raising and group bonding was being applied as a form of political organization in the women's movement, in 'black pride' and gay liberation. Its values can even be seen in therapy, educational, self-help and co-counselling groups.[33] All these different groups were finding that effective organization was not enough. The language and discourse of organization—the party, the institution, the army—were all loaded against them. It was not possible to be what they needed to be, to say what they needed to say, or to do what they needed to do, in these conventional contexts. New discussion formats like brainstorming, go-rounds and buzz groups, coupled with inclusive, sensitive, assertive language, created a setting in which new ideas could be expressed and old desires could find a voice.

My first experience of the affinity group was through direct actions like that at Whatley Quarry. We could meet the police and security not as an undifferentiated mob, fractious, jumpy, and slow to react, but as a diverse, intelligent and sensitive body, able to respond rapidly to local conditions. We could approach a site from many different directions, simultaneously arriving at several sensitive points, and taking swift, pre-planned and effective action. We could easily outflank the hierarchical organizations that confronted us, who looked in vain for a 'head' or 'centre' which could be neutralized. We could (within common ground rules, such as non-violence) take on different levels of confrontation. Some would remain within the law, demonstrating outside the main gates. Some would commit acts of trespass, risking injury by obstructing work inside the site. Others would carry out acts of sabotage ('monkey wrenching') in very small, covert groups. At the end of the Whatley action, most people who did not want to be arrested had avoided being arrested—and so much damage had been done to the plant that its operators ARC admitted that it would be a week before it worked again.

However, affinity groups are also the building blocks of workers' co-operatives, communes and local voluntary organizations—it is a way of working that has applications far beyond the context of protest. In Green Parties and in radical networks, the affinity group is the essential unit, and they function well or not so well in so far as they have access to the range of discourses they need to operate.

preferences—just as speculative as establishing their interests. Even if, as humans and as individuals, we do have an inner nature to realize, who can say what this is? I may feel that the present way of life of much of humanity is unnatural and alien, and that a life closer to nature would be more authentic. But there are many lifestyles lived by indigenous cultures that are close to nature—and they are very different. What is more, few of us would feel particularly fulfilled and 'at home' if we attempted to live them.

Although West has clearly said something important about the formation of identity, I am convinced that all these efforts to establish a counterfactual end in contentious judgement and selective blindness. We must accept that power is inherent in all human relations, to a greater or lesser extent, and that there is no possibility of a world 'free from power'. This means that we cannot simply regard power as a bad thing; it is what makes our lives possible.

Power is the tool with which we shape our lives. Maybe you think it only exists in government, boardrooms and battlefields. In fact, you use power in your dealings with others in hundreds of tiny ways every day. When we feel threatened or insecure, at any level from the individual or community to the planet, it is power we appeal to, use, or blame. Yet no matter how much power we gain, we always seem to be struggling, never really achieving the freedom and ease that we sought. It is as though the power that we invoke to aid us ends up turning on us; and we have no solution except to find another, greater power to rival it. The more we seek to control, the more out of control the situation becomes.

This might leave us in a vague and insubstantial world, where moral judgements on power are hard to make. However, I do think that although power is ever present, it takes distinctively different forms—an idea I shall explore more in Chapter 5. These forms are all 'real' power, but they are different in mechanism and appearance. Between like forms of power there is compatibility and resonance; between unlike, incompatibility and dissonance. Even if we can't take moral decisions over whether or not to use power, we can choose which form of power to use to meet our needs.

So power is everywhere; in this sense, the personal is most certainly political. Power relations exist between children and parents, between author and reader, between preacher and congregation, as well as between master and slave, soldier and civilian, and employer and employee. We cannot escape from it.

However, it is equally true that none of us is truly powerless. All of us have some capacity, some capability, to make our mark on the world. However diluted it may be in the sea of other people's actions, it is real, and no one's responsibility but our own. However shaped we are by our social context, we are also part of someone else's context, and capable of shaping them.

The greatest source of power is this diffuse network of power between people. No military force can long maintain an assault against the families and communities that nurtured its members. No wealthy tycoon can prevail if no one will accept his money. The taproot of power lies below the surface. It is obedience, co-operation, collusion: the social glue that ensures that each day proceeds much like the last. Every single one of us has the power to give or withhold our willing participation, to 'reproduce' or reshape society.

Alone, we may suffer for any break with the mainstream. But by reconnecting on new terms with those around us, our choice can itself be powerful. At one protest that I attended in 1996, a banner could be seen hanging from a building reading "We are more possible than you can powerfully imagine".

Chapter 2

In this chapter, we move from the 'what' of power to the 'how'. Since power relates to all our social interactions, this becomes a question of what the essential components of human society are. The two dominant theories of social organization are the individualist and the collectivist—one seeing society as the sum of its members, the other as being composed of unified blocks.

Greens have found both approaches wanting. Instead, they concentrate on the relationships and processes that connect individuals—an 'interrelationist' view. Strategies based on charismatic individuals or mass forces are inappropriate; it is networking that has brought results.

If power is a process, then the idea of the 'powerholder' is called into question. Technology, especially the nuclear industry, illustrates this well. Technology is not a neutral tool at the disposal of any group or individual that controls it. It has its own agenda and direction—it emerges from a process, and limits our actions to those consistent with that process.

If that is the case, then the old argument of means and ends is transcended; the means become the ends, whether we like it or not. The Green strategy cannot work by seizing the levers of power, but rather by rebuilding the whole machinery of power. Alternative technology is more than a good metaphor for this process; it is providing energy for a radically different lifestyle.

> The lines wait
> The trains wait
> The drivers are waiting
> Waiting for Power
> —W. H. Auden, *The Way to the Sea*

Power and the Individual

Individuals can exercise power in the most subtle ways, and even be unaware of it themselves. The last chapter shows us as capable of the most devious and deceptive forms of influence and control. And yet we seem, for the most part, unable to realize such intricate ploys in our everyday life. While working as a researcher in Westminster and in Washington, I tried to influence debates, to set agendas and to exercise power over events. I had resources available—informational, and the authority and legitimacy of the representatives that I was working for (often sympathetic to my case)—and yet it was not even possible to get heard. The agenda I had was irrelevant to discussions going on around me, to the extent that I might as well have been speaking in a foreign language. Of course, this was in part a matter of inexperience—but similar impressions have been reported by politicians reaching cabinet status. Faced with civil servants, opposed interest groups, budgets overstretched and over-committed, the weight of convention and of public opinion, their supposed power evaporates. The MP I was working for used all his experience to advance his particular cause (that of World Federalism) without ever being taken seriously. Their sense of being unable to pull these levers of power does not fit with the idea of a simple division of society into the powerful and the powerless.

In 1919, faced by the triple alliance of militant labour unions, Lloyd George met with some of their leaders. He said, "I feel bound to tell you that in our opinion we are at your mercy. The army is disaffected and cannot be relied upon. . . . if you carry out your threat and strike, then you will defeat us. But if you do, have you weighed the consequences? The strike will be in defiance of the Government of the country and by its very success will precipitate a constitutional crisis of the first importance. For if a force arises in the state that is stronger than the state itself, then it must be ready to take on the functions of the state, or withdraw and accept the authority of the state. Gentlemen—have you considered, and if you have, are you ready?" "From that moment on," recollected Robert Smillie, "we were beaten and we knew we were."[1] The apparent power of the unions failed to give the actual ability to influence events that they sought—or, to put it another way, they could only influence events within certain boundaries.

The story of multi-dimensional power outlined in the previous chapter has one overriding theme—that of the two enigmatic characters A and B. One the controller, one the controlled, they seem to operate in a vacuum. You might imagine the two of them seated in some anonymous office, one seated behind the desk, the other standing in front of it. This may be an accurate description of how most of us actually experiences power—but the office was put there by an organization, B is one of thousands of B's in the same position, and A is just one in a chain of command. . . .

Seeing power in a wide range of interactions between individuals expands our awareness of it, but within a very limited frame. This view treats individual human beings as the building blocks of society, and the actors in the power play. This seems intuitive—when we feel powerful, we may well associate this with a sense of feeling apart from or above those around us. Clearly, we are individuals, and even though we may share certain experiences or feelings we don't have a group mind or shared consciousness.

But the methodological individualist has a more extreme, atomized view of the world. Just as the early physicist might see only atoms colliding—fundamental particles giving rise to the complexity of the world we experience, the individualist today will seek to explain the acts of countries, societies, governments and economies as the effect of the individual decisions of those who comprise them. Individuals are seen as being free moral agents until power enslaves them.

Individualism needn't be a simple view: most individualist thinkers will acknowledge that some groups may be systematically allocated more or less resources, favouring or disadvantaging the individuals in them. However, they must still argue that those individuals are separate at the point of decision. For this to be meaningful, individualism also requires that individuals are autonomous, self-directed; they can rise above their circumstances to independently perceive reality.

The Theory of Collectivism

The individualist viewpoint immediately suggests problems. Such self-centredness would not normally be seen as a virtue; and when we think about what we want from life, other people feature prominently in it—we can't imagine being happy alone. Surely society is not just a casual association of individuals, but clearly has a pattern and form—its building blocks are groups united by some shared interest.

These feelings find their representation in political theory as collectivism—the belief that collectives are the active force in politics, being more than the sum of their parts. Individuals are shaped by the collective, picking up their values and behaviour from the needs of the collective. Although the collectivist may accept the way individuals can shape collectives, he or she would always insist that this rarely if ever involves a break with collective interests.

The implications of this would be that we simply do not have power as individuals. What influence we can exercise is a result of the functional role we occupy within the collective. It suggests that individual power is positional, associated with a location in the social hierarchy. Whether due to your political dominance, your economic role, or culturally determined legitimacy and authority, power is in the social mechanism, not the individual talent.

This is not so much a question of the forms that power takes, but rather a question of who is morally responsible for power—who could be said to be accountable. On the collectivist view, it is no longer A (the person behind the desk, in my previous example) who bears the responsibility for B's plight; if it had not been A, it would have been someone else. A's dominance and B's subjection are the consequence of the society that they live in; their roles in the collective.

Hannah Arendt argues, "Power corresponds to the human ability not just to act but to act in concert. Power is never the property of an individual; it belongs to a group and remains in existence only so long as the group keeps together. When we say of somebody that he is 'in power' we actually refer to his being empowered by a certain number of people to act in their name. The moment the group, from which the power originated to begin with, disappears, 'his power' also vanishes." Arendt's collective is the power behind the throne; the legions of police, the army or even the individual members of society who create the sovereign's power by allowing business as usual. The power holder may have some wish or intention, but can only implement it with the consent of the mass.

Some go further: Maurice Mandelbaum says, "By holding that there is a necessary direction of change in a society as a whole, and by holding that form of global law which states that the whole is so related to its parts that the parts are determined by the whole, a law of change concerning a specific institution follows."[2] In other words, he advises predicting changes in a part of society by observing the direction of society as a whole. According to this view, society has 'a life of its own'—so much so that it becomes hard to see any autonomous life in the individuals that make it up. Are collective groups more 'real' than the people who make them up? "Scientific method conceptualizes the perceptual data and treats them as if they were real and exact entities. This methodological process is essentially fictional. Its justification is to be found in the results to which it leads."[3]

The collectivist view sits uneasily with aspirations of freedom and liberty. Alan Carter has an idea of what the results of collectivist morality might be: "If the Party claims to be privileged in having the scientific theory which enables it to identify the real interests of the proletariat . . . it is but a short step to argue that the proletariat ought to obey the Party."[4]

The debate between individualist and collectivist has polarized the social sciences, as Michel Foucault describes: "People of my generation were brought up on these two forms of analysis—one in terms of the constituent subject, the other in terms of the economic, in the last instance, ideology and the play of superstructures and infrastructures."[5] The extreme positions of both have proved untenable, leading the exponents of both sides to assert their willingness to take on some aspects of the other. Alan Carter reports wearily that "the discussion has now become so voluminous that it is difficult to ascertain clearly what the respective positions in the debate actually are."[6]

It is an academic debate, but it is far from lacking in consequence. If we are concerned about the problems of society, and believe that these problems have resulted from a use of power, then we have to hold someone accountable—or believe that we could do better in their place. Otherwise, our efforts will be misdirected, and crises will seem like acts of God, coming out of thin air.

ATOM POWER

"Every night while you're asleep a miraculous power is at work in the land. . . . It cannot easily be explained. It cannot be seen or heard. It cannot be touched and yet it can harness nature. A most efficient and versatile power we can command as our servant. It is electricity. Energy for life."—'Genesis', CEGB Corporate Advertising Campaign (1986)

"1018 Rail tank wagons of 'low-level' nuclear waste are dumped every year in the USA, mostly in the North Atlantic (Statistical Record of the Environment). Semi trailer trucks nose-to-tail loaded with a years uranium fuel for the US's 113 operative reactors would stretch 86 miles (Uranium producers of America). The same trucks loaded with a year's Canadian production of radioactive uranium mine tailings would stretch 4,304 miles (Atomic Energy Control Board of Canada)."—Rowland Morgan, Planet Gauge

The origins of civil nuclear power are bound up with the push to develop nuclear weapons in the 1940s. In 1942, with a growing fear that German scientists would be first, all atomic research was placed under the control of a Military Policy Committee. With the end of the second world war, America was much more inclined to keep its knowledge to itself; the 1946 Atomic Energy Act (also known as the McMahon Act) surrounded nuclear power with a close shroud of secrecy. In the period 1945-60, US military research accounted for two-thirds of expenditure on nuclear energy. The need to construct reactors was driven by the perceived shortage of uranium suitable for bomb-making, and also to provide submarines with a power source that did not need refuelling. At first sight, only collectivism can explain such a massive diversion of resources. No individual could have guided this process, nor caused it to spread around the world. The collective power of the military and corporations was at work.

However, the role of the military alone is not sufficient to explain the growth of nuclear power as an energy source. The decision to develop civil nuclear power called for funding over and above that which was deemed necessary for military purposes, and countries which were constitutionally banned from the military applications, such as Germany, still pursued civil nuclear programmes. Nor was money-making the drive: even then, before the full scale of decommissioning costs was appreciated, nuclear power was not seen as a lucrative investment. The small military reactors gave little or no clue as to the viability of a commercial reactor. So what was the impetus behind civil nuclear power?

One explanation ascribes it to the 'military industrial complex', an amorphous network involving many agencies: "The principal actors in this coalition were the armed services, private industry and finance, the legislative and executive organs of government, intelligence organizations, and to a lesser extent the emerging atomic bureaucracy, sections of the scientific and technological community and even elements of the trade union movement".[7] Certainly some scientists, awed by the matter to energy conversion they had engineered, promised an electrical utopia; and politicians too became caught up in the excitement. The McMahon Bill in the US promised "wealth and leisure and spiritual satisfaction in such abundance as to eliminate forever any reason for one nation to covet the wealth of another." But despite all the inducements that government could offer, economists remained dubious: "In the short run at least, all available evidence supports the belief that atomic power will cost more—and perhaps considerably more—than will power from existent sources." Although many industrialists were involved, and many firms made profits from the immense state funding, nuclear power was not simply the result of a capitalist economy.

Britain's adoption of nuclear power is explained as being prompted by its excessive dependence on coal; Germany's the result of a lack of coal. Clearly both countries, like all industrial nations, were hungry for energy sources—but were they so desperate that they would ignore cheaper alternatives? In 1955 the British Government published a white paper, 'A Programme of Nuclear Power'. It said, "Our civilization is based on power . . . nuclear energy is the energy of the future."[8] In fact, future technologies result from present choices: we can choose to research nuclear power (in 1950, the US President asked Congress to raise the Atomic Energy Commission's annual budget to $3 billion[9]) or to research solar power (between 1980 and 1988, US budgets for developing renewable energy were cut by 80%[10]). One development implies another; constructing motorways will bring us to out-of-town-retail centres; building cycle lanes makes forms of local distribution possible. The path of technology is both a choice we can make, and a process with its own relative autonomy. There is a possibility of individual control, but only within a pre-existing framework and where the resources are available.

Easy answers that place power in one location, whether an individual or a group, are clearly inadequate. A process was underway that cut across institutional boundaries—a network of interconnected interests.

An Interrelationist Alternative

If individualism and collectivism run counter to reason, intuition and experience, then what is the alternative? Carter suggests that by rejecting the most extreme forms of both, a more tenable position incorporating aspects of both is revealed. "The methodological individualist is in error when he or she omits relevant relational features. We might call this 'the individualist fallacy'. At the other extreme, the illegitimate attempt to explain certain facts about social individuals in terms of their relations to the totality of which they are a part, we might call 'the collectivist fallacy'. As we have seen, such illegitimate attempts clearly arise when the totality is thought to affect causally or deter-

mine its parts. . . ." He proposes 'methodological interrelationism' as a perspective which focuses on the relations between individuals. He believes that
it is the way that individuals in a group relate to each other that determines
both the nature of the group and the common characteristics of the individuals in it. The table below shows how his methodology compares with individualist and collectivist approaches.[11]

Individualism	Collectivism	Interrelationism
The individual possesses supreme and intrinsic value or dignity.	The collective possesses supreme and intrinsic value or dignity.	Individuals possess value or dignity in their relation with others.
The individual is autonomous; he or she is self-directed.	The individual is subject to the totality of social forces and directed by the collective.	Individuals are self-directed, though influenced by others.
The individual can and ought to experience self-development and can do so alone.	The collective ought to experience self-development, irrespective of individual members.	Individuals can and ought to develop together, and not at each other's expense.
Only individuals can be the source of political authority.	Only the collective can be the source of political authority.	Only the relations between individuals can be the source of political authority.
The individual is responsible for his or her own destiny.	The collective is responsible for everyone's destiny.	Individuals are responsible for both their own and other's destinies.
The source of moral principles is the individual.	The source of moral principles is the collective.	The source of moral principles is interpersonal relations.
The individual is the only source and depository of knowledge.	The collective is the only source and depository of knowledge.	Related individuals are the source of knowledge, and it is dispersed.
The individual is the basis of all explanations of social phenomena.	The collective, with its own laws, is the basis of all expla-nations of social phenomena.	Related individuals are the basis of all explanations of social phenomena.
Only individuals really exist.	Only collectives really exist.	Individuals exist in relation to others.

This approach is more than just a compromise. It is a complete break, in
that it is concerned not with an object, but the processes between objects. This
has deep roots in Green thinking. Andrew Dobson says, "The general targets
of attack are those forms of thought that 'split things up' and study them in
isolation, rather than those that 'leave them as they are' and study their interdependence. The best knowledge is held to be acquired not by the isolated
examination of the parts of a system but by examining the way in which the
parts interact. This act of synthesis, and the language of linkage and reciprocity in which it is expressed, is often handily collected in the term 'holism'."[12]

This can seem like an obscure, almost mystical approach. We are limited by our human faculties, after all—and they seem best suited to identifying objects, not the connections between objects. Are we even capable of seeing the world holistically?

Laura Sewall believes we are. As a result of our intellectual traditions, "We readily perceive things, and are relatively insensitive to the relationships between them. . . . if we legitimize and practise a relational view, we act in response to a world that reveals forces and vibrancy".[13] She identifies five perceptual practices that develop the skill of relational perception. They are learning to attend, identifying relations, perceptual flexibility, re-perceiving depth, and 'visioning'. By learning to attend, she means to a state of alertness, readiness or heightened awareness in which we are open to suggestions of pattern or meaning in our environment. She refers to a number of indigenous people's practices as identifying relations. Inuit conversation includes a great deal of contextualization of objects and events that the Western ear would consider superfluous, and the Yoruba of Nigeria prize the shamanic ability to 'read the signs' and draw conclusions from seemingly unrelated events. Perceptual flexibility refers to the shifts of perspective that allow different patterns to emerge from the same sense data—like the way you can reverse the perspective on a drawing of a cube. We can change our attitude to the depth of our perception by seeing ourselves as being within the planet rather than on the planet; try imagining the atmosphere as a very thin ocean. Lastly, visioning is a way of using our imagination to visualize things consistent with our values and desires. These imagined scenes condition our perception and experience of the real world. The skill of seeing the world as interconnected is not esoteric, merely neglected in our culture.

Erwin Laszlo is a leading exponent of models based on processes (the 'systems theory' used by him is described in more detail in Chapter 8). He writes, "Some [social philosophers] have thought [society] to be an association entered into by free agents for mutual aid and benefit (e.g. the social contract theories of Rousseau and Locke). . . . Others assessed it as essential relationships formed by basically social human beings (e.g. Aristotle and Marx). With the rise of sociological theory in the work of Comte, society was recognized as something of an entity in itself."[14] In other words, individualists believe we choose to interact, collectivists believe we must form groups, but in reality our interactions are giving rise to distinct, almost autonomous phenomena.

Does this theory commit the fallacies which Alan Carter ascribes to collectivism? Certainly, Carter uses the term 'holism' as a synonym for collectivism.[15] Laszlo does describe the social system as an entity, raising the possibility of a part having a relationship to the whole (and hence having a relationship to itself, which Carter regards as a logical impossibility). In fact, the systems view suggests not so much that a system is the totality of its parts, but

THE NUCLEAR PRIESTHOOD

Camilleri offers four factors behind the 'technological faith of almost religious dimensions' that was sweeping the globe. An ideology of progress perceived nuclear power in Promethean terms, as bringing a brighter light to humanity. The bureaucratization of science put scientists in government posts in the wake of the Manhattan Project: Fermi, Oppenheimer, and Teller all found themselves on committees in the AEC, the Pentagon, Congress or the White House. The national interest was invoked as an unquestionable justification; no country, it was felt, could afford to be 'left behind' in the competition for global prestige. Links between state and industry were actively promoted so as to draw sceptical business into the 'nucleocracy'. Finally, the 1953 'Atoms for Peace' campaign heralded an attempt to break the connection with weapons manufacture and secure orders for the nascent US nuclear industry by offering to build reactors around the Western world.[16]

This is not exactly a result of powerful collective forces, nor was there any conspiracy behind it. This 'military industrial complex', about which even President Eisenhower warned his nation, was more insidious and inexorable than that, with no person nor group holding the reins of its power.[17] This dynamic process swept up and tied together not only the scientists and politicians but people with no conceivable interest; in Bradwell village, proposed site of the first British nuclear power station, an informal parish gathering expressed support for the development.[18]

The nuclear state that grew out of the drive for nuclear power has distinctive features. It is secretive and unaccountable, turning the members of the nucleocracy into a closed club with increasingly more in common with each other than with the people they claim to represent—voters, workers, scientists and shareholders. The British Atomic Energy Commission has its own police force; decisions on waste, safety and pollution are taken by quangos reporting to Ministers. "The features of devolved responsibility, administrative discretion and scientific expertise, combined with the secrecy surrounding nuclear activities, make public accountability nominal rather than a practical feature of decision-making."[19]

Furthermore, when the scale of a society's commitment exceeds a certain level, the secrecy, expense and hazard become more than a policy option; the relationship becomes one of dependency, and the nucleocracy becomes unassailable. "[French policy] has gone beyond 'nuclear substitution' . . . into a policy of 'nuclear electrification' under which the growth of electricity consumption has been deliberately encouraged. Between 1973 and 1981, for example, consumption rose by 51%, which is double the increase for the EEC as a whole." With all new homes electrically heated and all appliances electrical, the French have little choice but to accept the nuclear future. In fact, although French nuclear electric power is cheaper than other forms of electricity available in France, it is still far more expensive than using fossil fuels directly. There remains public disquiet, and some spirited opposition,[20] but it has so far gained little ground. "The public debate invited by Mitterand in 1981 raised scarcely a ripple. . . . In principle, the battle for 'tout nucleaire' has been won. Only its consequences have yet to be revealed."[21]

Effectively, the technology itself is beginning to exercise power over people. The servant has become the master. "No notion more completely confirms our technological somnambulism than the idea that technology has no political bias. . . . Nuclear energy cannot possibly move society in a democratic direction, but will move society in an autocratic direction. Because it is so expensive and so dangerous, nuclear energy must be under the direct control of centralized financial, governmental, and military institutions. A nuclear power plant is not something that a few neighbours can get together and build."[22] We can meet our needs with small amounts of energy delivered locally—better even, many would argue, than we can with large amounts of energy delivered long distances. As Illich points out, we are ruled by technologies when we make a fetish out of them; it is the unspoken assumption that faster is better that gives cars power over us,[23] and the goal of a high energy-use utopia that leads to nuclear power.

---

the totality of the relations between its parts. So the part has a relationship with this totality of relations, and not with itself.

Is there a danger of committing the other collectivist fallacy—that of the whole determining the part? Capra says that "self-organizing systems exhibit a certain degree of autonomy. . . . This does not mean that living systems are isolated from their environment; on the contrary, they interact with it continually, but this interaction does not determine their organization. . . . From the systems point of view, both free will and determinism are relative concepts. To the extent that a system is autonomous from its environment, it is free; to the extent that it depends on it through continuous interaction its activity will be shaped by environmental influences. The relative autonomy of organisms usually increases with their complexity."[24]

What I am suggesting is that instead of the mechanical view of simple building blocks in various arrangements (be they collectives or individuals) we see the world as phenomena arising out of processes. By being open to the dynamic and fluid interactions around us, we will be better able to see the patterns and make the connections that put us in control of our destinies. Process operates at every level. Our bodies are a collection of interconnected processes, which in turn build up communities, which interact to form society on a larger scale. At every level these processes are forming and regulating themselves—while at the same time being conditioned by the environment they are part of. Every way of looking at the world has some ethical consequences (see in particular Morris Berman's analysis, outlined in Chapter 8), and I believe that an orientation around process puts us in touch with both our power and our responsibility.

The Green Perspective

The Green movement has not fitted easily into either individualism or collectivism. Out of its efforts to work out its programme and practice, we can see an interrelationist approach emerging.

Greens have always asserted the importance of personal responsibility—a moral commitment to recognizing our own part in the total environmental impact of humanity. This is incompatible with a collectivist approach, which would place responsibility with structural forces. However, responsibility is not a concept that sits easily with individualists either: it would seem to dilute the political sovereignty of the individual. Individualists have always been more concerned with rights, which imply duties only to respect the boundaries of others' rights. The idea of an active responsibility to someone else's problems ties everyone together into a community—and yet simultaneously sometimes requires individuals to speak out against the community.

Greens' awareness of global crises are informed by science as much as by the humanities—in particular, the science of ecology. The interconnectedness of the biosphere has been powerfully demonstrated in research on biodiversity, which shows the collapse in the number of species in an area when a seemingly unconnected catastrophe befalls a neighbouring area ("[Species-area theories] have sprung up to explain the relationship between the area of a given place and the number of species found there . . . seen from ants through to zooplankton"[25]). The individualists' insistence that the parts of a community can operate independently is at odds with this observation. Of course, ecology is not the same as sociology; but then neither is physics, which dominated the enlightenment culture that nurtured individualism.[26]

Collectivists too find a challenge in ecology. The loss of a single species can have a knock-on effect throughout an ecosystem ("The eminent ecologist John Terborgh . . . has said that the removal of half a dozen carefully chosen tree species (mostly figs) from the Amazon basin could cause most of the rainforest and its species to 'collapse'"[27]); apparently, a part determining the whole.

Most of all, the Green movement's experience of social change has been at odds with both views. Greens have experienced a move from being considered cranks and eccentrics to being listened to, debated with—in other words, taken seriously. This did not happen by chance, but resulted from their own diverse activities. Some proved effective, and some did not. We can categorize these different tactics according to whether they relied on strong individuals, closely bonded collectives, or some other mode of interaction.

An individualist approach to social change is founded on the assumption that people take decisions autonomously and in their own interests. It is the talent and ability of the individual, and his or her ability to meet the interests of others, that determines their success in bringing about change. Many environmentalists felt that since everyone has an interest in a healthy environment, an individualist appeal for support would work. Is this strategy suitable for Greens, who seek to make society sustainable?

A political theorist named Michels raises one potential problem—what he calls 'the Iron Law of Oligarchy'.[28] As any movement grows, he argues, organizational structures become more formalized, in order to deal with the larger membership; within such structures, individuals gain a set of interests deriving from their role; a large part of their energies is devoted to securing their own positions. The make-up of the organization becomes more professional, motivated by selective incentives (protecting their own position); organizational survival rather than advancing the cause (e.g. promoting a Green Party rather than promoting Green Politics),[29] and a strategy of adaptation rather than opposition (operating with established structures and depending on them for support, rather than actively challenging or resisting them). What happens is that the interests of the party activists become distinct from the interests of the people they claim to serve. Greenpeace, who have used the image of the lone individual very effectively, could be said to have become more 'risk averse' during the 80s; in the last few years it has been largely grassroots activists that have brought new issues on to the headlines.

In order to appeal to an ever wider section of a population with which they can only communicate through mass media, radicalism is replaced with moderation. The German Green Party's Realos have identified the target group as that 40% in German society typified by "the urban, liberal, consumerist citizen, who is primarily orientated towards his (sic) individual plans for life. . . ."[30] This leads logically to part of the programme for economic restructuring which says that "ecological restructuring will be accepted only if it is guaranteed that it is possible without any loss in job security and income",[31] and to the abandonment of 'difficult policies' like a ban on vivisection.[32] Although this is evidence that the 'iron law' is already at work, I do not believe that it is really so rigid. The German Greens are still more driven by principle than by survival. Many Green organizations have avoided divisive hierarchies by dispersing responsibility rather than concentrating it in the hands of the most charismatic individuals.

Even if party hierarchies can be avoided, and compromise averted, there is no guarantee that change can be swiftly effected. It is simple-minded to see governments as all-powerful bodies standing above all other institutions (see Chapter 11); and any lone individual finds him- or herself at the centre of a complex network of forces. Even if the individual activist's role may be necessary, it is hard to believe that it is sufficient.

Individualism takes a pluralist view of politics: the task of Greens is to stand alongside rival candidates and present a more convincing case. Early ecologists standing for elections in the 1974 in Britain tried just this: Edward Goldsmith (then Editor of *The Ecologist*) wrote 3,000 words on his election leaflet, and employed a motley collection of stunts to gain press attention, including borrowing animals from a friend's zoo. He and the other four 'People' candidates received a derisory vote—the highest being 3.9% in Coventry. It could be argued that they suffered from a lack of media exposure (which they did), but when they contested the General Election in 1987, with 133 candidates and a party election broadcast, the average vote was 1.3% and the best result 3.5%. This was only two years before the 'eco-boom' of 1989.[33] The evidence is that voting is carried out without detailed knowledge of a party's platform, and with a strong awareness of context and the likely outcome. The dynamics of this cannot be accounted for in simple individualist terms.

What Worked?

This is not to say that Greens failed to achieve influence over this period. Was this because of collectivist strengths—a mass base? A collectivist strategy stresses the overwhelming public support necessary. In this light, Greens were doomed by their failure to address the needs and desires of 'ordinary people'. However, this option was never really available for the early ecologists; theirs was not a rallying cry but a warning, and one that many experienced as a threat to their affluent lifestyles (or their aspiration to have such a lifestyle).

The more closely we look at both approaches, the more the similarities become clearer than the differences. Both are mechanistic, with the effect following directly from the cause. In practice, we find that both negative and positive feedback are in operation; the effect can become its own cause. Both are ostensibly unbiased and even-handed, but inevitably favour some over others in practice. Both are anthropocentric, or human-centred, taking the actions of humans in isolation from the non-human environment. Both are more interested in the divisions between individuals and collectives, rather than the connections between them.

Greens had to find a way of spreading their message that relied neither on reasoned argument nor on sheer weight of numbers. Jonathan Porritt says that in Britain, "The central principle underlying the development of Green ideas in the UK . . . [was] strength through diversity, or 'let a thousand green poppies bloom.'"[34] They sought to make connections, to build networks, following the logic of communications technology—resources unavailable to the architects of past social movements. These connections were somewhat indiscriminate, but they began to bear fruit. Friends of the Earth and the Green Party built up lists of members and supporters, who formed themselves into local groups; readers' magazines like *Undercurrents* (later incorporated into *Resurgence*) and

NUCLEAR RESISTANCE

Despite everything, the nucleocracy has not succeeded. A report in the Guardian (12 Dec 95) says, "The sudden announcement came from British Energy—the holding company which after privatization next year will own the most modern reactors of Nuclear Electric and Scottish Nuclear. The future of the industry—at least for the next 15 years—will be nuclear free." In Britain, no more nuclear power stations will be constructed for a long time—possibly for ever. "The National Audit Office found in June 1993 that the bill for decommissioning existing stations had climbed to £18 billion. With the cost of reprocessing or disposing of waste added, the total undiscounted bill was put at more than £40 billion." It would be easy to say that the nuclear industry failed on simple economic grounds. But subsidies had been given for many years— and the prominence of the costs of waste and decommissioning would not have been an issue had they not been made into an issue by anti-nuclear campaigners. Breaking the consensus on nuclear power, and then winning the contest, may have been aided by economics; but we can still ask how the anti-nuclear movement prevented a French-style nuclear hegemony from becoming established.

Blowers and Pepper suggest a number of elements in this process. Firstly, legitimacy was lost as inquiries and investigations began to criticize the nuclear industry. Secondly, accountability and control became issues; in particular, leaks from Sellafield in 1983 exposed the secrecy and arrogance of the industry. A changing political environment was making concern about the environment and public health more pressing for government. Finally, the international disillusionment with nuclear power (following Three Mile Island and Chernobyl) weakened the position of the UK nuclear chiefs.[35]

Anti-nuclear groups could not effectively pursue conventional strategies to bring about this change. No charismatic leader could single-handedly overturn such a consensus; at the outset, all those who began to call the technology into question were cranks or eccentrics, operating outside the mainstream. To criticize the technocracy from outside is extraordinarily difficult when a state of consensus prevails. No mainstream political party would then break with nuclear power, since it would be an admission that they would not deliver the high energy utopia that then (and to a large extent now) was associated with success and progress.

But equally, no mass movement could be effectively galvanized. Certainly, the radical sections of the labour movement were active in the opposition—few missed the linkage between the miner's strike of 1983-84 and the proposed expansion of the nuclear industry. But other trade unions, those benefiting from the construction or operation of the plants, were equally vociferous in their support. There was no common interest among them—especially given the falling proportion of the population in conventional work, and the falling proportion of them in unions.

Instead, the organization of the anti-nuclear movement resembled a disparate network of individuals, groups and organizations who were prepared to express a principled concern. Every part of the network had its own tactics, but civil disobedience was always an important part—contrasting the commitment to non-violence of the protesters to the nuclear industry's connections with the military and its environmental violence. The image of the Greenpeace activists who were almost killed by barrels of waste being dumped at sea remains one of their most enduring images; if waste were still dumped at sea, the economic viability of nuclear power might be a great deal more healthy than it is.

At the same time, an alternative technology movement was emerging, based on renewable energy. The ubiquitous 'Nuclear power? No thanks!' stickers were based around the icon of the sun—the symbol of the alternative. The protesters did not demand democratic control of nuclear power, or an equitable distribution of its benefits. They called for a change in the direction of technology. At the festivals and Green Fairs where the anti-nuclear and Green movement gathered, practical demonstrations of windmills and solar panels stressed that a choice was available.

Green Line gave voice to the urgent conversations and debates. These were not conventional political organizations, since every contact was (at least to begin with) a dialogue—there was no central office, nor a party line to hand down. The autonomy of the network's various nodes has always been a key feature of the Green movement.

To say that they were effective, one has to accept that at that stage the goal was to reform the system, rather than change it fundamentally.[36] Nonetheless, this experience has shaped and informed Greens' understanding of political sovereignty, authority—and power. More recently, the same networked approach established the durable Green Student Network, and Earth First! in the UK.

Power as Process
Having established the methodology, we can now apply it to our study of power. Not only is power itself a relationship, but it arises out of relationships; wherever a process or system links people together, certain exercises of power become possible. The nature of this power is essentially determined by the system that gives rise to it, but the choice of whether or how to exercise it remains in the hands of real people caught up in that process. More important, everyone still has some choice—'relative autonomy'—over what systems and processes they become embroiled in. How much choice depends on the extent

to which they succeed in meeting their needs (material, environmental, emotional) independently of the dominant system.

If there is already an interrelationist view of power, it is in the work of Michel Foucault, the French 'historian of the present'. His definition of power has an oddly self-referential quality: 'the way that actions structure the field of other possible actions' suggests an unending chain of linked events. His work, which arose out of studies in the seemingly apolitical fields of madness and sexuality, led him to an awareness of power encoded in the most basic interactions between individuals. In his essay 'Disciplinary Power and Subjection', he establishes five methodological precautions for the study of power. The first is that it should not concern itself with legal powers but with power at the 'extreme points of its exercise'—the most local practice of power (see, for instance, the previous chapter). The second precaution is that the conscious decision or intention is of less importance than the mechanism that made the intention possible (a precaution observed in the previous chapter). The third is that there is no individual, group or class that holds power (however much they may seem to benefit from it)—these are the 'vehicles of power, not its points of application'. The fourth, that we can work back from these local mechanisms to see how they become organized into more global patterns (see Chapter 8). And the fifth, that the circulation of power in this way is so essential a part of our communication that it gives rise to a body of knowledge (see Chapter 10). Essentially, 'power is not a tool, but a strategy.'[37]

Foucault clearly rejects individualism ("The individual is not to be conceived as a sort of elementary, a primitive atom, a multiple and inert material on which power comes to fasten or against which it happens to strike."[38]) and collectivism ("Power is not to be taken to be a phenomenon of . . . one group or class over another"[39]). Rather, he argues that "power must be analysed as something that circulates, or rather as something which only functions in the form of a chain. It is never localized here or there, never in anybody's hands, never appropriated as a commodity or a piece of wealth. Power is employed and exercised through a net-like organization."[40] Foucault's analysis addresses many of the needs and experiences of ecological campaigners.

Going Behind the Façade

The task for Greens, then, is not to 'seize power'. Power is not what the referee or umpire has, but what the players are doing; it is a game that you are invited to join in. Perhaps this is not apparent if you are physically attacked (though see Chapter 8), but the exercise of force is only one link in a chain of power.

To conform to the expectations of established bases of power will not necessarily allow you to realize your intentions or desires, unless they are consistent with the flow and direction of that body. If a Green activist were suddenly to become a Secretary of State for the Environment, he or she might no more be 'in control' than if President of the Flat Earth Society. The post exists in a context which circumscribes the actions that may be carried out through it; unless that context is changed, the holder of the post is powerless to do anything else.

But having said that, there are other games in town. We can choose to make links, and build relations with people, that generate processes of their own. These processes then become opportunities for others to meet their needs in different ways—to become part of a different power strategy. The systems of action that we establish can come to have a life of their own just as much as the social relations that we oppose. The only relations that we should support and maintain in our lives are those consistent with the kind of world we want to live in.

This view of power, then, has an important implication for any social change strategy; the means cannot be justified by the ends. The means predetermine, or prefigure, the ends—the processes we become part of now are the society that we will live in tomorrow. Even our relations with enemies and opponents must not tie us into a pattern of aggression or violence, as that in itself constitutes a strategy of power. Gandhi's maxim that "There is no way to peace—peace is the way" is consistent with the view that no exercise of power takes place in isolation. Or, one might quote Bart de Ligt: "It is a fixed law that all means have their own abiding end. . . . It is impossible to educate people in liberty by force."[41]

Greens campaign for conservation, in defence of 'the natural world' (that is, complex, differentiated ecologies). Their aim has never been to establish a blueprint for society, or lay down some perfect human order. There is a sense in which Green Politics is almost conservative; Dobson says, "The Green aspiration to insert the human being in its 'proper place' in the natural order and to generate a sense of humility in the face of it is clearly 'right wing' in this context."[42] In Green theory, systems from the cellular up to the societal are capable of organizing themselves and spontaneously forming mutually beneficial interactions, and are beyond the wisdom or capability of anyone to control effectively. If our goal is not to establish some order but to facilitate the unending process of self-organization, then there is no end—only means.

To recapitulate: a Green view of power is one which recognizes the importance of technique and direction. Power is not an object, held by a person or a group. It is a social phenomenon arising out of successive and sustaining interactions between individuals. No one person can seize control of it, because it does not belong to just one person, but emerges out of the whole system. This means that it is all too easy to commit the error of believing that one holds power when in fact it holds us.

But if power arises out of our interactions, then we can change the direction of power by changing our place in the process. A process cannot be held,

ALTERNATIVE ENERGY

There is an alternative path. Schumacher describes it as appropriate technology, and Illich refers to it as convivial. Faced with a new technology, we can ask: does it enhance the skills of the user, or degrade them? Does it foster self-reliance in terms of skills and resources, or is the user dependent on experts and suppliers? Does it bring people together, or push them apart? Does it work with existing biological systems, or undermine or overload them? Does it use energy intensively, or extensively? Does it require control by a few, or participation by the many?

"Convivial tools rule out certain levels of power, compulsion and programming which are precisely those that make all governments look more or less alike. . . . To the degree that [an individual] masters his tools, he can invest the world with meaning; to the degree that he is mastered by his tools, the shape of the tool determines his own self-image."[43]

Appropriate technology (also called 'alternative', or AT) can be part of a social change movement in a number of ways. In one sense, it is the research and development division of the Green movement—developing the tools that will allow the Green society to function. This is necessary firstly because so many traditional and sustainable skills and crafts have been lost or driven underground. If overnight the land were handed back to the people and held in common—would they know what to do with it? It is also a transitional strategy. Since few members of industrialized societies are ready to become peasants, and since we may wish to retain many of the high energy technologies, something is needed to bridge the gap; to power our infrastructure without destroying the planet. Telling people that they can have their television provided it is solar powered is meeting them halfway. In particular, the millions who live in cities need ingenious solutions to meet their needs sustainably.

Some make greater claims for the strategic role of technology. Bookchin argues that the productive power of new technology has the capacity to drastically reduce working hours: once our desires are liberated from consumerism, we will see that work is not necessary. He calls this concept post-scarcity anarchism. It is certainly true that many observers of indigenous hunter/gatherers find that they seem to have immense amounts of spare time. Illich demonstrates that when the time spent in traffic jams, making unnecessary journeys, earning money to buy a car and repairing environmental damage is taken into account, the real speed of a typical car is about 2 miles per hour. In this light, working examples of AT should allow Greens to tempt the sceptical with promises of a true leisure society—not the postindustrialism of unemployment and overemployment, but a real liberation.

The Centre for Alternative Technology derives its power from a water turbine collecting water from a nearby reservoir, from wind generators and from photovoltaic solar panels. In addition, heat is collected from the sun, from degrading biomass and from the old quarry workings beneath the site. There is no mains connection. They have 80,000 visitors every year, including 20,000 school children. Since local authorities were directed to begin work on Local Agenda 21, many newly appointed environment officers have also been visiting and collecting ideas. Peter Harper, a founder of the Centre, says, "We still have to get across the hardest message: it's not simply a matter of picking on one technology or aspect of your lifestyle; it's your whole way of life." He also finds that people are looking for clean technologies that carry the same characteristics as the more conventional sort. "How much more exciting to put up a windmill which generates 1,000kWh a year than to install draughtproofing which will save the same amount of energy at one-tenth of the price."[44]

Alternative technologies are not just curiosities any longer—they are also the basis for viable businesses. "In 1982, Dulas Engineering was set up as an electronic design company within CAT, specializing in controls for small renewable energy systems. Over the years the work expanded to include total system design and installation both in the UK and abroad, until in 1989 it was agreed that the company should move off site and become independent from CAT."[45] Co-operatives are being set up to run wind farms such as 'Baywind' in Cumbria. There is increasing potential for community enterprises and co-operatives in alternative technology—it's hard to imagine a local, co-operative fast breeder reactor.

The technologies that groups like CAT have developed are making individuals and communities more self-sufficient, making low impact settlements practical, and liberating us from the 'energy slaves' that have become our masters. Viable Green enterprises are opening up niches in their local economies for conversions, sale of technology, or even sale of the energy itself. They are not dependent on high finance or synthetic materials; groups like Leeds AltTech scour scrapyards for the old bed frames that will become high-efficiency wood burners, the old hot water cylinders that will become solar water heaters, and the old starter motors that will become wind generators. In particular, it is groups living close to the land, as travellers or settled communities, that are enabled to live an authentic life without compromise with industrialism.

---

or possessed, but it might be diverted—or a new process established in competition with it. By linking our means firmly to the ends we hope to achieve, we can enable and empower a different way of life. The power games of A and B were always a myth; they took place in a context within which both were pawns. But A does not have to sit behind that desk, and B does not have to come as a supplicant. Both may be under great pressure to conform to their roles, but escape is not impossible. As long as there are people prepared to be

A, someone will always end up as B, the hapless victim of power. We need both A and B to become aware of their roles and to find a different script.

> The spectacle fades
> The tidy lives depart with their human loves
> Only the stars, the oceans and the machines remain:
> The dark and the involuntary powers.
> W. H. Auden, *The Way to the Sea*

Chapter 3

Within and Without

Take away every other resource, and what is left is our inner power—what might once have been called the soul. It is certainly shaped by the processes of power that operate through us, but there is also a wellspring of selfhood which can enable us to put our own stamp on those processes—and even choose which we engage with. Religion is the traditional guide to using this personal power, but the skills of spiritual reflection have become buried under dogma and doctrine.

It is not necessary to see our consciousness as resident in the brain, or in some intangible spirit; in fact, it is not a fixed or unified presence at all. Trying to pin down consciousness to just one place has led our culture to put up barriers between our selves and the outside world; even our own bodies.

Just as our behaviour is influenced by power, so our thinking often internalizes the authority around us. We begin to police ourselves, and accept the needs of power as our own needs. If we have real needs, they are those of love, community and identity as much as material needs. Getting in touch with our deepest feelings, beneath the habits of power, can be achieved through reflection, meditation and dialogue. When this is linked to political and social action, we become capable of taking control of the power in our lives.

> "It is a new spirit, a very strong power which grows in their own hearts and in their own heads. . . . By being side by side with others in the same situation— men, women, friends and strangers—who sit or stand or walk by your side, all moving together with the same life-protecting values and convictions. This creates a force, a peaceful power that is a spiritual power."—Gert Bastian, in Capra and Spretnak, *Green Politics*

I'm writing this in a police cell, after a protest at an open cast coal mine. A featureless yellow box, it is higher than it is wide, giving the feeling of being at the bottom of a pit. The daylight coming through the glass bricks is drowned by the yellow light left switched on 24 hours a day. In an alcove is a stainless steel toilet bowl (no door for privacy—it is visible from the observation hole). I am lying on a blue, plastic coated mattress on a raised platform, both marked with cigarette burns. The cell door is heavy, khaki and free from ornament except a small glass eye continually watching me. The absence of any door handle is disconcerting. I have been here 15 hours and I'm desperate to get out.

My needs are well enough catered for, measured on material terms. I am fed, watered—with this pen and paper I can even do some work. But even if the food were caviar and smoked salmon, I never cease to be aware that I am imprisoned. I have no control over my environment—the lighting, the heating (or lack of it), the endless meaningless sounds from outside. I eat when they please, and they set the menu. My only real choices are what to write and when to defecate (I discover later that some of my friends have to ask to go to the toilet). On a previous occasion, I remember that the police procedure was to lead you to your cell and then tell you to close the door after you—in effect, asking for your participation in your own confinement.

This is total powerlessness, and all around I can hear varying responses. From some cells there is dead silence; from others repeated appeals to our guards for food, water, blankets; from some, just terrible impacts as bodies are hurled futilely against the door. But in addition to the frustration, anxiety and claustrophobia, there is a general sapping of the will. I would not normally spend hours inactive, staring into space. Here it is natural and hard to resist. Where one acts, it is easy to get drawn into obsessive, repeating patterns, such as pacing or twitching. Considering the lack of stimulus, the pressure is strangely intense. I have to struggle to invent tasks, to keep my mind occupied—and the only tools I have are a pen, five sheets of paper, two plastic bowls, two broken plastic spoons and a brown paper bag with a sandwich carton in it. Anger burns inside me, but it has no outlet. If I were to let it out, I would most likely destroy the few useful resources I do have: briefly satisfying, but ultimately deepening the void. There is nothing else I can damage without injuring myself. There is a button on the wall I can use to summon someone—but if I do, the only thing I can do is reinforce my sense of dependency by asking for something. "Could you . . . Can I have . . . Please . . ."

An experience like this changes you, in unforeseeable ways. I am cut off from all the processes of power that I use and that sustain me. The only power I have left is that which I generate—that which comes from within. If I can see this through without hysteria, depression or fear settling on me, it is only through the resources I can find inside myself. This power-from-within seems small, but as the starting point of all the other processes of power it is worth isolating and studying. In a way, being in prison is a fine opportunity to do that. We all have it—even depression and fear are creative forces inside us. But it is resolve, positivity, love and compassion that are of more interest to me. If I can nurture them here, what can they not achieve when I am free? Many prisoners of conscience have spoken of feeling truly free only when imprisoned. This apparent paradox comes from the way this power within is enabled and unleashed by authenticity—by being true to ourselves. By living life without deceit or compromise, we build our inner reserves of self-worth and courage. By confronting power—even vastly superior power—you can liberate the power within. Resistance is therapy.

Power is a process—and it is one that operates through us. Human beings are capable of great feats of adaptation in order to survive in the world as they experience it. As Ken Jones puts it, "We each have our own way of coming to terms with life or, in other words, of convincingly masking and evading what we are. Most of us, most of the time, are hardly aware of this process; we are the process."[1] We have difficulty questioning or challenging power, because it means understanding ourselves. In other words, it is not simply that we are influenced or driven by the processes of power operating in society; our personalities, our preferences, our behaviour and even our awareness are constructed by them.[2]

That is not to deny us any independence. The operation of a process, and the chains of interrelation, are profoundly creative—much like a game of Chinese Whispers (for a more detailed discussion of free will, see Chapter 8). As we think about and analyse our experiences, our desires and our aspirations, we can favour, develop and pursue those aspects of our lives that seem to us most authentic, or most rewarding, or most right. A great deal of what goes on inside us is determined by what is going on around us, it is true; but a great deal of what goes on around us is determined by what goes on inside. It is a two-way process.

The decisions that we would like to call 'rational', or 'reasonable under the circumstances', are in fact a reflection of our insecurities and fears. Equally, when someone says of an action that seems exemplary to others 'it just seemed obvious at the time' or 'I just did what anyone would have done' they may well be describing their openness to compassion, or a strong moment of empathy. Either way, they are talking about the power within.

This personal power can be an active force, manifesting as ambition, desire, enthusiasm or anger. Equally, it can deaden or limit our responses, as depression, inadequacy, confusion or grief. None of these happen without reference to our context and our history—even our genetic history is part of a process external to us—but equally, none of them can fail to reproduce and continue that process, with our particular stamp on it.

The importance of our contribution is easily missed when we struggle to create an analysis that can reflect the interconnections of social structures. Gandhi comments on the foolishness of trying to create a 'system so perfect that no one would need to be good'.[3] There are always better and worse responses to circumstances, and we depend on people's inner strength to choose the better one. However, what constitutes 'better' may not be obvious to anyone at the time.

We can also tap into the sources of active power within us, and use them to offset the deadening force of despair. Passivity may be promoted by many means, but for few if any of us is it genuinely irresistible. As long as the brain is alive, it can respond to the processes of power it is caught up in, and amplify them, redirect them, or sap their energy.

Deep Inside

This does not mean that we respond to events with an objective, fresh analysis. Everything we consider comes to us through the filter of past experience, and is processed by the structured mass of assumptions, expectations and knowledge inside us. Some of this is genuinely fixed, like the basic structure of language,[4] but a great deal lies not in biology but is reproduced by long-lasting social structures. Roy Morrison calls these 'deep social structures' and describes them as 'nearly invisible cultural and social patterns that shape our consciousness'. He stresses that they are not an accumulating sediment in our minds that fixes us in certain patterns of behaviour, but are in fact highly plastic, formed and re-formed daily. We cannot be without becoming.[5]

There is clearly some sort of link between the socio-economic reality, as described in the last chapter, and individual consciousness. The ideas in our mind, on the most banal subjects and the most profound, come from the way that power has concentrated around us. Typically, social theory uses the word 'ideology' to describe the link between ideas and beliefs on the one hand, and material conditions on the other. Fiske defines it as "the social production of meanings".[6] The word has a hint of deception about it, and indeed it is commonly used to describe false ideas, believed to have been arrived at rationally, but in fact serving somebody's interest. However, this would be dangerously simplistic. After all, the best way to fool someone else is to fool yourself first; I suspect that the number of people circulating ideas that they know to be wholly false is in fact quite small. However, it is quite clear that we all seek to put our ideas about the world in such a way as to put ourselves in the best light. If, as I suggest, we are all to some extent complicit in the systems of power-over, that would naturally lead to widespread justification of that power. It is certainly true, as Collins suggests, that just as every discursive ideology fails to perfectly describe the world of objects, every discursive ideology has to deny that it might be wrong.[7] It isn't just the spin doctors used by the politicians—it is all of us.

Paradoxically, ideology is not just about ideas. Ideology can also be 'embodied' in material things or practices—a newspaper, a can of soft drink, a family, a charitable trust. These also 'carry' ideas or messages to us. When analysing the content of a cultural product, we need to look at much more than just what it actually says. Cormack offers the following checklist with which we can extract the messages carried in everything from bus tickets to blockbuster movies:

- Content: vocabulary, characters, actions, assertions
- Structure: chronological, opening/closing, doubt/clarity, binary oppositions

- Absence: avoidances, silences, unconscious taboos
- Style: how does it reinforce content?
- Mode of address: direct, indirect, specific, general, unified/fragmented[8]

Advertisers know that the message must 'call' an audience to which to address itself. We must position ourselves as the text asks, in order to receive the message—pick up the newspaper, turn the pages, read it. We have choices at this point: trust or suspicion; compassion or contempt. At each stage in the process 'noise' comes in, distorting or adding to the message.

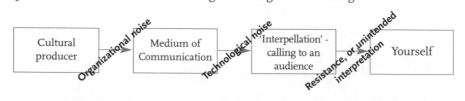

Althusser called this process of constituting an audience interpellation; a learned skill that develops as our self-consciousness grows. With the right skills, we can position ourselves so as to accept ideologies of dissent and resistance as much as ones of conformity. We also choose how to incorporate that text into the narrative of our lives. If I am 'called' by Kwik Save no-frills baked beans, it may reinforce my view of myself as an astute bargain hunter—or a penniless pauper. The text and its context carry a considerable amount of meaning, but the message can be read in different ways. In particular, when texts contradict each other or our experience, we choose to accept one or the other (or possibly neither). Parkin suggests three broad positions:

Deferential/aspirational	Buying into a dominant ideology
Accommodation/negotiation	Accepting a subordinate ideology as equally true, but still preferring the dominant
Rejection	Rejecting the dominant ideology[9]

Foucault argues a similar case, pointing out that the 'subject' that is the cause of social action is also an effect—constituted and brought into being by social power. Or, rather, social powers; the consequence of the many different ideologies around is that we are becoming increasingly decentred, with a complex and fluid set of social allegiances that we call on at different times. We may be different people in different settings, as we discard one pose and adopt another. Foucault denies that this process is one of repression, or limitation. He sees it as creative, and as unavoidable—would we be able to function in a society if we were unable to take on its logic? We are not free before power constrains us—we can act only insofar as we have adopted a network of power to act through.

This view has considerable grounding in recent research into neurology. It suggests that our brains are not 'hard wired' but that pathways are established and reinforced as they are used, gradually building up a network of well practised responses on the basis of trial and error. Our brains physically shape themselves according to our social experience, and reproduce that experience as a result.[10]

If this sounds like a fatalistic analysis, it is only because we have been conditioned to expect a level of individual responsibility that none of us can genuinely deliver. We cannot ask people to live their lives according to a fictional utopian setting—such behaviour is usually classified as madness, and raises real problems as you try to cope with reality. But we can ask people to be aware of choices between alternative 'deep structures', or contradictions and ambiguities within them, which can be resolved in one direction rather than another. We can be powerful by being aware of where we're coming from, or by developing an awareness of our motivation. We can choose to pursue a difficult or contradictory line of thought or behaviour, and become more fluent with practice. This must be a collective endeavour, because it is in social interaction that the crucial links are made. When such group interaction 'works', or proves viable in some way, then the processes are reinforced and reproduced. The positive feedback can be dramatic, leading to rapid change and the appearance of discontinuity, or a break, as old pathways are abandoned in preference for the new. As Gandhi suggested, to be 'good' is not simply a result of social structures, but also a practice—a devotion even—that is a precondition for maintaining and establishing such structures.

In most societies, one type of deep structure recurs: that of religion. The idea of God, and of a code of behaviour set by God, is one of the most common sources. However, the processes of power associated with it have changed dramatically. In this chapter, I will look at some aspects of religious experience to illustrate the way in which our internal sense of rightness interacts with social expectations.

The Search for Soul

The sense of an inner self who can be a source of will and decision may sound like a description of 'soul'. In fact, what I am suggesting is very different to traditional conceptions of 'animating spirit'.

Firstly, I do not believe that the distinction between mind and body can be sustained any more. Descartes' idea of a duality between body and soul was always problematic, given the need for an unbreakable connection between two worlds described as essentially different. How, for instance, could the control of body by mind be so much more effective than telepathy—communication between to minds which supposedly have much more in common than the mind and the body?

OUR FATHER IN HEAVEN

When we are wrestling internally with dilemmas or difficulties, we often appeal to God for guidance. Whether you consider this genuine divine guidance, or reference to a 'deep structure' that seems to reflect your values, is not that important. We can agree, I hope, that there is an awareness that we share in common which can help us to do the right thing. When this spiritual insight becomes codified and institutionalized, we call it religion.

Religion is quite distinct from spirituality. Historically, organized religion coincides closely with the rise of the city. This in turn is a development closely linked with the growth of military force—organized violence. The early cities could only be supported with a high level of extraction of wealth from the surrounding countryside; an army was required to police and maintain this steady flow of resources. The surplus accumulating in the cities provided the basis for the early priesthood, their temples and displays. The religions of the time reflect this: cults of warrior gods, proving their divinity in battle, building heavenly cities. The artworks recovered from these civilizations show the warrior caste as the height of nobility, but they could equally be viewed as operating a protection racket on the surrounding countryside.[11]

We can go back further. In the archaeological record there is a noticeable shift towards a rise in the status of male graves relative to women, and of some men relative to others. This is a clear sign of the emergence of patriarchy. It is in this context that we see male gods becoming dominant in urban belief systems—either as head of a pantheon, or as a unitary, omnipotent god. The hard distinction drawn between 'pagan', pantheistic multiple deities (like those of the Greek or Romans) and the Judeo-Christian monotheism is hard to maintain. Zeus and Jove prefigure Jehovah as male, ruling sky gods—it is their characteristics, rather than those of any of the other earth-identified gods and goddesses, that have been carried over to the monotheistic tradition.

This is the third big change resulting from the shift to organized religion— Gods move out of the earth and into the sky. Even as their worshippers adopt more dominating relationships to land and to domesticated animals, building larger farms to produce greater surpluses for the growing cities, their gods retreated from the forests (as they were felled), left the rivers (as they were diverted) and fled from the land (as it was ploughed). They did not just move into the sky in the sense of the wind and the sun, but into a quite distinct realm—a world of the spirit which traditional spirituality did not recognize. This Heaven was more than 'up there', it was unreachable by any means other than the mind—specifically, the minds of the priests.

So although the social function of the priesthood remained similar to that of the traditional pagan elder, they became part of a different set of power relations. The moral guidance that human societies both generate and require became distorted by that changing role. Rather than reading it intuitively from the landscape, with the advice and guidance of holy men, it was delivered exclusively from the mouths of the priests, with the threatening authority of a warrior god. Old taboos concerning the spirits in the earth were replaced by the logic of arbitrary domination. Intuitive or reflective insight into the natural order became a hierarchical competition to rise to a more 'civilized' (from *civis*, meaning city) and hence godlike state. The role of the elders in mediated conflict resolution was replaced with a set of religious justifications for the military establishment.

Taken by themselves, these practices of piety might have seemed the same: but they were part of a new order, and were directed towards new ends. The goal of priests was no longer to listen to the many indicators of the health and dynamics of the ecosystem, but instead a struggle for acquisition to raise the church closer to the sky and further from the earth.

The extent of the break becomes clear when the organized religions turn against their persistent predecessors—as in the assault on the 'wise women' or 'witches' of the middle ages. By supporting a different route to inner power, the witches became an enemy: their knowledge, and their culture, had to be wiped out.

"Gradually men moved into cities. And they loved the display of people better than the display of a tree. They liked the glory they got out of overpowering one another in war. And, above all, they loved the vainglory of their own words, the pomp of argument and the vanity of ideas. . . . Till at last the old Pan died and was turned into the devil of the Christians."—D. H. Lawrence, *Pan in America*

In the last century, dualism has been far less pronounced, but the 'seat of the soul' is still there. Today it is not the pineal gland but the cerebral cortex where thought is commonly believed to originate. In reality, experiments have shown that in many cases, our responses happen before thought. Tennis players, for instance, have returned the ball across the net before they have actually thought about what to do. To avoid confusion, our brains create a fictional account of the decision to return the ball—after the event. The narrative of our consciousness is largely fictional. In fact, 'thought' is taking place throughout our body—not just in the mind.[12] Physiologists have found receptors for neuropeptides (which create much emotion and feeling) all over the body, not just in the brain: we experience life all over.[13] Why do we even impose a boundary at the extremities of our body? Many of our memories of feeling and awareness have actually come to us via other people, or even via empathy with our non-human environment. We have to deal with the disquieting thought that our consciousness is embedded in flesh—or perhaps it is only disquieting because we are so unused to considering the world in that way.

The fact that the brain is physically located behind the eyes leads us to believe it is the only source of awareness.

If our experience and our personality are formed so fluidly, with input from so many interconnected sources, then we should be capable of a much stronger sense of empathy and community than most of us experience. Ideas of self-interest, self-reliance and selfishness are transformed by the awareness that our 'self' need not end at the boundaries of our body. Traces of this awareness are present in the close bonds in family, for instance—it does not demand so much that this 'other love' or 'circle of compassion' should be extended to our community, to the land, to the other members of the ecosystem we inhabit. Universal love is not beyond us, but is simply the less well-trodden path in our minds. I would argue that this is because it is so ill-rewarded by the powers of industrial society.

So instead, our sense of identity retreats further and further into our bodies, seeking to treat everything outside of itself as 'other' as it goes. The idea of the individual, detached soul is the final refuge—even the body is other, and an object of control. We see this reflected in the 'bodyshaping' movement, and an obsession with physical perfection. Dieting, bodybuilding, cosmetic surgery: we respond to the power of conformism by 'attacking' our own bodies. Only those with considerable strength of will can accept themselves as they are and be at ease with their bodies. The material substance of our bodies is not our enemy; in fact our mental powers could not exist without it.

This is not to say that materialism is the only explanation that we require, or that to speak of spirit or soul is meaningless. Another consequence of the new science is that we have become more aware of the way that complex systems generate behaviour that cannot be reduced to the components of those systems. The whole is greater than the sum of its parts (Chapter 4 considers the Gaia hypothesis in this light, and Chapter 8 goes into more detail on systems theories). These additional characteristics of living systems, which are undetectable in the dead, dismembered parts of the system and which cannot be predicted or understood except by knowledge of the whole system, certainly possess some of the attributes of spirit. It is intangible and essentially mysterious, and it is entirely reasonable to adopt a mystical reverence when trying to understand its powers. However, this has not stopped rationalism from claiming the ability to make accurate predictions in every area of knowledge. The remarkable effectiveness of such analysis of simple systems has boosted our confidence in it, and made such materialist analysis the bedrock of our search for answers in the modern age.

The Government Within Us

In many political conflicts, the role of belief and social cohesion is more important than material factors. In the riots in Paris in May 1968, among the slogans on the walls was one that read "L'état c'est chacun de nous", which means 'the state is each of us'. Our obedience to power is much less to do with the force of arms or other coercion it can muster, and much more to do with our own co-operation. Laws depend crucially on a broad social consensus in support of them; when this is lacking (as, for instance in the case of the prohibition of cannabis) the law cannot be enforced, but can only give rise to a set of unintended side effects (organized crime, for instance). Where public protest is met with armed repression (such as in Moscow in 1991, or elsewhere in Eastern Europe) the use of force has, if anything, served only to weaken the regime—the last shreds of legitimacy gone. An examination of successful authoritarian governments invariably shows an extraordinary level of participation in social control. The people registered with the old Stasi (secret police) of Eastern Germany as informers constituted a significant percentage of the population.

In Western liberal democracies, this is even more clearly the case. The state depends on its revenues, earned and paid by millions of people. The occasional breakdown illustrates the truth of this: when people simply failed to pay the infamous Poll Tax in late 80s Britain, the government was humiliatingly forced to abandon the tax altogether.

The point is that most of the time this does not happen. Even when we are clear that we oppose a policy, and dream of a world very different to this one, there is a 'policeman in our heads' that tells us to do as we are told, and makes us feel guilty or 'bad' if we do anything 'naughty'. The barrier that holds most people back from protest is not specifically the fear of punishment (for low-level protests, at least) but the sense of being naughty, or disobedient. We may even feel shame at the thought of breaking the law.

There is only this barrier of respectability and social expectation between ideals and uncontrollable protest—the reluctance of human beings to disrupt united communities. This awareness has led to the frustration of radicals through the ages, expressed as variations of "Why can't they *see*!?" Why can't people simply put the expectations of society behind them and live their beliefs?

The answer is the same as the answer to the question of why those same radicals could so easily shed their radicalism and conform to society so soon after. The deep social structures they were advancing simply did not deliver the results in people's day-to-day lives—they were at odds with lived experience. Equally, the willingness to resist authority depends heavily on whether that authority is delivering a stable and secure existence. Our inner sense of direction will become more pronounced in any setting where rigid social order has softened or been widely ignored. Resistance happens in communities, just as conformism does.

This is why radical subcultures can be developed in student ghettos, or among communities of the long term unemployed, without ever really threatening to extend beyond them. The sense of possibility and authenticity that we can experience in such heady settings is hard to sustain outside. Away from that milieu, beliefs subtly change. Excuses and denials along the lines of "I haven't shifted, but the Party has", or "I still hold the same values even though my lifestyle has changed", are comforting explanations that conceal a real loss. True power lies in finding viable ways to sustain a more authentic or ethical practice (consider the examples of Mondragon and Radical Routes in Chapter 7). Under these circumstances, we can find ways of living that feel closer to our ideals and we can find greater courage to resist what we see as evil.

Without such a sustainable practice, the policeman within us (and the parent within us, the judge within us, the boss within us, and so on) is the only source of effective action. The power here is not the power of deceit, but of harsh social reality: we are not tricked into believing that mutual exploitation is in our interest, but rather we make the very reasonable discovery that survival is based on conforming. We internalize oppression because we need to know every detail of its functioning so that we can find our proper place under it. It is not a 'false consciousness'—it is true in the world that we must live in, even though that world is daily reproduced only by that consciousness itself. Even seemingly immutable concepts like property, law and hierarchy are simply shared deep structures that have evolved from the continual dialectic between internal will and external experience.

Are there any needs that people have that are inherent in being human, and not shaped by society? The most common error that such lists of needs fall into is an economistic one, defining needs in strictly material terms. For instance, it might seem logical that food and water are our most basic needs, and such things as community and empowerment mere luxuries to be added after the essentials have been satisfied. In fact, there is a good deal of evidence that human beings find it hard to maintain mental equilibrium when deprived of community and company; such emotional or social needs are necessary to our survival, whether or not we have sufficient nutrition. And where there is a strong community, material needs can almost invariably be met, even in very harsh conditions. It is only true that material needs are paramount when an individual is considered separately from society. After all, our very first needs were for love and support from our family and community.

The other error is to suggest needs that only exist in our society—such as money, position in a hierarchy, or voting rights. Power being the endless process that it is, the answer to the question, "How can I meet my needs?" tends to be "With further use of the powers that established them as needs". Power is a circular process. It poses us questions to which only it can provide the answers. All our patterns of thought are echoes of the acts of power that placed them in our minds. This is not to say that we have no capacity for creativity, since we can always play off one internal power structure against another, by noticing the contradictions and conflicts inside ourselves and choosing to resolve them in favour of what we believe to be right. This 'right' comes from deeper needs which don't depend on social setting.

SACRED AND PROFANE

Do we need spirituality? The process of belief is often described as an irrational or pre-rational one, or as superstition which is unnecessary today. But superstition is essentially about the breach of taboo—it is the shock at hearing the unsayable said, or seeing acts that are off the communal agenda carried out. This taboo is equally present in modern, supposedly rational society. For instance, anyone giving away capital or forgoing a larger income is regarded as foolish, imprudent and maybe even a threat to their community. It is regarded as a dangerous act that threatens good order, and as a criticism of everyone else. It is not just an attack on the collective, but also a very personal challenge to anyone who has internalized these taboos and built their lifestyle upon them.

All acts of taboo-breaking are in a sense calling a bluff, since any taboo carries sanctions, either implicit or explicit. It threatens vengeance, and if the vengeance does not materialize, the taboo is fatally weakened. The taboo is powerful not because of who holds it, or the evidence for it, but because it is so widely upheld. There will always be taboo, and there will always be superstition, because there will always be a dominant culture and an identifiable set of shared practices arising from it. When two spiritual belief systems clash, it is invariably because each transgresses the other's taboos, and so threatens it with change. The roots of their beliefs may be in very practical sources; for example, a place may be taboo because past experience showed that hunting there caused a collapse in the food supply, perhaps because it interfered with reproduction. Such properties of a complex ecosystem can't be predicted in advance, nor can you say how many times they can be damaged before they lose the ability to recover. So, a pre-rational taboo may be more effective in protecting the community than a rational form of management, and spirituality comes into its own.

Rediscovering a spiritual belief system is not possible; few are capable of the mental leap of suddenly accepting as true a library of myths, legends and allegorical stories that come from a totally different culture. However, one can adopt a different set of taboos, and regard certain classes of action as ill-advised, dangerous and lacking in respect for the sacred. This process of resacralization can draw on ancient traditions without implying an insincere imitation or a suspension of critical faculties. Indeed, it is a necessary counterweight to a rationalist belief system that has desacralized living things. However one tries to argue rationally about different policy options, and from a position of equal power, the argument is bound to touch on the mysterious, the unknowable, the unpredictable—and the debater who can call on the most strongly felt taboos will win.

Maslow proposed a hierarchy of needs: physiological, aesthetic, safety, belongingness, love, esteem, self-actualization, knowledge and understanding. This is a more balanced view of our internal drives, which recognizes that emotional and psychological comfort are a vital part of our lives. Although physiological needs come higher in Maslow's hierarchy, it is often the non-material needs that pose the biggest challenge to us—whether our materialistic culture acknowledges it or not. Erich Fromm suggests that in addition we have certain existential needs, to deal with the human problem of realizing that we are mortal, that the world goes on without us, and that there are limits to our knowledge. He describes these as rootedness (relationships), a unified worldview, stimulus and effectiveness.[14] It is the last which suggests a 'will-to-power', an inherent drive to make a difference. All of these are detectable in ourselves, and I will resist the temptation to suggest any kind of order.

The Political Persona
Since Nietzsche, many writers have commented on the 'will-to-power'; it may go back further than humanity, coming from the part of us that has changed little in the evolution from reptile to human. This burning desire to build our life-force is present in all of us—not necessarily as a destructive urge, but quite possibly as a creative or preserving drive. With this will-to-power balanced (as, for instance, is described in the Indian concept of chakras) between denial and excess, it is possible to use it as the basis from which to engage in more self- or community-conscious projects. Out of balance, our attempts to reach fulfil-ment take the form of a series of overcompensations, lurching between excessive restraint and arrogant aggression.

The will to power has no moral content, no matter how we might pretend otherwise. Bahro, in a brave passage, writes of the outcome of a discussion based on the koan 'Who am I?'. "Dismayed, I realized how much will-to-power had driven me to resist the conditions in East Germany, and how much it was bound up with my desire for woman, which in my childhood and youth had long been unsatisfied."[15] Can any of us be certain that our acts of seeming altruism are not coming from a deeper drive? Writing a book is as much a manifestation of will-to-power as robbing a bank. The point is that this urge to make our mark upon the world is not in itself harmful—provided it is balanced and not obsessive, and provided it does not operate at the expense of others. Outcomes are determined both by the power structures available for us to work in, and by the way our personality responds and interacts with them.

We cannot separate the processes of power we are involved in from the contours of our persona. At its heart is our ego, our sense of self and identity. Threats to our ego are threats to our sense of self, our autonomy and self-worth. When something becomes very important to us, we include it within our ego boundaries, and identify with it so closely that any criticism of it becomes a criticism of us. We may also build strong oppositions in our mind, a shadow that contains everything that is definitely not-us. We may raise strong boundaries around the ego if we feel threatened, or lower those boundaries as we feel more trusting or secure. M. Scott Peck suggests that the healthiest state is one of universal love—not by extending the ego boundaries, which would imply that we must own or control everything we identify with, but by gradually lowering our boundaries altogether.[16] It is a fair criticism of this view that such an open, trusting approach to the world exposes one to betrayal—in a world of hardened ego boundaries, such betrayal is certainly more likely. Maybe we can achieve such a state of universal love—but it will be much easier as a whole society than alone.

The boundaries around our identities are formed and reformed continuously, but this process is by no means assured. We can close ourselves off to challenges to our worldview and experience, and harden ourselves against exposure. As our lives progress, and we make increasingly hard choices that deny love and compassion, it becomes harder and harder to rediscover the compassion. We have to justify and deny the past to protect our self-worth—when only an honest reappraisal will allow us to lower the barriers.

One of these denials explicitly concerns power. The hardened ego must believe that it is isolated, independent, objective and not in any way subject to outside pressure. And yet it is precisely the attacks by power that have hardened the ego. Endless challenges to authentic development can only lead to a persistent sense of insecurity. One of the dynamics of power is that it covers its tracks: the more we are shaped by it (and as the lifeblood of social interaction, we are all shaped by it to some extent), the less we can be aware of the process.

By meditating on our motivations and by examining our actions in an environment free of guilt or judgement, we can open our eyes to the processes we have become part of that have led us away from what we really need to be. The difficulty is finding that safe place to work from. The policeman in our heads, ready to punish us for any weakness, and our day-to-day lives, may allow few moments of stillness. Even alone, we can be subject to the condemnation of the mass. In many ways, it is better to expose ourselves with the assistance of a witness: someone who is neutral, and able to listen without approval or disapproval, superiority or inferiority. Co-counselling is one such technique; a good friendship might be another.

Spiritual liberation is not something that happens to a collective of passive receivers, nor is it an individual leap of consciousness. Like any process of power, it is something that arises out of a relationship. This may be an intimate, personal relationship—a internal dialogue leading to a revelation, which may feel more like the 'inner work' of the spirit. But it may also be connection with and openness to an experience—a change of context that opens up pos-

GREEN SPIRITS

There is a growing movement calling for a 'Green spirituality', one which centres around the sacredness of the living world. It is essentially an argument about values—what is good, what is precious—and it tries to tilt the humanist obsession of most religion towards a more ecocentric view. This movement has been growing since the post-colonial crisis of confidence allowed a collision between eastern and indigenous beliefs and the increasingly faithless Western industrialism. When an alternative lifestyle movement provided the material basis for the realization of these new values, new belief systems began to gain a foothold.

Buddhism and Taoism have both been very influential; neither is tied to a systems of deities, and both stress practices of meditation and reflection that effectively met real needs in a population inheriting a strong work ethic. Their stress on cycles and processes, rather than on hierarchy and individuals, also fitted well with an emerging 'new politics' of decentralized and spontaneous resistance.

At the same time, within the Christian churches, a rediscovery of creation-centred spiritual teaching was underway. The Franciscan tradition, linked to the practice of 'liberation theology' in developing countries, became more viable in a church less and less closely linked to the institutions of industrial society. Although the church is still a significant landowner, and a wealthy organization, it has not been able to stay with an increasingly materialist (in the sense of exploitative materialism) mainstream without veering into open contradiction. Nonconformism, with its congregational and non-hierarchical practices, provided a good resource for Christian reformers.

Pre-Christian Western traditions have also been rediscovered in Celtic paganism—a self-consciously earth-centred spiritual path. Despite an almost total lack of continuity, making it highly unclear and unfocussed, paganism has brought together a range of people concerned about the exploitation of life and alienated from traditional religion. Its language and imagery has influenced the direct action movement in particular, although a very wide range of people practising alternative lifestyles can be found marking its festivals and combining it with other indigenous people's spirituality.

At the same time, religions from Islam to Judaism were discovering that the faith which their forefathers used to support the political powers was now in conflict with them. Only where fear and insecurity heightened the strength of their taboos were religions not moving into an oppositional role.

All these different traditions find themselves with little stake in the technological, economic and political structures; those who have made them their priority experience a sense of their moral and ethical concerns drifting to the margins at exactly the time when they are most needed.

The practice of Green spirituality is still emerging. Outside of a few ecumenical gatherings, it has no real centre or connection. But a combination of different pursuits, ranging from seasonal festivals, complementary therapies and meditative prayer meetings to community work, fair trading overseas links and treeplanting, are bringing the people together. The term 'New Age' is often used to describe esoteric spiritual activities, and in some contexts this is a useful term. However, writers such as Monica Sjoo point out that there is a significant contrast between the dark, earthy immanence of Green, pagan beliefs and the white light, heavenly transcendence of the New Agers. The belief that individuals can shape their destiny through their thought alone is an individualist heresy for process-orientated Green spirituality, and it shades into economic relations that are highly acquisitive. Any Green spirituality that is trying to establish moral codes for sustainable existence must be cautious that its critique of traditional religion does not merely help it to adapt to dominant industrial power structures, but rather prefigures the emerging political economy of empowered, co-operative communities.

Most of those practising this kind of empowering spirituality have created a wholly original synthesis from a number of sources—a blend of Buddhism, nonconformist Christianity, Celtic Paganism, Hinduism, Taoism . . . This kind of syncretism risks incoherence, and as yet has not proved capable of binding communities together. But linked to new forms of social organization, it could become an increasingly potent force.

---

sibilities and presents you with a choice. Both are processes of power which take place alongside each other, and may contribute to each other. But we can't say that our material environment determines our culture any more than we can say that our beliefs will unproblematically translate into social change. Even the power inside our heads is a process we are caught up in—neither a beginning nor an end. Bahro writes, "There has been much meta-political abstract talk about a paradigm shift to the 'new age', and much of it is twaddle. 'New thought' becomes practical if political forces constitute themselves to develop a politics of Turn-around. The 'new thought', the new subjectivity, must first of all get itself together. But it is important that this occurs with a political intention, right from the beginning. Otherwise the spiritualization adapts itself once again to the status quo."[17]

Authenticity: the Process Inside
What is the authentic? Power, as Joanna Macy puts it, can be seen not as an object to be held or passed around, but as generated from within. This power coming from within us comes from more than the cultural heritage we inhabit—it comes from our place in the living earth. It is a drive to be what we

can be, and it can challenge the boundaries imposed on our lives by a culture or society that wants us to be something else.

Rupert Sheldrake suggests that the 'animist physics' of the Middle Ages and Renaissance was based on the idea of organisms pursuing their own internal purposes. The English word animal comes from *anima*, meaning the soul—not in the sense of a detached 'pilot' of the body, but a creative essence permeating the whole organism. An acorn grew into an oak because it was drawn into the shape of its soul—the soul of an oak. Modern science today still has only a limited understanding of how the genetic information in all living creatures causes them to develop in certain ways. It has followed the mechanistic ideas of Newton and Descartes to their limit, insisting that there is no animating force within, but only a series of mechanisms driven by external forces. At the same time, a religious orthodoxy has focused the animating force on a more and more narrowly defined external entity—God. This dualism has reduced us, and the earth, to passive tools of power.

Rudolf Bahro suggests that this effort to make an artificial divide between the conscious mind and our inner nature has contributed to our alienation from authentic social organization and created a modern society of rationalist, anti-nature institutions which in turn reify abstract thought over raw matter. Even without Bahro's somewhat extreme idealism and belief in rediscovering a spiritual/tribal lifestyle, one can accept that repressing and denying the unconscious is at least a powerful analogy for the subjection of the environment by industrial technology.

If we have an inner nature (to use a Taoist phrase) that can guide us through moral dilemmas and provide a route to authenticity, how does it arise out of material, animal instincts? The study of fractal geometry has given us insights into how simple information can give rise to ordered, complex and highly differentiated systems. The key idea is that of an 'attractor'. Like a ball bearing rolling around a bowl, a system can 'home in on' a steady state. However, the study of complex systems has described attractors far more intricate than the point at the bottom of the bowl—complex, even chaotic vectors that map out a huge range of evolving possibilities, but within boundaries. These dynamical attractors are a modern reinvention of Rupert Sheldrake's *anima*. If you want to speak of soul, there is perhaps some justification for doing so.

No one can tell anyone else what is authentic for them. No measurements nor analysis can predict the exact course of a 'strange' attractor, because its various pathways are too many and varied, and the slightest change in the initial conditions can totally change the result. Our searches for right livelihood involve testing our experiences against the anima within us to find a way forward. This inner nature is not limited to the individual aspiration, but speaks to us of the environment that is right for us and the ways in which we can sustainably interact with it.

We have, then, the power within us to be more than pawns in the greater scheme. Just as the relations between people can be creative, so can the inter- actions inside us. This is not a return to a kind of individualism, but a recog- nition of the creativity of interrelation. The power of law and institution is not all there is—in fact, it is a more superficial level of power that depends for its effectiveness on the unstated, implicit power of social interaction. As I will show in later chapters, this power can take many forms, not all of which are in tune with our inner nature; this is because society is an organism in itself and can develop its own logic. To be powerful, then, is to be self-aware and true to your self. Without this reflection and intuition, we can only reproduce social power, and not shape it creatively.

[Transcript of 'Hugging Demons', a BBC Radio 4 Documentary on alcohol addiction]
Presenter: After the drink and drugs have gone, there's a vacuum. Step 2 [of the rehabilitation process] is an invitation to consider a power greater than our addiction to fill this void.

Reformed Alcoholic: Yeah, I had trouble with the word God. I think the word God drove me back out there. I went to meetings in fear, initially, and as the fear subsided and I got sober I thought, well I've learnt a lot from you good people, but I'm not like you . . . What I did was to go out and suffer some more, lose a lot more . . . Then I was on my knees, and then I was prepared to look at this word God and see that it doesn't have to be associated with religion; it can be a God of my understanding.

Presenter: I quite liked it as an acronym for Good Orderly Direction . . .

Reformed Alcoholic: . . . or Group Of Drunks . . .

Presenter: The Broadway Lodge programme is full of paradox for me. One of them is the serenity of prayer—'God grant me the serenity to accept the things I cannot change/The courage to change the things I can/And the wisdom to know the difference.' As a fully paid-up pagan it always works like a miracle.

Chapter 4

Earthly Powers

Power is not a human invention. In this chapter, I aim to see humans as one of many species on the earth, using and directing flows of energy and resources—power in the most material sense. I introduce energy flow diagrams to illustrate the patterns in energy use, and contrast 'natural' and 'unnatural' energy flows. Consumerism is an example of an unnatural pattern, in which the rise of the commodity causes a destructive and unsustainable use of energy.

The Gaia hypothesis illustrates the complexity and importance of the earth's powers. How have humans drifted so far from co-operation with them? To understand energy flows in human society, we have to add the 'backforces'—the symbolic systems that drive our use and abuse of power. This in turn raises the question of the relationship between material power and social power. How are resources and regulation connected?

In fact matter and culture can be reconciled. Power—the flow of energy—is always self-organizing, and never takes place without pattern or order. Neither matter nor culture should be regarded as the driving force; they are interdependent. Our strategies must respect and draw strength from the powers of the earth, matching organization to ecological reality. Access to land will be essential, and permaculture is a sustainable way for humans to harness the solar power which falls on it.

> She sustains cruel delicate care
> For all her daughters feathers and fur
> Unite as one to march at our side
> To find the place where is to lie
>
> Leaf and bark, bone and hair
> Turn to seed 'neath her stare
> Seed to burst, soar and rise
> Ours for love is the care
> Tending each everywhere
>
> Timelike pulse shakes fierce through chain
> With banks spread calm to reach her flame
> And all is hushed through foul and dim
> Save for the whirr and chime within
>
> —Cardiacs, 'For Good and All'

Since I am concerned to show the connections between the worlds of natural science and social science, it should come as no surprise that the 'scientific' definition of power holds special importance for me. This is the definition of power as the rate of flow of useful energy. Energy is measured in units such as the calorie and the joule, and can be calculated in a number of different ways. The famous equation '$E=mc^2$' shows that energy can be derived from mass and the square of velocity, and that mass is directly related to energy in proportion to the square of c—the speed of light. It can also be defined as 'force through a distance'. Since force is mass times acceleration (for instance, a 1 kg mass in earth's gravitic acceleration, 9.81 m/s^2), then energy can be derived from mass times distance per second per second times distance. Defined in electrical terms, power is measured in watts—voltage times current. Voltage is joules per coulomb (how much energy each 'block' of electrons carries) and current is coulombs per second—so power is the product of these, which is joules (of energy) per second.

What scientific language does is to give us a common language for measuring a number of different forms of power in the same terms—the rate of flow of useful energy. Energy can neither be created nor destroyed (provided we are not converting energy to matter or vice versa), and the laws of thermodynamics tell us two things about the way it 'flows usefully'. The first has to do with entropy—the tendency of all systems to move to states of greater disorder. As energy becomes dispersed, it is less and less available to do useful work. So the only possible processes—the only ones that will take place in the real world—are those where, at the end of the process, the universe is more disordered, more random, than when it started. The whole universe is gradually moving from ordered concentrations of hot and cold to a 'heat death'—an even, random spread of useless background warmth. In gambling terms, you can't win.

The second law of thermodynamics states that in any real process, some energy will always be lost in the form of useless, low quality energy ('waste heat'). This might result from friction, resistance, or accidental radiation. You can minimize it, but never eliminate it; in gambling terms, you can't even break even.

But this begs as many questions as it answers. Surely, what we see around us is not decay and disorder. We see disordered cloud patterns apparently resolving themselves into ordered spirals in tropical storms; we see disordered wasteland bursting into life as plants take over. Where is the entropy here?

These systems of sustained order are known as 'dissipative structures' because they achieve localized order by 'dissipating' waste heat outside the system. In a sense, the earth as a whole is a dissipative structure, receiving high quality solar energy, using it to build ordered living systems and radiating a dull heat. At the end of the day there is only one source of power for the earth—the heat of the sun.[1]

Mapping Energy Flows

For human beings, then, power is experienced as coming from a source (ultimately, the sun, but it may appear to be coming from a fossil fuel, or be matter-
energy conversion such as nuclear power) and moving through a series of
transformations ending in ourselves. At every stage in this process, some
waste is generated—much of it reused in some other process. The scientific
language may give the impression that this is a matter of known, unquestionable facts. In fact, full knowledge of all the pathways and flows in the biosphere—and particularly, how changing one energy flow may affect
another—is beyond us. It would be a mistake to assume that those energy
flows that we have succeeded in identifying and measuring are the only ones
that matter.

A diagrammatic way of representing these flows has been built up in the
life sciences. A number of symbols represent different aspects of the system,
while the lines connecting them show the flows involved. For the study of a
particular system, figures would show the size of the flows; however, as important as this quantitative science may be, our concern is more with the qualitative information—how these flows bring about stasis and change in a system.
It is the arrangement and interconnection of flows that we need to be able to
follow: although change also comes about when a flow grows so as to overload
the system, only in very simple systems can we predict when this will happen.
James Lovelock asked a group of climatologists in Amazonia which they
thought would happen first: the destruction of the Amazonian rainforest, or
the understanding of the consequences of destroying the forests. They replied
that the forests would go first.[2]

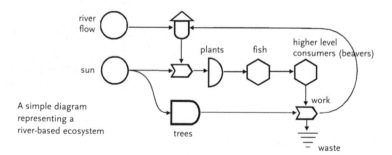

A simple diagram
representing a
river-based ecosystem

For example, the figure above shows a simple energy diagram for a river inhabited by high-level consumers—e.g. a colony of beavers. The sun provides the
main energy input; but the flow of the river is also important, because along
with trees it helps the beavers dam the river and so regulate the fish stocks.
There are two kinds of connection here: the first is the large flows of power that
represent energy, materials and resources being moved and transformed. The
second is represented by the line that doubles back from the beavers' construc-

tions to the fish; it is a relatively small flow of energy—we might see it as the stress in the dam across the river—but because of the effect it has on the size of the lake, it is a controller. Sometimes these flows are not measurable as such, or the level of energy is irrelevant: on other occasions, the controlling effect is a consequence of the large size of the energy flow. Whichever is the case, this flow is not important in itself, but rather as a regulator of another flow. In other cases, it is not a regulator, but a switch—either a flow of energy is enabled, or it is not. Below is a range of symbols used in energy flow diagrams.[3]

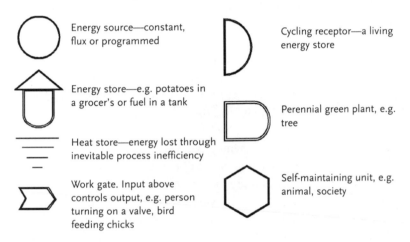

Energy source—constant, flux or programmed

Cycling receptor—a living energy store

Energy store—e.g. potatoes in a grocer's or fuel in a tank

Perennial green plant, e.g. tree

Heat store—energy lost through inevitable process inefficiency

Work gate. Input above controls output, e.g. person turning on a valve, bird feeding chicks

Self-maintaining unit, e.g. animal, society

The living creatures in the flow diagrams are distinguished between the primary producers, or autotrophes (that is, the plants) which simply receive energy and store it, and the consumers (sometimes referred to as heterotrophes, or respirators; in simple terms, animals) which consume stored energy, store it themselves, and use this stored energy to look for more. These are not hard and fast distinctions; the same system can be represented in very different ways, depending on how it is analysed. I have shown fish grouped together separately from plants and beavers; this grouping is arbitrary, and made on the basis of what I want to communicate. I could equally well have grouped together the fish with the beavers and the herbivores, as respirators—or divided up individual species partly into herbivores and partly into carnivores, according to the main constituents of their diet. The divisions and the boundaries are unimportant; the flows are what makes the system stable and living.

Humans and Gaia
Does this have any connection with the conception of power used in the social sciences? In simple terms, it certainly does; replace beavers with humans, and the same diagram describes a pre-industrial fishing village manufacturing nets from hemp. Take it further, and replace the river flow as the source of

power with fossil fuels, and you have a very crude representation of an intensive, industrial farming system. But from the previous chapters we have seen that social power—the switches, controls and regulators on the flow of human energies—is immensely complex and subtle. Can this lifeless scientific classification really tell us anything about a global, industrial, human society?

Undoubtedly human beings cannot escape their biological nature. Energetics commands that in order to do useful work (that is, in thermodynamic terms, to exist) we must transform high value energy into low value energy. In the bounded system that is the earth, that means that we depend on primary producers to continue concentrating the dispersed energy of the sun. In practice, there are other energy sources that we can tap—stored energy in the form of fossil fuels, or the direct conversion of matter to energy in nuclear reactions. However, these are not even close to generating the energy that the sun provides—and if they were, we would have other problems (the greenhouse effect, in the case of fossil fuels, and the considerations in Chapter 2 in the case of nuclear power).

Why should we want to rely on living, evolving systems rather than (for example) a giant greenhouse collecting the sun's energy under controlled conditions? An artificial system is unstable for a number of reasons. If a system is maintained by simply repairing its injuries—a kind of immortality—chance dictates that sooner or later an error will creep in, and the organism will die. If simple reproduction (or cloning) is adopted, without variation, then again chance takes over. Eventually, an error creeps in and the reproduction is increasingly imperfect. Only a diversified system of random variation and natural selection allows indefinite reproduction—not necessarily identical, but always adapted to survive.[4]

The diversity and interconnectedness of different species is the source of our biosphere's stability. Recent developments in ecology have led us to see the world differently: not as an arena for struggle between species, but rather based on interdependence and symbiosis (relationships where two interacting species both benefit). Ecologists have known for a long time that diversity increases stability, though a rigorous proof is hard to find. It is intuitively clear that a highly differentiated system will be better able to adapt to crisis and change, as it has more potential pathways to manage resources and to process energy, and more regulatory mechanisms to respond and adapt.

The Gaia hypothesis has added to this intuitive insight a large-scale model of how it might work. James Lovelock's theory suggests that just as life evolves to fit its environment, so it shapes its environment. As well as the physical environment (climate, oceans, atmosphere, rocks, soil) determining the life forms that can exist, living organisms also shape their physical and chemical surroundings. The implications of this are very far-reaching because they introduce a range of control processes that had not previously been expected.

For instance, scientists had long assumed that since sulphur was washed by rain from the land into the sea, there must be a corresponding physical process that replenished it—for instance, by the oceans emitting hydrogen sulphide. In fact, it became clear in the 1980s that the regulation was being carried out by a number of marine organisms—in particular an algae called *P. Fastigiata*. The process goes even further: the dimethyl sulphide produced by the algae may well be the main cause for the formation of clouds over the ocean. This process works like a thermostat. As the temperature rises, the algae become more active, generate more cloud cover and reflect back more heat from the sun. Experiments in the 1990s confirmed that these processes are taking place, and correlate with global temperature changes (if this seems to the reader like a miracle cure for global warming, I should warn that the full story is not a good one—whether it responds with an ice age or with accelerated warming up to 10 degrees higher than now, there is no reason to believe Gaia will be patient with us).[5]

In short, the power of the earth is not only massive; it is exercised in a very controlled manner, for all that it is exercised unselfconsciously. I would go so far as to say that it lends credence to traditional and pagan spiritualities that revere 'the spirit of the earth'. After all, if it looks like a duck, walks like a duck, and quacks like a duck we would say that it was a duck. This network of self-regulating feedback processes certainly possesses all the essential characteristics of, for instance, the 'Great Spirit' of native American folklore.

We depend on it not merely for the life that stores energy for us to consume, but for the geological and chemical conditions that make life possible. Our social controls are the way we regulate our role in the flows of earthly power; if they clash with the many other control mechanisms predating our own, we will be subject to severe negative feedback. The complexity of these pathways and mechanisms is such that we will never have a definitive scientific statement on what degree of encroachment on other species activities is 'safe'. A better guide might be the culture and practices of indigenous people, adapted to adapting their environment, and a habit of reverence and respect.

The reverse of this fallacy of assuming that human control of power and energy is large enough to give us 'dominion' over the earth, is to assume that our activities are small enough to be lost in the planet's flows. To fell a tree in a vast forest seems insignificant; to tip waste into an ocean that stretches from horizon to horizon seems harmless. But the reality is that human impact is not just measurable, it is dominant.

Net Primary Production is a measure of how much of the sun's energy is captured and stored by plant life (less the energy used by the plants themselves). It is, pretty nearly, the sum total of new energy available for all consumers and decomposers—the earth's shopping basket. "It is estimated that 39.1% of terrestrial NPP . . . is pre-empted or destroyed by people." Pre-empted means that it is

OPPOSING CONSUMERISM

Consume' [-syoom'] vt. eat or drink, possess; use up; destroy -**consu'mer** n. buyer or user of commodity; one who consumes -**consump'tion** n. using up; destruction; wasting disease -**consu'merism** n. the creed of increasing consumption.

Everywhere in the West, people are driven to purchase things they cannot afford, do not need, do not understand or are ignorant of the source of, trying to satisfy themselves as fast as the advertisers can breed dissatisfaction. It seems that we can never have enough; the product that yesterday would bring eternal happiness, is today mundane and commonplace, and tomorrow will be obsolete and inadequate.

Why should Greens oppose consumerism? There are three main reasons: the drive to accumulate, the substitution of technology for nature, and the way that consumerism increasingly sells not just a product, but an image or identity.

The most obvious aspect of consumerism is the drive for 'more'. By definition it does not seek to satiate our desires, but instead to indefinitely increase our consumption, meaning that needs must be created rather than merely responded to. On a finite world, this makes no sense. It is hard to believe that our capacity to experience pleasure has kept pace with the abundance of commodities. What is really happening is that more resource-intensive ways to provide pleasure are replacing the existing ones. Our lifestyle must be made increasingly complicated in order for our levels of consumption to be increased further. In ecological terms, it is a determined effort to maximize the amount of energy lost to the 'heatsink' in respiration. Any act of consumption to maintain an organism involves a transformation of stored energy, and entropy demands that some energy be 'lost' (i.e. dispersed, degraded or otherwise made less useful) in this process. Consumerism seeks to increase the flow of energy and materials with no benefit to the organism. Consider the manufacture of packaging; the energy of the sun and fossil fuels, and the work of people, go into creating something that is a dead end—it cannot easily be used or digested by the biosphere.

The expansion of the consumerist machine demands that natural, self-reliant communities be replaced by controllable, 'productive' and dependent technological systems. Since biological processes of supply are based on 'enough' rather than continuous increase, technology must be substituted for biology. An example of this might be the baby milk market. The vast majority of mothers are quite capable of feeding their babies on breast milk; it contains the appropriate amounts of protein for the human baby, all necessary nutrients, antibiotics, and the mother's immunity to diseases. Bottle feeding, outside exceptional circumstances, has little or no value: and yet it has become so widespread as to be considered the norm. This 'infant formula', made from cow's milk, is much inferior to breast milk, and if not carefully made up under hygienic conditions can be extremely dangerous. Above all else, it is not free. Indeed, in Third World countries it is very expensive; and yet 'bottle baby syndrome' is becoming more and more a cause of illness and death.[6] This process of commodification—the creation of new product lines—obstructs and destroys biological processes that are not only invariably superior, but also important in other ways in regulating the biosphere.

Commodification is a subtle process: an apple in itself is not a commodity—anyone can pick it off the tree and eat it without having to purchase it. To make it into a commodity a range of institutions are needed—access to the tree must be controlled, the number of trees can be limited, the social importance of apples might be increased (or the importance of apples packaged as a commodity), etc. etc. Ideally, the knowledge that apples come from trees would be suppressed.

Indeed, the clean, sterile, high tech image is one which consumerism promotes, denying any natural or human history to the product. Inquiry into the source, method of production, byproducts or other external costs is carefully discouraged. Brands and labels develop associations and images that will reassure the consumer. It is as much the image as the product itself that is on sale: buying a product, we buy an identity ('Flora man', 'Marlboro Man'), a lifestyle (McDonalds=company, fun, acceptance by your peers), and a set of myths (the good mother, the nuclear family). Almost as important as the products on sale in shopping centres are the other events that take place that give them an image. Recycling facilities suggest environmental awareness, celebrity visits suggest glamour . . . Shopping centres are promoted now as a 'family day out'; the importance of 'providing for your family' makes a good lever, and never forget that the children of today are the consumers of tomorrow . . . The increasing number of shopping centres that have cinemas, bowling alleys and other 'leisure facilities' illustrates two things: firstly that shopping is regarded by many as a leisure activity in itself, not merely a means to satisfy needs; and secondly that culture is becoming a collection of commodities to be consumed.

In short, consumerism is a complex system for disconnecting us from biological mechanisms, disconnecting our control over our own consumption, and disconnecting us from each other.

---

used directly by people or in human-dominated ecosystems. About half of this takes place in the conversion of ecosystems—forest to pasture, pasture to agriculture, agriculture to built environment. The other half takes place in the form of pre-empting in systems already modified: principally harvests and grazing.[7] These flows of stored energy represent a seizure of power by humans from other species, and cannot be achieved without the destruction of innumerable control mechanisms. It is not that the power to modify the earth is being lost, but that it is being applied randomly and chaotically. Huge concentrations of output in one place constitute a crisis for an ecosystem, where evenly dispersed they would be resources. Inefficient use of stored energy creates low quality wastes that provide no opportunities for other species. Synthetic materials block processes, over-stimulate other processes, or constitute unregulated processes in themselves. The ways in which humans are meeting their needs today seem increasingly to depend on these 'unnatural' flows of energy.

The Nature of Nature

Is it possible to speak of a system as being 'natural'? As many writers have pointed out, humanity has shaped its environment in so many places that it is hard to see anywhere that is genuinely natural. Natural moors and heaths have been created by patterns of clearance and grazing. Natural grassland was once forests. Natural rainforests have been seeded by generations of itinerant hunter-gatherers. How can we appeal to nature, if nature is artificial?

Such a conception of nature was always doomed to collapse. If the oppo-site of nature is artificial (i.e. created by humans) then we are defining humans as separate from nature—as unnatural beings. But clearly we are as much of this earth as any other mammal. Only a tiny percentage of DNA separates us from chimpanzees. We eat, we breathe, we defecate. Anything we do is natural; anything we create becomes part of nature. Is it then meaningless to speak of acting 'against nature'?

I do not believe it is. To regard nature as an object makes it impossible to draw a distinction—in that sense, everywhere is natural. But there is a way of describing nature that does not collapse into meaninglessness: as a process. In the many different processes underway in the universe—the life cycles of stars, the expansion of galaxies, the weathering of planets under planetoid impacts—nature is the one process that we have a particular interest in. It is the growth and diversification of life on earth, and it is a process that we depend upon for survival. Indeed, our own reproduction, life and activity is potentially a part of it. I say potentially, because not all human activity takes this process forward; it can also—and does—hold it back or even reverse it. Agriculture could be described as an artificially immature system. A natural process operating on it would increase species diversity, add canopy and bush layers, recycle nutrients and add grazers and predators higher up the food chain. The movement from grassland to brush, brush to woodland, and wood-land to forest, is called succession. Nature as process is remorseless in doggedly pursuing this route; in the course of human history we have shown ourselves capable of furthering it, by planting trees, distributing seeds, cop-picing, and raising our families.

Nature as a process is continually developing along several clear lines. There is a progressive increase in biomass—living matter—as the growth of more and larger organisms becomes possible. There is an increase in species diversity:

each new species that exploits a niche in the system creates further niches for others to occupy. The number of interconnections and pathways through the system multiplies as the system matures.

Even if there is a 'natural way', why should we follow it? As living creatures, we owe our origin to it. It may well be that we depend on healthy natural systems to survive as well. We are inevitably tied into the processes that reproduce air that we can breathe, water we can drink and food we can eat. Although some or all of our needs can be met by technological systems that would provide new pathways from energy sources to our consumption, it requires a great optimism in human ingenuity to believe that we could ever satisfactorily replace highly stable and differentiated systems that have evolved over millions of years with our own—and more to the point, why should we want to? Furthermore, by removing or competing with natural processes, we risk a breakdown of processes we had previously taken for granted. Finally, a way of living that is at odds with natural processes will invariably be at odds with people also. There is no choice between looking after people and looking after the earth; the same tools, ideas and institutions that destroy nature also oppress people (see Chapter 6).

How Society Directs Energy
Throughout this chapter I have referred to humans as the agency of 'unnatural' development. There is a problem with treating humans as a discrete block in the biosphere; just like the ecosystem described above, it is an arbitrary division. Humans are not the only consumers; nor are all humans consuming on the same level. It might make more sense to categorize humans by their lifestyle—a tribal hunter-gatherer is, in ecological terms, indistinguishable from any other omnivorous predator. The changes they make to their physical environment are little greater than the equivalent biomass of beavers or termites. Even some individual humans in industrial societies have a very small practical impact—though they are in a tiny minority. And the humans living a highly destructive lifestyle might be categorized alongside the non-humans playing a destructive role. A number of island ecosystems have been devastated by species as diverse as rabbits, pigs, cats and rhododendron being introduced without natural controls or predators; and their impact on biomass, diversity and ecosystem stability is just as destructive of nature as the human developers and destroyers.

There is one difference. An unemployed, itinerant human who purchases cheap food from a supermarket is, as an individual, having a very small impact. He (for the sake of argument, I assume a male) is collecting resources from the very end of a number of pathways of energy and materials. His actual act of consumption degrades an already highly processed form of energy that was not available to any other part of the ecosystem, and is no greater in size than any other similar animal. However, his purchase has consequences of its own. Money flows back to the producer of the food, and with it information about demand. As profits, it continues its flow back to the shareholders, with a new kind of information—profitability. And that leads to decisions about investment and development that are potentially destructive on a scale far beyond the individual's consumption. This 'backforce' that is the money system is included in flow diagrams by the ecologist Howard Odum. He describes it as a 'loop reward selector',[8] by which he means that production by one person is immediately rewarded; it is a form of positive feedback loop. This leads us to a second level of modelling, in which economics is accounted for as a backforce on the energy flow.[9] This would not be explainable in energy terms alone, because there would be no explanation of how the 'switches' worked, controlling the flow of materials into the industry and the flow of materials out.

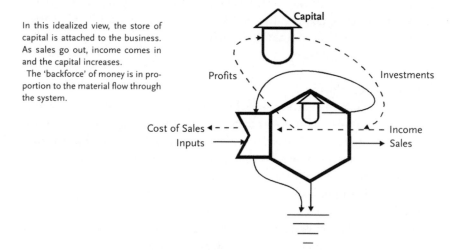

In this idealized view, the store of capital is attached to the business. As sales go out, income comes in and the capital increases.

The 'backforce' of money is in proportion to the material flow through the system.

However, there are problems with this depiction of economics. There is a tendency in Odum's writing to equate money and energy as though the latter was always reflected in the former. Although he points out that the 'ratio of money to energy' increases downstream (that is, as the product reflects more work and less raw materials and is increasingly processed), he does not account for the energy and material flows that take place without regard for money. An industrial process takes in energy and materials, and produces a product; but there are a great many other inputs that are regarded as 'free goods' (such as air and water) and outputs that similarly carry no cost or profit, such as effluent, waste heat, gases, unwanted packaging, valueless byproducts and so on. These may well have economic effects—if the water table drops too far, life becomes expensive for everyone. But this energy input carries no cost. They are 'externalities'.

Odum shows that economic backforces can be a useful way to regulate a human community; credit allows us to ride out temporary shortages of goods, and it is a regulator of individuals' consumption. But there is more than one way of doing this, and the Western conception of money and property is not necessarily the best. The issues around this are explored in more detail elsewhere; in Chapter 6 I consider the particular character of property and money in industrial culture, and in Chapter 12 LETS (Local Exchange Trading Systems) provide an example of an economic system founded on different values and working in a different way. In reality, money often does not operate as a backforce: most flows of energy and resources taking place today are to a large extent detached from this feedback. Money comes from a variety of sources to a managing body, which directs how energy and materials should be used.

In this more realistic model of a business, the capital store is more of a determining force. It can redirect its investment to other businesses if the return from this one is unsatisfactory. It can control the functioning of the business to increase its returns.

The backforce is not simply shadowing flows of matter, but has a symbolic power of its own.

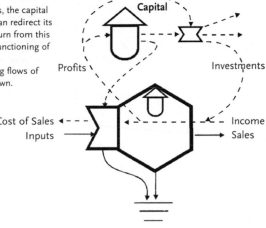

Is Power a Material or Cultural Phenomenon?

Money is of course only one of a great many controls acting on humans. As we have seen in the previous two chapters, language and technology are also important. Energy flow diagrams have difficulty depicting the more subtle influences that shape us and our actions. If we use the three categories of power suggested by Boulding and Galbraith (see Chapter 1)—threat, exchange, and communicative—then we can see that they are ideal for describing the first two, but less effective for the third. And yet most of the power that we experience is a result of our interaction with people at this more insubstantial level. How do we reconcile this with the importance that material flows along the earth's energy pathways have for our survival?

Since the ancient Greeks, this question has been posed as a choice between materialism and idealism—two different theories of what is real and important. Materialism asserts that matter determines ideas: our thoughts are just effects produced by the mechanisms of our brains, responding to

CONSUMERISM IN THE NORTH OF ENGLAND

Like any cult, consumerism has its temples. Meadowhall shopping centre is one of the most obvious in the North of England. As big as a fair sized village, it stands astride the river Don by the side of the M1 motorway. Its central dome reminds you of St Paul's Cathedral, its covered arcades and galleries suggest a vast monastery, its various chapels are dedicated to deities such as Marks and Spencer, and the vast expanses of car parking suggest the squares and court-yards of holy cities. Yet at night it is lit like a funfair, and inside you can hardly see the surfaces for the sparkle, and you are bombarded with disorientating dis-tractions. Meadowhall was the largest shopping centre in Europe when it opened. In its first year its turnover exceeded £500 million.

Consumerism in the North of England is closely linked with local govern-ment: Meadowhall had to obtain planning permission from Sheffield City, and was carried out in co-operation with the Development Corporation. 'Landmark Leeds', a project to convert the city centre into a prestige shopping district attracting more consumers to the self-styled 'regional capital', has been strongly promoted by the Council. Indeed it has earned the name 'Trickett's Folly', after the then Council leader Jon Trickett.

The metropolitan councils increasingly measure success in terms of attracting investment, in the belief that this will create jobs. Also, with central government reining in expenditure, and the Poll Tax all but uncollectable (despite bullying and cajoling those unable to pay), income from local business is a vital source of revenue. This revenue can then be spent on high profile developments that promote the city as a centre for investment, and so on. This has led to increasingly direct competition for consumers: as the size of shop-ping centres grows, so the area from which consumers must be drawn in grows. Meadowhall was advertised as 'just down the M1 from Leeds' shortly before the big push for 'Landmark Leeds' began.

What are the costs of this competition? Local economies suffer, as big capital is prioritized over local capital. Shopping Centres start as collaborations between the local authority (which must provide planning permission, techni-cal assistance and infrastructure), the backers (often multinational—the people who brought you Meadowhall are currently at work on another in Germany, leading the German Green MEP Berbel Honn to visit Sheffield on a fact-finding tour), and the big chainstores, who provide a ready-made image, guaranteed customers and big money. This, plus the high costs of moving into a prestige shopping centre, ensure that most businesses operating there are national or multinational concerns. A sizeable part of money spent there flows straight into the corporate account rather than circulating more quickly, accountably and productively in the local economy. Since Meadowhall opened,

Sheffield has seen a loss of trade in the city centre; combined with the recession, this means bad news for local small businesses. The initial swell of jobs
that was promised has failed to materialize, suggesting quite possibly a net
loss in employment. Meanwhile, the local community stores are reduced to
corner shops and video rentals; hardly the basis for local self-reliance. It is not
simply that the local shops cannot compete in terms of price (though they
can't, given the bulk purchasing and distribution of the large chains, and the
ability to run loss leaders) but that the branded, packaged commodities in the
superstores offer benefits in terms of identity, status, prestige and image in
addition to any material worth they may have.

    This means that even if they weren't impressed with the advertising, the
need to buy essential goods prompts people to travel considerable distances to
do their shopping. The size of the car parks around Meadowhall bear witness
to the scale of the endeavour; the environmental costs are staggering. The
increasing road traffic figures lend justification for road building projects such
as the completion of the Leeds inner ring road, or the upgrading of the A1.
Meanwhile, the deaths and pollution continue to mount.

    Finally, the slick packaging and short life goods, not to mention the pro-
duction wastes, must all be disposed of somewhere; areas of moorland around
the North are being targeted for landfill sites. Recent investigations suggest
that most wastes are failing to break down in these gigantic shallow graves,
with lettuces several years old being exhumed intact. The endless cycle of consumerism cannot go on forever.

---

external physical events. Idealism argues the reverse: that thoughts, spiritual
forces or ideal forms are the determining force; material reality is just the
outcome of this higher power.

    At first sight, materialism might appear to be the most suitable approach
for those concerned with sustainability. It suggests that there is nothing very
special about us which sets us apart from nature; we are physical creatures,
products of our environment. While that link is still there, materialist thinking
can actually be seen most clearly in right-wing philosophies of 'enlightened
self-interest', or in nihilistic, hedonistic behaviour.

    But this is not all it has given us. It has given us a desacralized world, an
inert planet with no intrinsic value; a collection of resources to be exploited
according to our desires. Even the living creatures that populate it are just
automata, driven by animal instinct. This can apply to people too; as workers,
they are treated like robots. For the individual materialist, there is no higher
morality to aim for, just gratification of the senses. The individual is alone,
with nothing but species or self-interest in common with other people, and
nothing at all with the rest of the natural world. Materialism cannot concede

the meaningfulness of anything that cannot be seen, touched and measured. In politics, materialism was in the past associated with Marxism. While this remains true, its main offspring is probably the idea of technocracy: rule by élite teams of managers, administrators, neutral and unideological, fine tuning the machine of industrial society.

Does idealism provide the answer to this uninspiring vision? In its most extreme forms, it argues that the material world is an illusion produced by our minds; however, it is more commonly found as the idea that ideas determine matter, as in religions with an interventionist deity or Hegel's dialectical progress towards an 'ultimate idea'.

In the Green movement, idealism is represented by the New Agers, who are confident that the dawning of the Age of Aquarius will cause people to see the error of their ways, becoming global-minded, unselfish and benevolent. There are no physical barriers to human achievement; with liberated minds we can do anything.

But this view also is loaded with dangers. A philosophy that reduces everything to ideas can lead us to ignore the very real material pressures that force people into a destructive role. We end up blaming people for the consequences rather then diagnosing the root causes. It can also produce élitism in 'the enlightened': just as materialism reifies the 'experts', so idealism creates a hierarchy of priests and gurus. It sees only intentions, not actions; it doesn't matter if you're a merchant banker or a director of ICI, provided you're spiritually pure. By turning our attentions inward, it can lead to neglect of the palpably real outside world.

Dualism is presented as the solution to the problem of an undeniably important material world and the undeniably important world of ideas. The two exist together, but are separate save for the interaction of our bodies with our souls. Since in dualism the 'I' is the mental, thinking part (as in Descartes' famous "Cogito ergo sum"), the spiritual sphere is generally seen as dominant, or higher. Dualism has been very influential in modern Western culture.

But dualism is another highly individualist philosophy, regarding our souls in perfect isolation, removed from the physical world. Indeed, by combining introvertedness and a desacralized material world, it combines the worst features of materialism and idealism. Moral and ethical laws operate only in the world of the mind, a personal, private sphere: in the profane world, pragmatism reigns. By seeing our body almost as clothes for the mind, it is the philosophy of the plastic surgeon and cosmetics industry, not to mention allopathic medicine and narcotics abuse. The total divorce of the sciences (all about matter) and the humanities (all about ideas) makes the former heartless, callous and arrogant, and the latter unreal, irrelevant, and academic. Physical work is scorned in favour of mental labour; a 'higher' plane of creativity. A hierarchy is justified, with the 'civilized' human at the top (the mental worker;

manager, planner, thinker) and the 'primitive' less-than-human below (the manual worker, peasant or housewife).

There are signs that a different view of reality is emerging, which does not treat matter as inert and predictable, or spirit as supernatural and detached. This can be seen in the new sciences of the last century. Quantum theory has introduced the idea of uncertainty, and destroyed the previously clear distinction between matter and energy. Ecology, along with cybernetics, has given us the idea of interdependence, and systems as wholes rather than the sum of parts. Finally, chaos theory reintroduces mystery; where the God of the Gaps merely constructed and tinkered with an automatic and predictable machine, we now have an unpredictable, unstable flux of matter and energy, out of which complexity and order emerge and collapse constantly.

The riddle of the material and the ideal seems to end not in the domination of one or the other or the separation of both, but rather in their reconciliation. The Universe is material, real, tangible; but it is also sacred and mysterious. Whether it is predictable or unpredictable, self-directing or directed varies according to which part you study, at what level you study it and at what time you are studying it; the flow and flux of energy and the dance of matter form their own patterns, and every part of the universe may be affected by every other.

Materialism, idealism and dualism all provide an insufficient basis within which to define a strategy, in part because they are among the ideas that legitimize this domination. Materialism encourages us to tackle only effects, without seeing their ideological basis; idealism breeds apathy and empty rhetoric—the belief that if we simply point out to people what is happening, they will mend their ways. Dualism promises spiritual purity, while endorsing the expoitation of anything and anyone outside 'civilization'. It achieves the worst of both worlds by denying the links between the two sides: without an ideological and ethical basis, our practical actions play the political game by existing rules, meaning that we must either lose or become like the competition; while ideas, values and theories become academic and irrelevant.

The Relationship between Nature and Culture

We do not have to choose between seeing power as the flow of energy or as the interaction of human beings. It is in the nature of entropy that concentrated energy 'wants' to flow, to disperse itself. The charge on a cloud in a thunderstorm wants to flow to earth; the rain falling on the highlands wants to flow downhill. What we learn by observing the way they achieve this, is that flow is quicker in an ordered system. The static charge in a thundercloud doesn't seep out evenly, but discharges along a pathway which (we can see from slow motion film) almost 'feels' its way to the path of least resistance. Similarly, water doesn't just spread out on a hillside, but cuts itself a gully and establishes a riverbed. These are examples of entropy—the universal tendency to

THE CAUSES OF CONSUMERISM

A key question in analysing consumerism is one of human nature. Many begin (and end) with the premise that people are greedy, and have always sought to maximize consumption, and will always seek to do so.[10] I would argue that this is oversimplistic, and regardless of whether or not it is true, cannot be sufficient to explain consumption patterns. Firstly, too much consumption is directed to activities people don't actually enjoy: many, for instance, dislike driving, but consume huge quantities of resources in owning and using a car. Secondly, much consumption is of things that could not possibly be instinctively demanded: teenage mutant ninja turtles, for instance. There have to be reasons why people buy such highly specific things, without having previously wanted them. Thirdly, much of what is purchased is very rapidly being thrown away; people are consuming not only things they want, but also many things that are of no interest to them, such as packaging. Fourthly, the continuing success of charity demonstrates that people are quite prepared to make material sacrifices, even on a regular basis, to tackle a social or environmental problem; even if people are generally greedy, they are also generally compassionate. It is undoubtedly true that, as Irvine and Ponton say, "an attitude of 'enough' must replace that of 'more'",[11] but it is still insufficient to explain why people consume so much.

There are questions of ignorance, in terms of people's inability to conceptualize the circumstances which make an act of consumption possible—for instance, people are unaware that oil is so cheap because America supports despotic rulers in the Middle East who exploit their populations, or people's lack of knowledge about the grim pay and conditions of people harvesting tea in India. Often this ignorance is connected with myths or comforting illusions—when people buy eggs, they think of a few chickens strutting around a yard pecking at seed, rather than thousands of debeaked and crippled birds in small cages stacked on top of one another. Thirdly, there is a failure to connect problems of excess with one's own contribution. Because a traffic jam is so huge, the individual driver can ignore his or her own contribution; people are acutely aware of the consequences of overconsumption in their own back yard, but continue with a lifestyle that creates identical problems in someone else's back yard. In all cases, the separation of cost and benefit, cause and effect, production and consumption, supply and demand, is sufficient to insulate consumers from the consequences of their decisions. The separation exists in geographical distance, in time (through the delay before the consequences become apparent), and in the complexity of the processes leading up to the act of consumption.

While fundamental needs are ahistorical, ways of meeting them have changed dramatically; similarly, while there have always been 'wants', their nature today is quite distinctive. Andy Dobson argues that marketing is a significant factor, drawing our attention to "the role of advertising the habits and practises of consumption that [the Greens] seek to criticize".[12] Firstly, marketing stands accused of encouraging irresponsibility: with its raison d'être being to increase and diversify sales, it is directly in opposition to any attempt to reduce through-put of resources. The principal defence of this is that advertising only seeks to encourage a choice between rival brands: however, this hardly stands up to scrutiny. There is a distinct ideology that emerges from the requirements of any promotional campaign: the elevation of the importance of commodities to an unreal level, coupled with a progressive superficiality that first denies any history or separate components to the commodity, then denies the importance of the commodity itself relative to the brand, image or corporate identity associated with it.[13] Beyond selling us objects, consumerism now sells us an entire alternate reality, including self-image, aspirations, wish fulfilment and comforting preju-dices. The original analysis of reification and commodity fetishization came from Marx; today, however, the dominance of consumerism goes further. Where capital accumulation led to the selling of particular commodities, consumerism sells conformity to a way of life based on self-realization through consumption.

Marketing is not only about the creation of desires, but also the creation of needs. Where there are 'free' goods—the result of biological processes—consumerism is unnecessary. In order to gain a competitive advantage, marke-teers need somehow to introduce artifical products in competition with these natural ones, often with fraudulent claims about their superiority. It is not suf-ficient to blame the 'profit motive' for such substitution of inappropriate com-modities for appropriate natural processes: it requires an ideology that views such natural systems as 'dirty', 'unhygienic', 'uncivilized'. While it is the case that many corporate marketing divisions strengthen this ideology, it is also true that the assumption that natural systems are chaotic, messy, unplanned and uncontrollable, and require the intervention of technology and commodities to allow their 'commodification' and hence ownership, sale and marketing.

The change of needs does not take place only in response to advertising campaigns, but also in response to social, political and economic changes. Once we have established a society in which workplaces are large in scale, the shopping centre is the main outlet for goods, and amenities are centralized in a few locations, then a car moves from being a luxury to a necessity. Affluent lifestyles create role models: the riches of the few, then, become a motor of con-sumption for the many.

disorder—generating order as it proceeds: the dissipative structures referred to earlier. Power creates dissipative structures in just the same way, and just as it is impossible to say whether the river created the gully or the gully created the river, there is no hierarchy of importance between the flows of power or the mechanisms of control. Both are necessary, and rarely if ever is a flow of energy seen without ordering dissipative systems. This is the same as Foucault's belief that that there is no power without knowledge. No material fact can fail to generate cultural systems, just as cultural systems create and regulate the flow of power. Ultimately, they are the same thing.

However, just as lightning never strikes along precisely the same path, there are any number of possible forms of organization for human society—and for the biosphere as a whole. Just as rivers divide and meander and shift their course over time, so different systems of power rise and fall and dissipate energy in different ways. A clear and sustainable pathway may endure; another may generate its own blockages and fail.

A sustainable system builds up biomass, in order to make the most use of the power available—every bit of light that hits the earth is collected and stored, every output an input somewhere else. Similarly it becomes more diverse, with interconnected units allowing the system to be responsive and adaptive, adjusting to changing circumstances. Loss of biomass happens when a blockage appears—diverting the flows of energy needed to reproduce the system, or support other parts of the system. Loss of diversity takes place when the collective regulation of the different species is interrupted, and an external regulation imposed. It is normal enough for one species that is particularly well adapted to conditions to be dominant; but other species, even those seeking to fill the same ecological niche, should still be present to some extent. In general, a sustainable system exhibits self-regulation, and an unsustainable or unstable system is other-regulated.

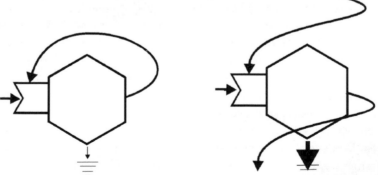

Any strategy for social change must be aware of energy flow—power in the most basic sense. Power is not an exclusively human phenomenon, and only by understanding its flow through all species can we distinguish sustainable

CHALLENGING CONSUMERISM

'Green consumerism' has been a useful starting point; by raising awareness of the histories of products, and the records of companies, it has cracked the consumerist veneer. Boycotts and demands for Greener goods will continue to be important. However, for the less well off, cost and access make Green consumerism a game they cannot play; and companies are adapting fast to the new conditions, separating Green consumers from the rest. Non-consumerist ways of meeting people's needs will have to be promoted and practised. These include self-provisioning through allotments and permaculture, and skills exchanges; co-operative purchasing, such as Food Co-ops and Local Employment and Trading Schemes; and co-operative production and retail.

Advertising is the medium through which consumerism's myths are re-established; the creative defacing of advertising hoardings has been used to turn the advertisers' weapons against them. Economic sabotage of the consumerist machine slows its expansion; this can be done by denying it access to land, and resisting the construction of the roads, landfills and power stations that accompany its growth. Encouraging people to boycott the most destructive shopping centres, and publicising planning battles, may help to frighten off likely investors, or persuade them to invest elsewhere.

Local government will be a crucial area; the development strategies adopted will determine whether the local environment is orientated towards consuming, or towards living. Audits of local communities will identify areas needing development; basic infrastructure, such as local markets and small workshops, will increase local trading; and many of the campaigns described above will benefit from local government backing.

The alternative is not just piecemeal opposition, but a struggle to establish a completely different way of meeting needs. Permaculture is the term coined by Bill Mollison for the design of sustainable systems, and it provides a framework for a non-consumerist society.

The term is a contraction of 'permanent culture' and is concerned very much with flows of power and resources. A number of design principles guide the permaculture practitioner, relating to the ways in which different elements should be ordered. The goal is a productive, sustainable, ecosystem—the most efficient use of the energy and resources available to the system.

These principles include the idea that every output should be an input. In terms of an energy flow diagram, this has the effect of minimizing the energy loss to the heatsink, by including in the system elements that can collect and use even the most degraded and diffuse outputs, and themselves have outputs that are usable by other elements.

Permaculture achieves levels of efficiency achieved in natural systems because, for although it is based on human designs, it follows a natural process. It mixes diverse species, uses biological regulation and maximizes biomass by encouraging perennial plants and trees. Plants are stacked—herb layer, shrub layer, bush layer, up to the canopy created by the highest trees. Every permaculture system contains a zone of wilderness—not as a token 'set aside' but as a resource. Wilderness is the teacher, suggesting new arrangements of plants, new ways to conserve energy, and harbouring new species.

Every element in the system has multiple functions, and every function is served by multiple elements. This creates a highly stable system in which the needs of all the plants and animals are met—including the human designer. Indeed, the human residents are designed into the system; a mature permaculture design should require little intervention, being as far as possible self-regulating. The humans simply harvest to meet their needs, contribute seed distribution and composted wastes, and maintain structures.

The original idea of permaculture as 'permanent agriculture' rapidly mutated into 'permanent culture'. Bill Mollison realized that principles of cycling, diversity, relative location, energy conservation and small scale were applicable to non-agricultural technology, to economics, and even to social order. Permaculture is underpinned by an ethical core—earth care, people care, and fair shares—and this applies to people's dealings with each other as much as with the earth.

So economic systems that are favoured are those that encourage rapid, even, local trading, and do not take more from the biotic community than it can spare. Organizational structures are designed to be responsive to local conditions, co-operative, open and participatory. These are not merely consistent with the permacultural lifestyle—they are a necessary component for it to succeed.

In contrast to the rule of the commodity in consumerism, permaculture puts people directly in touch with the source, allowing for local, democratic regulation. This alone ensures that natural flows of power develop and are maintained—which contrasts with the destructive, lethal power of consumerism.

---

systems from those which have no future. This is not to say that power in human society can only be understood in terms of energy flow diagrams—any more than the understanding of power relations between humans can tell us whether it will rain tomorrow. All these systems have their own internal dynamic, and over the short term it is study at that level that will tell us the most. But anyone concerned with long range planning to avert human and ecological crisis and insecurity needs to be able to link both together.

Access to land will for this reason be crucial for any strategy for social change. There may be millions of dollars controlled by corporations, and millions of votes held by politicians, but they are ultimately just symbols. What they refer to is real flows of energy—almost all of which comes from the sun and is captured at the surface of the Earth. A third of that—and the most easily accessible third—is on dry land. This is why land has always been the rallying cry for so many social movements. The power bases of the rulers can always be dispensed with, provided our connection with the land is secure.

OXBOW, NY—The residents of Sylvia Lake blew up a beaver dam this summer, but dynamite proved no match for America's most industrious rodent. Within four days the beavers had rebuilt their dam, stopping up a crucial outlet and raising Sylvia Lake to problem levels once again. On the fourth of July, people barbecued on docks under six inches of water. "You come out here, you want to cook your dinner, and you take your shoes off," said Gale Ferguson, a commercial printer who in nearly five decades on Sylvia Lake had never seen the water so high. Branding beavers as "the enemy", Mr Ferguson sounded an ominous call. "We've played their game for five years," he said. "Now that they're winning we have to get serious."

Nearly wiped out by trapping and farming in the 19th century, beavers have come back. "Beavers have no social life," Mr Ferguson sighed. "They had 24 hours a day to do this. They're near impossible to keep up with."—*New York Times*

Part Two

Social Change

Chapter 5

The Source of Hope

Although power completely permeates our lives, it is not seamless or undifferentiated. Intellectually and intuitively we can identify different kinds of power. Our experience is dominated by the dominant 'power-over'—external regulation or control. There is also 'power-to' ('power with' and 'empowerment' are broadly similar concepts) which corresponds to ecological self-regulation. These two forms of power are incompatible, in the sense that the spread of one must be at the expense of the other.

The Green movement has for some time been aware of the need to discriminate between these different forms of power, but the difficulty of pinning down empowerment in a culture so wholly dominated by power-over has caused confusion. By removing modifiers and amplifiers of power from the picture, we can see more clearly the distinctive categories.

This has considerable implications for the agency of Green social change—the Greens' 'class analysis'. If the commitment to empowering relations, and the opposition to power-over, are the distinctive features of the Green constituency, then those movements arising from resistance to the most oppressive and overt uses of power-over will be a key audience. Because they will all be developing empowering alternatives, there is a commonality of interest between them.

Byrom Mann of the Powder Posse
Exp 7 Years minimum 5/7/93

Steve Green is a grass

Daz Brown ere
18/4/96
19/4/96

RD ON DA SASS
EXP 3-5 YRS
SEC 20 GBH
WOUNDING
BEEN OUT 5 WEEKS
FROM A 3 YR

DID 20 MONTH NO BOVA!

 Robbo ov Derby 96
Got 2 yrs Derby Crown

RD GEANELLY
EXP 3YRS AGAIN!

FUCK THIER LAW
SMOKE YOUR DRAW

GOD GAVE ALL THE SEED BEARING PLANTS AND HERBS TO USE

Robbie McBeath 96 You're all Fucked Northern Gypos

Don't know what you saw but you know its against the law and you know you want some more

Keep Buzzin Lads

—Graffiti seen in Chesterfield Police Station cells, October 97

We are bound together in a web of power—a flow of energy from source to dissipation, out of which we build the order and pattern of our lives. Yet, this is not a seamless web, but one in which we can see contrasts and boundaries between the different patterns formed.

I'm sitting in my room looking out over Chapeltown, Leeds, with power flowing all around me. The sun is beating down, ripening the pears on the tree. In the drive, someone is working on a van, hauling on a spanner. My stereo's speakers are vibrating, driven by the potential difference between live and neutral in the wires. Here, at the extremity of the national grid, it is small, but somewhere else—let us say nearby Ferrybridge—a huge, rapidly spinning turbine is generating the current that I and countless others are using. The turbine is driven by energy released by coal—perhaps the coal dug from the vast opencast mines near Leeds. The plants collecting the power of the sun and the creatures living in the soil have been scraped from the surface and a vast black hole dug, releasing a fine choking dust into the atmosphere. The people doing this are only aware of a fraction of the consequences of their actions; they are preoccupied with the belief that they have to do these things in order to build their own power, in order to realize their aspirations.

The building I am living in represents a huge store of potential energy, and also a space within which order can be generated and maintained. The structure of the building is itself maintained by the Housing Co-operative which owns it, which is a symbol that tells us that we all, equally, own and control the property we inhabit. Of course, we also have the symbol of a mortgage from the Ecology Building Society, which helped us buy the houses. This building society gets its power from investors, who pass on their power on the condition that it will be ethically invested while it accumulates. This is one of many ideas presently in my head as I sit here. Of the energy flowing through my body, that needed to sustain and generate these ideas is a very small amount. But it is the tiny ideas that regulate small actions that have large repercussions of the kind that established all these flows of power.

Intuitively, we put value on power. We believe that there is good and bad power, and that we can make good or bad choices—not just clever or stupid, or profitable or wasted, but morally right or wrong. I hope the previous chapter has shown that this is not just a pious fantasy, but a real consequence of the way life uses energy. Some systems of power—those I described as 'other regulated'—show a tendency to accelerate the disorganizing effect of entropy. Others, characterized by self-regulation, have shown the capacity for establishing 'dissipative structures' that locally sustain more ordered systems. We are ourselves ordered systems, and we depend on the ordered system of the biosphere to maintain us. So we there is a definite sense in which power is necessarily laden with values—working for life or against it. Of course the power of living things is such that it can often survive despite such interference. But beyond a certain point this homeostasis becomes impossible, and the stress leads to a failure to function properly. We see this most clearly in our society in those people who struggle to survive from day to day, and who have lost almost all power over their own lives—the poor.

Poverty manifests itself as an absence. It appears to be a lack of power, a lack of resources flowing. In fact, there is no shortage of power in poverty: there is mutual aid, there is regulation and control, there is force and violence, there is the struggle for survival. All these powers establish the sophisticated structures and cultures of poverty.

Different Powers

Of course, the lines are not drawn as clearly as these simple categorizations might at first suggest. Real life presents us with tangled nets of power which defy easy categorization, and I do not mean to suggest that self- and other-controlled are the only two possibilities. I will explain shortly why I think those two are worth concentrating on, but the number of possible patterns of power is quite possibly infinite. Some will be rare or even theoretical possibilities only. In many cases patterns will be mixed together, and the overall character of a given power structure hard to establish. Nonetheless, these are the kind of judgements that we already make—that we have to make—and that I think we can make better with an analysis of power flows.

In the passage at the beginning of this chapter, I contrast the power of opencast coal mining (destructive, coercive) with the power of co-operation and natural growth (positive, constructive). It would be tempting to say that

BREADLINE BRITAIN

"The [Benefits] officer returns with a supervisor, a young, moustachioed man in blue shirt sleeves who does not sit but stands, leaning over intimidatingly. The client cannot believe what he tells her.

"'Fucking ten quid for a week? What am I supposed to do with that? Fucking cheek. My book says £24 a week. Why did they cut my money then? Could you live on £10 a week?... And when they send my hospital fares they don't send the proper money, they send £1 less, and they say they've included for a cup of tea on the way, the fucking liars . . . This'll be the last time I have to come here because my husband's coming home next week, thank God.' She is overcome with emotion, with offended pride, and finally decides on a gesture of futile, self-destructive rebellion. 'I'll tell you what you can do with your fucking £10. You can stick it up your fucking arse!'

"It is always like that. Submission or rebellion is the choice: there is no question of dealing as equals."[1]

Such is the nature of poverty in a European social democracy. Since that was written, the arcane benefits system has been adjusted and modified, the presentation and the packaging much improved. My visits to benefits offices have always been rather more banal. But the undercurrent has always been there; asking for the means of subsistence on a daily basis can never be anything other than humiliating.

And this is meant to be one of the more enlightened ways of dealing with that persistent embarrassment, the poor. Elsewhere, their lot is to survive on food aid, to beg on the streets, or simply to starve. Leeds Child Poverty Action group, asking people what poverty means, came up with these replies: "Sitting with my coat on when the kids go to bed to save fuel . . . Standing in a department store and almost stooping to shoplift because I want my kids to have nice clothes and things. . . Endless drudgery. . . Living off egg and potato, having to sew up holes in my tights. . . Having constantly to say no to the kids, never having a holiday."[2]

Even if the poor are relatively few in number (and in 1995 one third of the world's working population were unemployed or underemployed, the worst situation since the 1930s[3]), there is a part of our minds that is always with them. Not necessarily in the compassionate sense, but as a caution—if we are not careful, it could be us at the bottom of the heap. Somehow, it seems that every effort to eradicate poverty has failed, irrespective of the sums of money poured in or the good intentions of those involved. Sometimes—as in the eager construction of housing projects that turn into slums—they only seem to make matters worse. Between 1940 and 1960, a period during which Brazil was undoubtedly a very poor country, infant mortality in the Sao Paulo region fell by more than half. But between 1962 and 1975, a period of 'economic miracle' when the economy expanded to rival industrialized nations, the same infant mortality figures rose by 45%.

Even more puzzling, not all poverty seems to matter. A peasant farmer in South-East Asia may have income and amenities far below those of, say, an unemployed man in Harlem. And yet, in terms of the degree of pain, the self-esteem, the awareness of poverty, the farmer seems much better off. Mari Marcel-Thekaekara was part of a team of Indian development workers who visited the Easterhouse housing estate in Glasgow. "These people had assured housing, electricity, hot and cold water, refrigerators . . . by Indian standards this was middle class luxury. . . . Then suddenly we were hit by the reality of the poverty surrounding us in Glasgow. Most of the men in Easterhouse hadn't had a job in 20 years. They were dispirited, depressed, often alcoholic. Their self-esteem had gone. Emotionally and mentally they were far worse off than the poor where we worked in India, even though the physical trappings of poverty were less stark. . . . Our host in Easterhouse had shown us underdeveloped Scottish children—a whole generation were growing up a head shorter, smaller than their grandparents."[4]

Throughout history, voluntary poverty has consistently been equated with spiritual wealth—such as St Augustine saying 'All plenty which is not my God is poverty to me', or Thoreau writing 'Give me the poverty that enjoys true wealth.'[5] How can material possessions be at the same time a blessing and a curse?

Charles Peguy puts it this way: "Destitution is almost always confused with poverty; this mistake comes from the fact that destitution and poverty are neighbours. No doubt they are neighbours, but situated on either side of a boundary. All is misery within this boundary; misery of uncertainty or misery of certain destitution. . . . if one evaluates according to quantity alone, a rich man is much farther removed from a poor man than a poor man is removed from a destitute man. But between destitution and poverty a boundary arises. And the poor man is separated from the destitute man by a difference of quality."[6]

This boundary is one of power. The poor man may still be powerful in that he may be in control of his life, whereas the destitute have lost control over even the most trivial requirements, as they have to ask for everything. The poor farmer still has the land, the seed, the sun and the forest around; all of these things mean that self-provision, self-determination and self-direction are possible. But it is not the case that this power is simply another way of measuring possession. Even the affluent can be destitute if they owe all their riches to forces beyond their control, if the goods they possess tie them down, or require servicing, or were purchased on credit, or were obtained to meet insatiable aspirations, or in some other way demonstrate desperation rather than satiation.

It is not the quantity of power, but the quality. What the woman quoted above is missing is not so much the £14 she has been refused, but the ownership of her whole life.

one of these is real power and the other an aberration, or an absence of power. For instance, Dahl's definition of power is: "A has power over B to the extent that he can get B to do something that he would not otherwise do."[7] The power that I gain by joining a co-operative could pedantically be said to be that of making the mortgage lender lend money to a project that otherwise would not have happened. But this surely misses the more numerous effects on our ability to develop ideas, manage our own finances, improve our dwellings, pool our resources and gain from sharing. The effect on my life is surely one of power—but not as Dahl describes it.

The reverse example comes from Joanna Macy, who says: "Power, the ability to effect change, works from the bottom up more reliably and organically than from the top down. It is not power-over, but power with . . ."[8] If only this were true. The open cast miners could have got together with local people and tried to establish a consensus for exploiting the coal, and maybe even found a way to do so that left wildlife unscathed, but it is hard to see how this is a more reliable way for them to achieve their desired outcome. In fact, if you have a given objective—let us say, to get a roof over your head—the use of power-over in some form is probably a lot more reliable in this society than the co-operative route. Power-over, for all its destructive tendencies and denial of diversity, is a profoundly creative force. The impulse to control lies behind the transformation of the earth wrought in the 20th century—an act of power in every sense.

Attempts to define these different forms of power out of existence will not work. There really is a range of different patterns and pathways through which potential can be realized as power, and through which power can be directed to meet a need. They are different not merely in the detail, but more fundamentally in the quality of the process.

Conflict or Compatibility?

Of course, every example of power is different; my justification for grouping them together is in the interaction between them. There is a sense in which we might say that two examples of 'power-over' are compatible, or that one might lead to another. By digging up the land for the open cast mine, the ability of the micro-organisms in the soil to maintain the soil structure is harmed, and the farmer has to work harder to keep it fertile. Setting up our Housing Co-operative has given us the skills and resources to set up a worker's co-operative. The institution of land ownership, based on individual control of land, makes possible mining without the consent of the community. Every time a power process is established, it makes possible other connections. It leaves assumptions and expectations in people's minds, it leaves a mark on the landscape, it teaches skills and patterns of behaviour. This is a zero sum game—not in the sense that every choice is an either/or choice, but in the sense that establishing one model of power undermines other possible models.

Many researchers of 'empowerment'—which is a term I will take as referring to the quality of 'power-to'—have argued that in fact it is perfectly compatible with 'power-over'. Croft and Beresford, and also Holmes, argue that if
one group is empowered, it does not necessarily take power from another
group—it is possible, by being 'assertive', to actually add to the total power
available.[9] Up to a point, I agree with this; the whole point of empowerment is
that being empowered yourself does not prevent someone else from being
empowered. In fact, the example you provide, and the knowledge that is developed as you become empowered, may very well make it easy for others to
follow. Empowerment is simply a self-regulated power flow—it does not interfere with anyone else's self-management.

However, that is because like power is compatible with like power; self-
management cannot interfere with further self-management. If, however, we
imagine a system in which other-regulation is controlling many of these circuits of power, any unit that becomes self-managing must do so by blocking
some other form of regulation. When discourse theorists such as Foucault say
that we all have the option of engaging in a different discourse[10] (see Chapter
1), I agree, but note that the more people adopt a discourse of empowerment,
then the fewer are the opportunities to regulate and control them in a discourse of 'power-over'. This is why empowerment so often arises out of struggle, and why patterns of power-over are preceded by violent attacks on
self-reliant lifestyles. One cannot be both obedient and self-directed.

Green Choices
Within the Green movement, 'power-over' and 'power-to' are both well understood concepts. Discussion of power has been dogged by the ambivalence of
Green activists; on the one hand they are clear that they want power for their
ideas, and power over their own lives, and power to live 'authentically'. But
equally, there is a strong sense that power corrupts, and is oppressive, and is
at the heart of the problems they are campaigning on. For many, this has led
to an avoidance of the use of the word 'power'. Michael Allaby, for instance,
wrote: "Ecology activists are not concerned with power: they have no wish to
take political or economic power from one section of society and give it to
another."[11] In contrast, Sara Parkin wrote in 1988, "Greens will have to stop
being squeamish about power. . . . Greens are after all deeply concerned about
power . . . only by becoming experts in the nature and dynamics of power will
Greens be able to applaud when it is being used in ways that they approve of,
and to shout 'foul' when it is abused."[12] Guy Dauncey, in the same year, goes
further by offering guidelines to what is 'foul' and what is fair play: we should
be "going beyond domination, and beyond having power over others . . . [and]
actively seeking the empowerment of everyone, both personally and in communities."[13] Even when (as in the UK Green Party in 1991) those sceptical

CRIME AND PUNISHMENT

Walking home through Chapeltown (the poor district of Leeds in which I live) after dark, it's hard not to get spooked. Thinking about it, very few of the occasions I've walked through Chapeltown alone have ended in my being mugged; but those few occasions have a powerful effect on expectations. I fear my neighbours; anyone I meet whom I do not know, I mistrust. Once I was accosted by someone I had met at a credit union meeting, who just wanted to say hello. I almost panicked before I realized who he was.

Who are the muggers? There are a lot of them—in the last five years the annual rate of incidence in London has risen to 22,000. They are disproportionately drawn from the unemployed, poor, badly housed and badly educated urban youth. Most white people in Britain are mugged by whites; most blacks are mugged by blacks. The black community is known to be significantly more at risk from assault, threat, robbery and theft. In the US, this has led to Jesse Jackson speaking out about the need for the black community to tackle this threat from within. In Brixton, a consultative committee drew up a profile of the typical mugger—a style-obsessed young man with expensive habits.[14] This fits with my experience, and that of people I know: we have been assaulted by people almost twitching with self-consciousness and lack of self-confidence, desperate to find some status in their ideal of the well-dressed robber. Sadly, they fail. Among criminals, muggers are regarded with contempt; burglars are only slightly better.

But the poor continue to prey on each other regardless. Knight and Stokes, writing in *The Guardian*, say: "There are now at least 40 areas in Britain where civil society has broken down. We interviewed residents in one of these areas and they described it as a 'war zone'. Burglaries, car crime, violence, threatening behaviour, all-night parties and drunkenness in the street were the norm. Problems were caused by a minority of 29 residents from 13 families who together possessed 395 convictions. . . . One young family called the police after their fourth burglary. Minutes after the panda car had left, all the windows in the house were smashed. . . . When crime attacks civil society in this manner almost all 'social capital' is destroyed. People can think no bigger than dealing with their immediate problems, adopt a siege mentality and withdraw from the public stage."[15] The most visible form of this process is when tension—and boredom— explodes into riot. One such riot was that in Luton North, in which a shopping centre was looted and three schools seriously damaged. One parent said of his sons, "They shouldn't have been doing it, but there should be somewhere for them to go. They were loving it. It's a bit of excitement. They were safe. I had my eye on them. It's only the police who are not safe around here." Another riot participant said, "They build us road humps but no community centre. There are so many young people here but there is nothing for them", and another, "Rioting is a cheap way of livening up hot summer nights."[16]

Not only is there nowhere for them in the community, there is little space in the home. For parents struggling to make ends meet, the 'little sods' are an inescapable source of stress. Often they are driven on to the streets. They see enough of the mainstream to know what is expected, but given no access to any of it. One fourteen year old says of his repeated car theft, "It's just Hackney. It's the atmosphere. I never did it cause I needed money. I just did it because it was there."[17] Another thief says, "I got no plans, I just take it as it comes. What's the worth of thinking ahead? The only time you can think ahead is if you've got the money. If you made plans, you'd only be disappointed. They wouldn't work out anyway."[18] The culture generated is one in which you would have your car broken into one day, and next day see someone on the street offering to sell your radio back to you.

There is nothing heroic about this incestuous crime. No matter how much people suffer at the hands of domination and power-over, still they seem to find no answer beyond using their own physical power to gain dominance over someone else. "It's all because I'm a bit small. They always kept me down. I ain't got no push, see, that's why. If I'd been a big bloke, they'd have taken notice. If you're small, they walk all over you."[19] No one is at the bottom of this heap; every battered mother has a child to shout at, every destitute thief has a passer by to rob, and no one will seriously question whether goods are stolen if they can only afford the discount price. The dominance of power-over seems total. It is not wholly surprising. After all, building up the connections and structures that would empower depend crucially on having "a surplus of mental and physical energy over and above that needed for work and survival".[20] In the absence of that, power-over is all that is left.

The judicial system seems unable to deal with crime; prison only makes matters worse, as convicts come out hardened, better trained and with even fewer alternatives to crime. The dynamic of power cannot cure its own problems. Clearly no one would choose this arrangement. Yet it is equally true that everywhere power-over is employed, it reinforces and reproduces the use of power-over elsewhere.

Just sometimes it is possible to break the circle. Mediation and Reparation services are pioneering alternatives to punishment—replacing the predictable response of power-over with a 'reasoning and rehabilitation' programme which helps offenders develop skills for self-management—how to solve problems, negotiate for what they want, control their anger and addictions. Californian criminologist Mark Lipsey has found that for 50,000 offenders, constructive community-based schemes reduced re-offending significantly, while punitive sentences actually increased re-offending.[21]

about power clash with those seeing it as necessary, there is a surprisingly high level of agreement. The former can be found calling for 'power for ideas' leading to 'power to legislate', while the latter can be found warning of the consequences of unaccountable 'power-over'.[22] This view of power as a choice between domination and liberation has deep roots. As a choice between an anarcho-syndicalist 'personal power' and bureaucratic capitalist 'functional power', a similar idea can be found in Andre Gorz, writing in 1980.[23] Another source is the 'Aquarian' mysticism of 70s California—Marilyn Ferguson describes a shift from 'power-over' to 'power for'.[24]

This intuitive idea has gained theoretical flesh more recently. Erich Fromm, in his 1977 book *The Anatomy of Human Destructiveness*, describes the sadistic character as follows. "What the sadist is striving for is power over people, precisely because he lacks the power to be. Many writers in order to smuggle in praise of power-over, identify it with 'power-to'. Lack of control does not mean lack of organization, but only of those kinds of organization in which the control is exploitative."[25] He argues that the features of sadism/power-over tend to occur together, that they form a 'syndrome'. To justify this, he analysed anthropological surveys of 30 primitive tribes and shows how the coincident features group them into three clear categories—life affirming, non-destructive aggressive, and destructive. The life affirming tribes displayed sexual equality, permissiveness, limited personal property rights, trust and confidence—though they existed in settings of both abundance and scarcity. The second type was individualistic, competitive and achievement orientated, but within limits. The destructive societies exhibited all the features of power-over: violence, cruelty, pleasure in war, private property, hierarchies, and sexual repression. Fromm notes that Spinoza argued that greed and ambition are not merely failings but forms of insanity; today, they are not even considered to be failings.

Riane Eisler, in her book *The Chalice and the Blade*, terms the two models of social organization 'partnership' and 'dominator', and provides a wealth of examples of dominator relationships in our own culture, and partnership relationships both in ancient cultures and in social change today.[26] Starhawk, in *Truth or Dare*, identifies three types of power: power-over, power-from-within and power with.[27] Her approach is primarily psychological, and she connects power-over to a sense of estrangement (an idea I return to in the following chapter). She describes power-from-within as "akin to the sense of mastery we develop as young children with each new unfolding ability. . . . It arises from our sense of connection, our bonding with other human beings, and with the environment." She also identifies another form of power—power with. This might also be called leadership—the power to inspire, and bind together a group in common purpose. This Starhawk sees as the bridge between the dominating impulse of power-over, and the immanence, or spirit, of liberating power-from-within.

I'm not convinced that she adequately makes the case for this three-way taxonomy. After all, power-with (as she describes it) cannot exist on its own, but is an amplifier of the other two. As she describes it, it has no character or moral content of its own. I would rather say that what Starhawk describes as power-with is simply the way in which power forms increasingly extended processes; it is the tendency of social beings to connect, and to reproduce and extend structures of power.

A more recent and more philosophical exploration of this theme is Karen Warren's essay, 'Towards an ecofeminist peace politics'.[28] She is concerned with the sources of violence, and argues that the meaning of violence is highly dependent on the position of the actor in the hierarchies of industrial society. 'Power-over power' is the power of 'ups' (that is, those actors dominant in the patriarchal system) over the 'downs'. Though it may be malicious or benevolent, it always maintains the power structure. Then there are three forms of power which are 'neutral' in the sense that they may liberate or maintain oppression. Power-with power is described in terms much like those of Starhawk, while power-within power is seen as just as likely to be a source of neurosis as a source of empowerment. The third of these 'two-edged swords' is power-towards power, which describes a transformation of life—potentially towards a more authentic existence, but also potentially towards a lifestyle of over-consumption and greed. Her fifth category of power is that exercised by 'downs' against 'ups', described as 'power-against power'. She sees it as a distinctive form because it is the power of the resourceless, and provided it does not serve to reinforce oppressive relationships, then it may be justifiable in a way that power-over power cannot be.

Again, I feel that Warren shares with Starhawk a tendency to put distinctive types of power alongside the distinctive ways in which those types are manifest. So, for instance, a given example of power could be both power-over and power-with, although no exercise of power could be both power-over and power-against. This is unsatisfactory because it surely calls for two different kinds of classification—types of power, and methods of propagation.

I also cannot agree that 'power that serves to perpetuate relations of domination' has a 'key feature . . . that it is exercised by Ups over Downs'.[29] Power-over is as commonly used by 'Downs' as it is by 'Ups'. Warren seems to regard power as a phenomenon influencing relations of domination rather than being (as I would see it) the very substance and subject of those relations. Empowerment is something which may be possible through power-with, power-within, or power-towards, but Warren does not regard it as a distinctive category in itself—mistakenly, I believe.

The concept that there are qualitatively different forms of power, linking together different features in a 'syndrome', is now well established, and has been thoroughly researched. The difficulty is to communicate this concept to

HOMES FOR HEROES

Housing is at the heart of issues of poverty. Not only is it near the top of our 'hierarchy of needs', but it is also the precondition for so many other needs— it is where food is prepared, it is where children are raised, it is where we might establish a workplace, it is where we begin building community. Without the main force of feudal power, there was no one to say who owned or did not own a piece of land. As recently as the eighteenth century, there were many people living on common land—and in a few pockets of rural England, there still are today. The commons were not, it should be stressed, just empty, or unclaimed, but managed by the community.[30]

Today, the landless poor are contained in the sprawling slums of the world's megacities. In the industrialized countries, these slums are typically vast public housing schemes, built in a spirit of social democracy and managed by the municipal authorities. That these attempts to provide homes for the masses have largely proved to be failures is widely accepted. From Pruit Igoe in the US to Quarry Hill in Leeds, the dreams of social reformers have all turned sour.

Why is this? Partly because the architecture and standards of construction bore no sense of respect for the dignity of the people who would live in them. Partly because the maintenance of these properties, entirely in the hands of the municipality, was invariably late, slapdash and partial. Partly because the administration was remote, impersonal and unfriendly. Alison Ravetz writes of Quarry Hill, "Tenants were excluded from the little official machinery that existed to deal with the estate as a whole."[31] Partly because allocation became a battle to escape the 'sink estates' and a political tool of the authorities.[32] But there was also something more: "The usual balance of power between landlord and tenant is everywhere upset by the condition of housing shortage. But the problems are even more acute in council tenancy. It is not only that the council tenant is even less free to move than the private tenant. The private tenant can at least hate his landlord for taking advantage of the conditions of shortage for his own financial gain. The council tenant knows that he is fortunate in having his house, and feels that he has been done a favour. . . . In the long run, power employed paternalistically provokes far greater resentment than power employed selfishly or even antagonistically. Because there is no satisfactory outlet for it, the resentment accumulates. . . . "[33]

Private self-interest and public provision have both failed to alleviate the desperate squalor in which millions in so-called 'developed' countries still live. The cause is the failure to genuinely empower people, but instead to control them out of poverty. This will never work, because poverty simply is control, or vulnerability to control. Where people have been allowed to take control of their lives, they may have been materially poor, but never normally destitute or deprived. Using power-over to repair the damage done by power-over is no cure, but only more of the disease.

people who in their lives have only ever experienced one of them, and who cannot conceive of any other way of functioning.

The Triumph of Power-over

The description of a society in which all our relations with others are tinged with hierarchy, and in which we are always either looking up or looking down, will fit closely to the experiences of many—particularly those ecofeminists who have experienced systematic oppression as blacks, as women, as poor, and as 'close to nature' (see following chapter). It must be clear that if we regard power-over and empowerment as two equally potent, but clearly distinctive, ways of meeting our needs, then one is clearly predominant in our experience. Our world is saturated with hierarchy and control. Empowerment, self-management, autonomy, self-reliant liberty; these things are exceptions, the subjects of social experiments and wistful anecdotes. Is this because they call on unusual human talents? Hardly: in fact, some of the most successful experiments in empower-ment have taken place among the least 'successful' members of our society.

However they have been achieved, it is a social reality that the forms of power to which we have the easiest access, which have the greatest support, which command the greatest resources, and which account for the largest human transformation of energy, are those of power-over. It is no surprise that placing empowering relations on an equal footing with disempowering ones is at best visionary, at worst wishful thinking. Although I believe that the wish to oppose power-over and support power-to is deeply entrenched in the Green movement, the issue remains a source of controversy for precisely this reason. "Greens want to use as a guideline for the new society 'power with' or 'power-to' concepts as opposed to 'power-over', but no one has yet defined what a gov-ernment based on this power prescription might be."[34]

By establishing this contrast, I do not mean to suggest that these are the only options; or that power-to is the only route to sustainability. I am keen to avoid the dualisms and dichotomies that have plagued Western thinking. The choice is not 'black and white', 'good and evil', 'yin and yang', 'male and female' in some new form. Ken Jones reminds us that movements based around antithetical bonding (in other words, uniting against something) lead to blinkered ideology rather than creative, inclusive theorizing.[35] Bahro is scep-tical about "final struggle fantasies about 'white' against 'black' power".[36] They invariably rest on subconscious projection—identifying some 'other' to carry all the aspects of ourselves that we do not want to acknowledge.

I accept that we must immerse ourselves in power-over in order to realize power-to (see Chapter 10). But I am not seeking merely to restore balance. I argue that sustainability demands that self-management become the dominant form of human (and ecological) organization, but I am not engaged in a witch-hunt against all control or other-regulation. The moral world we live in is strictly 'greyscale', and every initiative of empowerment can be found leaning on the structures of domination—if only because they are too pervasive to avoid. Similarly, the incongruence that I believe separates these different forms of power does not preclude connection and co-operation. Often it will be hard to tell the difference, or say where empowerment ends and control begins. But that does not mean we don't have to try. It is the possibility of such a shift that is the source of our hope.

The New Powerholders

This approach to social change has considerable implications for the question of agency. As I have written elsewhere,[37] the question can be posed in a number of different ways highly relevant to power. We might ask: who has an interest in this new society, in that they would gain power? Who already embodies the power relations of a new society? Who is making demands of power that can only be met in a different society? Which group has the power to bring about the new society? Which group has the standpoint from which the route to a Green society is obvious?

By drawing this cleavage across the field of power relations, some answers become obvious. If we agree that empowerment is the essential dynamic of an ecological society, then we might well expect that empowered people, or people aspiring to empowerment, are the obvious category to look for. This is similar to the argument that working class consciousness 'prefigures' the culture of a socialist society; in the same way, those choosing empowering relations are an obvious audience. The argument of 'trade union consciousness' has undermined this assumption of class unity, suggesting that the aspiration is for 'shorter hours and better pay' rather than any challenge to alienated labour. This is a view shared by many Greens, who look for a 'historical subject' distanced from the power-over system of work and consumerism. Andrew Dobson argues, "It is the distance from the process of consumption and the degree of permanence of this isolation that currently determine the capacity of any group for Green social change." This points us to the underclass, or the long term unemployed, a group described by Andre Gorz as having 'radical chains'. They have needs that cannot be met under hierarchical relations of power, since they are trapped at the bottom of the heap.

But there is a sense in which there is no bottom in power-over; everyone lacks control over their own destiny and environment. It is also true that every individual has access to power in the discourses they reproduce, in their acts of consumption, and in the actions they take to survive.

That is not to say we are all equal. Some compete more successfully than others in the free for all, and the way power accumulates makes the gap between winners and losers grotesquely large. There are Greens who argue that we should refrain from 'shopping for a historical subject'. Bahro says, "If we want to keep to the level of the overall interest of humanity . . . we must once again take the species interest as our subject." But the clear disparity between the winners and losers in this universal competition surely suggests that some members of the species will be more interested than others.

Very often, the universalist approach becomes an appeal to the middle classes. Porritt explains why: "The reasons are simple. Such people not only have more chance of seeing where their self-interest lies, but they also have the flexibility and security to act on such insights." However, this security is also a problem. Saral Sarkar points out that when the German Greens took as their target audience "the urban, liberal, consumerist citizen",[38] it led naturally to a policy protecting their interests as consumers.

But it does not imply that the very poorest are automatically going to support the Green agenda. As well as exclusion from structures of domination, there must also be a positive commitment to building structures of empowerment. If you reject a position of dominance, there is no guarantee that you will not simply move to a lower position in the same hierarchy. The poor of industrialized nations are in a highly disadvantaged position; treated so brutally, there is every evidence that they become brutalized themselves—recent crime surveys, for instance, show a strong correlation between long term youth unemployment and crime rates. Can the Green movement "make the marginalized class aware that [aspiring to affluence] has no future?"[39] Perhaps—but there are other groups far better placed to hear this message.

These are hard to define, but are generally held to include peace activists, feminists, ethnic minorities, community campaigners, unemployed activists (rather than the unemployed as a whole), communards, squatters, environmentalists and civil liberties campaigners. Although they are a disparate lot, in practice there is a lot of cross-fertilization, and they prove to have much in common. This takes us to a third possibility: the 'new social movements' as an agency for change. Some see this as stemming from a 'post-materialist' outlook, a belief that issues of quality of life are more pressing than those of material abundance. James O'Connor sees it as being a shared economic interest in the conditions of production, and hence in the democratization of the state that regulates access to them (see Chapter 8).[40] Yet another explanation for the common thread in these social movements is David West's idea of 'authenticity'. He focuses on the idea of 'personal politics' common in many new social movements' discourses, and sees their common interest as that of liberation from inauthentic interests.[41]

TENANTS TAKE OVER

The first step towards empowerment on the estates is the formation of grass-roots bodies such as tenants' and residents' associations. These may be very informal bodies, even just an extension of neighbourly chats over the garden fence. Researchers in Britain have found that, "Once established they tend to last, and to concentrate on welfare work for their community. . . . Their method is to organize social events first, and later serve as a consultative committee for the estate," and that "The great number of these autonomous, self-formed organizations are not 'grievance' bodies, but non-political associations formed for the purpose of creating some sense of community and neighbourliness."[42] Reactions to these bodies by the authorities vary. Some see 'troublemakers' and some see a useful 'consumer council'. This depends of course on the particular circumstances, but I would argue that in all cases the formation of such an association restricts the power-over of the Council, even if only potentially. There may be no overt conflict, but it may alter the preferences of the Council regarding the estate, or set limits on their agenda (note the correspondence with Lukes' dimensions of power—see Chapter 1).

Tenants can then begin to enter into a planning process for their future. On the Buttershaw estate in Bradford, a single parent in the residents' group canvassed 600 homes on what they wanted. "Vast things need doing. There are hardly any shops, the laundrette's just closed down. I have to get four buses to go to the doctor's. There are no playgrounds for the kids. What we'd like to do is have a park for the area." Six months later the residents' group had funding to employ professional consultants to follow up the survey and produce a detailed plan based in people's expressed desires. "We'd create a village centre in the middle of the estate. New community facilities, a health centre, laundrette, library and shops." Bradford City Council quickly moved to support the plan, and to find government money to support it.[43] Now the residents were actually setting the agenda.

Planning for Real is a participatory planning device that takes this a step further. A scale map of the area is taken to public meetings around the area, and local residents are encouraged to stick flags into it showing what they would like, and where. Then, with expert input, the pooled responses are combined to include as many as possible of the ideas in a viable plan. This makes a powerful tool with which to put pressure on the planning authorities. Similar ideas allow participation in the details of architecture and construction, and the institutional basis of a plan. There is nothing that cannot be decided in an empowering, consensual, community-based process.

In some cases, tenants' groups are formally involved in a tenant participation process by the Council. However, their motives for doing this often fail to correspond with the desires of the tenants, as different dynamics of power conflict. "These proposals seem to be essentially methods of improving communication with and representation of tenants from the top downwards, rather than building up from the bottom. . . . Tenants are being asked to decide on matters affecting a group of estates . . . rather than what is necessary for their own individual estate."[44] The Council may think that they are doing the tenants a favour by inviting them to participate in power-over; they do not understand that the tenants are seeking something qualitatively different.

This is tenant management. An early example of this comes from Oslo in 1962, where a pre-war estate was progressively transferred into the ownership of the tenants' associations. This 'problem estate' was transformed when the housing manager and the tenants agreed that housing co-operatives should take over the estate. Interestingly, they chose to pay rents higher then those against which they had protested before.[45] In Britain, only a vigorous squatters' movement came close to the same kind of tenant control. But in the 1980s, a change in legislation encouraged a number of residents' groups to bid for self-management. In Leeds, two estates have undertaken this: Halton Moor and Belle Isle. The management board at Halton Moor was set up in 1993, and the Council Housing Director said, "The management board has brought self-help and self-management to the estate. The estate did have a bad image, but the tenants themselves are turning that around." Crime levels immediately began to fall.[46] In Belle Isle, the experience of self-management has changed the people as well as the estate. "I never thought in a million years that I'd do this. My life since I left school has revolved around working in a sewing factory. Now I've been to night school, learned word processing. I know quite a bit. It's given me real confidence," said Kath Lonsdale, the Secretary of the Management Board. The gains are not without conflict, as Housing Officers ask them to implement their cuts, and withhold vital information. The Chair of the same Board said, "[Council Officers] tend to try to forget that we're here. They are scared of releasing that little bit of power. It takes them time to realize we've got to be informed. We're not trying to tell them what to do, we want to work with them. But if they want to do anything on this site, we've got to be involved."[47] The experience has led them to pursue more initiatives to develop the area—a community-owned business to create local employment and a credit union. Overcoming years of expectations of control and paternalism does not happen overnight. But these tenants have shown that it is possible to meet the same needs with a completely different form of power: one which denies power-over and spreads autonomy.

Movements for Empowerment

All three of forms of agency seem to have part of the answer, but none of them is wholly sufficient. O'Connor's suggestion, for instance, that 'the urban-based new politics of identity have to do with the new international division of labour', seems like a bit of a long shot. West's conception of authenticity is pushed to account for the peace movement, or for environmental action. Post-materialism is hardly evident in the literature of anti-poverty campaigners. And yet there is surely a common thread. For all their diversity, and even taking into account the local disagreements, the examples of co-operation across these new movements are too many to be coincidental. Two weekends before I wrote this, environmentalists, peace campaigners, libertarians and road protesters gathered in Liverpool for a weekend of demonstrations and awareness-raising entitled 'Reclaim the Future'. Their hosts were a group of dockers, on strike for a year with little recognition or support from the official unions. Everyone I have spoken to who was there stresses how their seemingly disparate concerns dovetailed into a common vision.

Campaigning organizations find increasingly that as their researchers move beyond slogans to more detailed demands, they find common cause with other groups. Homelessness groups find that they are speaking for young gays and lesbians excluded from the patriarchal household. Environmentalists find themselves concerned with access to housing and the 'fuel poverty' of the urban poor. Campaigners on ozone-destroying CFCs and greenhouse gases find that the military is one of the largest and most indifferent sources of pollution. The campaigns against the Criminal Justice Act in 1994 brought together an unprecedented coalition of ramblers, radical unionists, environmentalists, animal rights protesters, peace activists, gays and lesbians, civil libertarians, black community leaders against a united front of Westminster politicians over the issue of trespass and access to land.

I believe that the nature of the cleavage we are seeing here is a clash of discourses of power. The networks of power-over have constructed a dominant culture that is placing people and planet under intolerable levels of stress. It is not merely that it is unsustainable in the future, but that it is untenable and indefensible now. The new social movements are made up of people—from many different sectors of society—working or living at the most overstressed points on the network. The common language they have found in their resistance is one of empowerment—an alternative set of practices and knowledges that negate and bypass the hierarchies of industrial society.

This power analysis for the emergence and co-operation of new social movements provides a link between culture and political economy. The state's regulation of access to land and labour is critical, because it is the interface where biological, self-regulated systems are co-opted and pre-empted into other-regulated structures; it is the 'front line' of this clash of powers.

Authenticity is an issue for a similar reason; it invites the release of generative, creative power-from-within instead of conforming with the hierarchies of power-to. If post-materialism is a common theme in new social movements, it is more symptom than cause. Those concerned with empowerment are seeking self-reliance, and are becoming less and less dependent on other-produced commodities. It is not so much that the movements are post-materialist (many have very material needs and concerns) but that they are anti-consumerist. Recognizing this helps to get us past what may appear as contradictory demands for both less and more material goods.

In strategic terms, then, a movement for survival is one that is choosing and building empowering relations, based on the power to control one's own destiny—to be no one's slave and no one's master. These movements are emerging from the points of greatest stress where power-over connects with biological reality and sustainable cultures. While these are not the only possible dynamics of power, they pose a real choice for us today. No one concerned with detailed analysis likes to face a black and white choice. But the ubiquity of power, and the scale of the danger, makes this one impossible to duck. Which side are you on?

Chapter 6

The Colossus

In this chapter we examine the mechanisms of 'power-over' in more detail, trying to answer the questions: What do different forms of oppression have in common? What are the mechanisms which consolidate a dynamic of power-over?

Naming oppression is only the start of the matter; oppression survives because we are unable to unpick it from the everyday dictat of power. To suggest that all 'single issue' liberation struggles can increase their effectiveness by making common cause does not deny the local requirements of a particular form of resistance.

The collaboration of power plays takes place through common practices, common technologies and common experiences. As power-over becomes established in a community, it can break up patterns of empowerment and colonize our lives.

Using Wingrove's metaphor of 'currencies of power' gives us a way to understand the way in which status in a power hierarchy can 'buy' us our needs—material, emotional and spiritual. The more such currencies are exchanged, the more dependent on them we become.

Ultimately, power-over is about denying the rest of the world an autonomous identity, but treating it as though is were merely a collection of passive objects. This 'objectification' has highly damaging psychological effects—not least when we objectify ourselves. One of these effects is to deny the existence of the very interrelations that allow power to function.

We cannot be free from domination ourselves unless we approach the rest of the living world without dominating. Our co-operation and coalitions must resist the temptation to recreate authoritarian structures. This is everyone's struggle—a struggle for life.

"The assassination of Kirov, that was the key date. Shot in the back with a Nugen revolver in the headquarters of the Leningrad Communist Party on the 1st of December 1934. Stalin's friend and ally, Stalin's comrade. Therefore, as we innocently used to say, therefore the one person who could not possibly have wished or hoped for it, let alone ordered it, was Stalin himself. This was an impossibility in all known political and personal terms. For Stalin to have ordered Kirov's death was not just 'out of character', but beyond our understanding of what character might comprise. Which was precisely the point. We have moved into an era in which 'character' is a misleading concept. Character has been replaced by ego, and the exercise of authority as a reflection of character has been replaced by the psychopathic retention of power by all possible means and in mockery of all implausibilities. Stalin had Kirov killed: welcome to the modern world."—Julian Barnes, *The Porcupine*

There is a colossus towering over all of us—a figure always looming large in our mind. Not so much any one judge, policeman, employer or politician, but an abstract sense of authority. It makes us feel small, insignificant—not just helpless but actually worthless or unimportant. My more fortunate readers may not recognize this, if they have hardly ever been on the losing side in a power struggle. However, for the purposes of this chapter, I hope I can assume that every one of us has at some time experienced this sense of frustration as someone smiles condescendingly or crushes our plans casually. This is not the fate of the few; this is a common experience—and although the moments of power may be separate, and may come from different sources, there is something systematic about them. Every exercise of power-over is connected to every other; behind the individual, the circumstances, and the occasion, there is the fact of power and the opportunity for its use. Hence the imprint in our minds of power as domination.

Am I justified in forming a pattern out of this? I would argue that a pattern forms quite naturally in our expectations and in our beliefs, as our past experiences of power shape our behaviour. Even if we develop sophisticated defences—not exposing ourselves to betrayal, outmanoeuvring potential opponents, not taking on battles we know we cannot win, or strengthening our own position—we are reacting to a society riddled with hierarchies. Hierarchy is not always sinister, or illegitimate: but democracy and meritocracy (for instance) are still ways of appointing rulers, fairer though they may be.

Perhaps this ubiquity also explains the prevailing assumption in political theory that power is power-over—that no other form of power is possible, or that power should be defined in terms of domination (see, for example, Lukes' definition in Chapter 1). The theorists are describing the society they experience, which offers opportunities for achievement principally at the expense of others. But as I argued in the last chapter, this is not necessarily the case in any society; it is possible to conceive of empowering social structures that meet the same needs in different ways.

I can't deny certain advantages to the competition of power-over. Although I noted in Chapter 4 that Gaia—or, if you prefer, the biosphere—functions primarily through self-regulation at every level, that is not to say that other-regulation has no part to play. Within a community of deer, for instance, competition may play a functional role; but only because it is kept within limits, and because it contributes to the overall self-regulation of the herd. The bulk of deer

POWER INCORPORATED

Imagine 'power-over' institutionalized; an agency with no physical body, with no life of its own, with no corporeal form but simply a network of relationships of control, authority and exclusion. It would be driven to extract matter from ecosystems, refining and processing it into symbols of power and possession. Within its boundary, there would be a pyramid of roles and positions which, although they might be fluid and at times co-operative, would always be struggling to gain ascendancy. Competition between them would drive them to extend control over more and more of the self-directed world—in other words, over life. Some of them would feed on each other—but ultimately, the biosphere would have to carry the full load.

It may have become clear that I am describing the modern incorporated company, and the economy created by the activity of many thousands of such corporations. Although they are sustained only by our laws, we treat them as though they were living entities, giving them rights and obligations. They represent more than just people working together on some enterprise; their existence gives rise to patterns of behaviour that would be meaningless without them.

As early as the 14th and 15th centuries, joint stock companies were used to bring together the finance for expeditions seeking new lands, new markets, and slaves. These were temporary affairs; when the ship returned, the profits were shared out. Meanwhile, from the 1500s Royal Charters of Incorporation were granted by the Crown on the advice of the Privy Councillors to give trade associations a monopoly over narrow areas of trade. The Dutch East India Company, formed in 1602, was just such an association for trade in the Indies. But its members chose to sell all their stock to the company, in exchange for a share. This gave it a permanent capital fund—the first step towards becoming a legal entity in its own right.[1] The South Sea Company was formed in 1711 to similar ends, but wild speculation in shares led to the first stock market crash, and was followed by restrictions on trading shares which lasted for over a hundred years. Even during this time more and more operations requiring centralized management structures (such as canals, railways and utilities) were needed by the industrializing nations. The power to register moved from the Crown, through Parliament, to a public body. This last move happened under the 1844 Joint Stock Companies Act, of which Gladstone said, "Under this bill there would be a power for the first time, for persons to associate themselves in companies for the purpose of commercial pursuits, without the fear of interference from any human being whatsoever." Today, I can register a company for fifty pounds by filling in a few forms.

What is the significance of this corporate persona? Since 1855, the shareholders have had limited liability. The debts belong to the corporation, not to the individuals. This encourages risk-taking with accumulated capital, and more adventurous economic activity, which in turn brings higher returns and further accumulation. Limited liability companies are almost certainly a driving force behind the economic expansion of the industrialized nations, and their spread around the world; anyone wishing to borrow money for some foreign trading expedition could do so knowing that, provided no dishonesty was involved, they would not be liable for any losses. In this way, the shareholders and creditors (in effect, the wider society) underwrite the risks in the growth and expansion of industrial activity.

Secondly, the corporation achieves what individual entrepreneurs can only dream of: immortality. Individuals may come and go without disturbing the long-term schemes of the company. Although inheritance may be used to pass capital on, it does not guarantee any drive to accumulate further. Only companies are capable of this indefinite, relentless growth. Decade by decade, the economic power of companies is steadily gaining on even the larger nation states. This growth can only be maintained by colonizing areas of human activity, since humans managed fine until the corporations came along.

Corporate longevity might not matter were it not for their freedom of action. We take this for granted, and yet it was only in 1966 that a Court ruling allowed a company to register with objects including "[to] carry on any trade or business whatsoever", and in 1989 that a Companies Act was passed allowing objects to include "power to do all such things as are incidental or conducive to the carrying on of any trade or business". But even when many corporate activities were 'Ultra Vires' (that is, not permitted under its constitution) there was rarely any challenge in the courts. Only now are the dangers of this unlimited power becoming apparent.

The hierarchy that has characterized the corporation since its emergence is not the only way they can be organized. Indeed, many co-operatives have since the nineteenth century combined incorporation with egalitarian practices, breaking the chain of domination (see Chapter 10). The early companies raised capital from a group of shareholders, who were not the disinterested investors typical today, but were closely involved in the project, and wanted to play an active role. They wanted a hierarchy with themselves at the top. Even when capital did not have such a large say, the businesses were established to protect an established individual trader or manufacturer; the model of top-down control stemmed naturally from property laws encouraging accumulation. In general, as Rolf Osterberg suggests, this culture of 'instrumental rationality', controlling property to achieve productivity, is highly compatible with hierarchical organization.[2]

behaviour—responding to threats, deciding when to eat and when to move on, grooming, crossing rivers—is self-determined; it would spell disaster for the herd if it were otherwise. In the same way, a certain amount of competition and even authority in human societies may well prove functional, or just harmless fun. But the evidence of the impact of 'power-over' structures is that the balance has been left a long way behind, and their total hegemony is unsustainable.

Slings and Arrows

I have already noted that conventional political theory treats exercises of power in isolation. In Chapter 2 I tried to show that power was not static but was part of a process—that before each exercise of power comes a series of connections that make it possible (or even inevitable), and after it come further power relations caused or implied by it. I now want to ask whether exercises of power that are causally separate—that is, where there is no direct connection between them—can also still affect each other.

This idea of 'systematic power' is most fully developed in feminist writings, and in other areas where an entrenched social prejudice gives rise to domination—against black people, gay people, disabled people, travellers and many other oppressed groups. Here, the subjects of this oppression have found that the individual abuses they experience are visibly connected. The link is the legal, political and cultural belief in the lesser status of the oppressed group, whether explicitly or implicitly stated. To say that a woman getting lower pay than a male worker doing similar work is connected to a completely different woman being beaten by her husband is no longer controversial. A fair amount of consensus exists that something—call it sexism, call it patriarchy—links these two apparently unrelated acts. We have gone beyond simplistic prescriptions based on the individual case—give up that job, leave that man—and recognized that something wider is required: structures and attitudes that treat women as having the same right to decide their own lives as anyone else.

This makes the connections between separate incidences of power, but it is limited to one oppressed group. Power is more wide-ranging than that. I have said that 'power-over' is a distinctive and particular way to manage and relate to the world around us. We might expect to find the same kind of underlying pattern characterizing all its manifestations. The issue arises most clearly when different forms of domination or oppression are considered alongside each other. Is it a coincidence that the oppression of women and black people have similar justifications, similar technologies, similar economies? The arguments against women's emancipation were based on women's presumed lack of reason, knowledge and intellect—much the same reasons as those used to deny black African countries self-rule, or slaves their freedom. The clubs, colleges and public buildings that were explicitly or implicitly designated 'men only' were tools for social exclusion much like the apartheid of the white South African regime. The patterns of ownership of land, the limited opportunities for employment and the differential earnings for jobs of equal worth, all exist for black people under racism as much as for women under patriarchy.

Consider these testimonies from women fighters in the Tigrayan People's Liberation Front. In 1989, after a prolonged campaign of building resistance among the many ethnic groups in Ethiopia, they overthrew the military regime which had systematically attacked them. The TPLF had to recognize that they were weakened by power struggles among the people they were trying to empower, across lines of ethnicity and gender. The first challenge was to ensure everyone had a voice. "We [the Kunama] were oppressed by Tigrayans, who degraded our culture and insulted our language. . . ."[3] Among Tigrayans, "Women could not be called as eyewitnesses to give evidence in court . . . In fact, she was not allowed to speak in public at all and so had no voice in affairs."[4]

Other parallels are evident. "The Kunama . . . could be sold like cattle, and when a son or a daughter was married a barya [black person] could be given to them like a cow or an ox."[5] This is powerfully reminiscent of statements like, "If someone wants to marry they have to give money to the bride's family [among the Afar people]. We women are treated like commodities."[6] Economic oppression took the same forms too: "To declare that land belonged to the tiller . . . we had to break the law that women couldn't own land";[7] "[The Kunama's] land was taken by the landlords so we had no land to farm and had to eat roots and plants."

There are of course plenty of differences between experiences of social inequality—as you would expect, given the very different needs that the oppressors sought to meet through these power structures. What they want from women is very different to what they want from black people—so different, in fact, that it makes these similarities all the more striking. It suggests that it is more effective to apply the same mechanisms of exclusion, deprivation and control to very different subjects than it is to develop particular forms of domination according to the particular group to be dominated.

The significance and meaning of these parallels has been a source of controversy and tension as, for example, black women encounter racism in the women's movement and patriarchy in black organizations. Similarly, the Green movement has seen an active debate over the relationship between anthropocentrism (human domination of other species), feminism, and social justice movements (domination of one economic class by another).[8] Although I have used the examples of racism and patriarchy here, the increasing awareness of liberation struggles and discrimination in the West recently has revealed a myriad of dominations: straight over gay, able-bodied over disabled, orthodox over heretic, homeowner over traveller . . . Is one form of oppression the cause of another, and hence more important or more significant? Are both phenomena merely the symptoms of a deeper, single cause? Do those experiencing both have a privileged viewpoint? Is one a genuine oppression, and the other not?

All of these explanations seem unconvincing to me. Attempts to find a causal link between one form of oppression and another tend to be connected with 'first oppression' theories, going back into history to establish whether racism, sexism or wealth was the first basis for systematic domination. This is an understandable approach—it is possible to measure the status of women in a society by the conditions of their burial, and divisions of labour and wealth with archaeological research—but it creates problems when applied to the present day. Manifestos abound claiming that 'when our oppression is ended, yours will surely follow', and arguing that in the meantime someone else's oppression should not be considered a priority. The 'root cause' theories have a similar problem. By denying any autonomous existence to the dynamics of oppression, they may be highly aware of an abuse that is clearly connected with the root cause, but be blind to another. Murray Bookchin argues, "All our notions of dominating nature stem from the very real domination of human by human. . . . As a historical statement [this] declares in no uncertain terms that the domination of human by human preceded the notion of dominating nature."[9] This view leads him to oppose groups that prioritize the defence of nature, leading to conflict with those who should be his allies.[10]

Maybe, then, we should continue to treat them as wholly separate. This would mean that one could never truly appreciate discrimination unless one was subject to it; and hence that someone experiencing it from multiple sources has a 'privileged viewpoint', being able to see the world from a much less morally tainted standing. This kind of belief led to a joke in the British National Union of Students that a candidate's prospects in internal elections depended on the amount of 'oppression points' they could collect—one for being black, one for being a woman, one for being working class, and so on. If we accept that an Afro-Caribbean man's experiences are different from an Asian man's, and those of a man from Azad Kashmir different from those of a man from Bangladesh, then the logic of privileged viewpoint suggests that each must have their own liberation struggle. By this logic, we are left alone in our resistance, subdivided so far that no collective movement can arise.

The position I intend to adopt is that the autonomy of these power struc- tures does not imply that there is no interaction between them. As the systems theory described in Chapter 8 has it, all wholes are also parts of a larger whole, and all parts are themselves wholes made up of parts. bell hooks says, of fem- inism, that it "must exist apart from and as a part of the larger struggle to erad- icate domination in all its forms. We must understand that patriarchal oppression shares an ideological foundation with racism and other forms of group oppression, that there is no hope that it can be eradicated while these systems remain intact."[11] Uniqueness exists at every level, and no one can claim that by experiencing one kind of oppression, they are then experts on the

BRINGING HOME THE BACON

To see corporate power exercised in a more naked form, we need to look at the point at which business finds its raw material—communities and ecosystems that are in some way self-managing. It is here that power-over has the opportunity to widen its bounds and bring more energy into its circuits by facilitating control, disrupting self-sustaining systems and building cultural dissonance.

It would be easy to regard these situations as an attack by the powerful on the powerless, but as *The Ecologist* has commented, this view "is one to which corporations and governments themselves—at least those that have lasted—have never subscribed. . . . [They] are aware of the many different types of power they do not possess, although they might well wish to—the knowledge and skills that enable small farmers to look after millions of scattered agricultural plots . . . the power inherent in different cultural tastes and values that stand in the way of corporate plans to secure new markets or sell uniform product lines . . . the social networks that enable local communities to organize against a factory or a road; and the power of mobilization based on face-to-face conversations in dialects central actors find utterly impenetrable."[12]

So if this is the case—if corporations find the self-reliant community a challenge—how can they 'colonize' it with the structures of power-over? Recently, the activities of Shell in the Ogoni lands of Nigeria gained intense media attention. Here the local branch of Shell has begun acting almost like an additional government—to the extent of funding the local police. Nationally, the multinational argues that 'Western ethics should not be applied uniformly'. This attempt to make Shell look like anti-imperialists works only as long as you ask whether the executions of those resisting oil companies are part of traditional Nigerian ethics. In reality, Ogoni ethical standards are considerably higher than those of the corporate executives, with their contempt for the Ogoni and their homeland. Do they think it is justified because the protesters are black, because they are poor, or because they are closer to nature in their lifestyle? We may never know—but the same behaviour in the West is inconceivable.

Nor was this an isolated case. Texaco and Total have been working with the Burmese government, which is forcing indigenous people to clear their own forests to make way for oil and gas exploration. One report describes it as 'ethnic cleansing'. Meanwhile in Nigeria, 32% of the UK's 50 largest companies had operations there in 1996.[13]

However, brute force is not enough. Ultimately, the corporations need people to work for them and buy their products—they must be willing participants. They must really come to believe that 'what's good for General Motors is good for America.' For employees of the corporations and their families, this is not hard. By using the fear of redundancy, employees can be turned into grassroots activists just as effective as those of environmental or public health groups. As one lobbyist puts it, "The public is completely convinced that when you speak as an industry, you are speaking out of nothing but self-interest. The pro-industry citizen action group is the answer to your problems. It can be an effective and convincing advocate for your industry. It can utilize powerful archetypes such as the sanctity of the family, the virtue of the close-knit community, the natural wisdom of the rural dweller . . . and it can turn the public against your enemies . . . "[14]

There are also a number of economic tools for justifying exploitation of a resource. Cost-benefit analysis is a way of supposedly weighing up the gains and the losses in some proposed project. But because it uses financial values, ecological goods rarely carry the same benefit as, say, five minutes off some executive's journey time. In this way, emotive issues of life and death are reduced to harmless sums. As Peter Montague puts it, "It's a process the goal of which is to obtain permission to kill people and to destroy the environment. . . . The whole thing is unconscionable, it's immoral, it's a form of premeditated murder."[15]

Companies know that they cannot meet the accusations of environmentalists head on—that to simply say, "Profit is more important than lives", would not be effective. Instead, a two-handed approach is used. There are a great many corporate sponsors for organizations like the World Wildlife Fund, Nature Conservancy, Environmental Defence Fund, and so on. But the same companies provide funding for about a quarter of the 37 organizations listed in the Greenpeace Guide to Anti-Environmental Organizations—groups dedicated to opposing environmental campaigns.[16]

Why does this happen? Why do more companies not just quietly accept the need to clean up their act? The answer is that they would have to find a way of effectively competing with other companies that did not. Within companies, the more unscrupulous executives will always be able to show better returns. It seems that their most effective strategies are those of converting their enemies into their supporters. The currencies of power they have to wield allows them to buy off support, and even to win true believers. Corporate power does not happen at the level of boardrooms as much as at the grassroots—in the hearts and minds of the general public whose lives and values they have colonized.

"The trade ought not to be abolished. . . . It ought to be preserved and protected as well as any other."—Lord Maitland. "No other measure could inflict so deep and lasting a wound on the commerce of this country."—Mr Rose. "We must not sacrifice to . . . benevolent emotions the dearest, and most valuable commercial interest to this country, and thus rashly and precipitately extinguish a trade so essentially advantageous as a branch of our national commerce."—Alderman Newnham. "[Abolition] would fill the City with men suffering as much as the poor Africans. It would render the City of London one scene of bankruptcy and ruin."—Alderman Newnham.
—Arguments advanced against the abolition of slavery in 1789. Slavery accounted for 18% of GNP at the time.[17]

oppression experienced by others. We shouldn't assume that a West Indian will automatically empathize with a Pakistani simply because they are both black, or that a staunch feminist couldn't possibly be racist. However, it is equally true that where there is a basic congruence in the forms of power experienced, then there will also be real connections and interactions, with each power process reinforcing the other. Even types of power that may appear quite distinct from our traditional notions of oppression, such as hierarchy arising from wealth, or a hierarchy of human over other species, should be recognized as following these connections. As Plumwood puts it, they are 'cut from the same cloth'.[18]

Birds of a Feather

We need to look more closely at how one process of power-over can reinforce or even create another. There may be a facilitator; something which was established principally to enable one instance of domination, but which also provides a convenient mechanism for others. By more convenient, I mean that there is a new 'path of least resistance'. Where before, a system may have been self-managing, the facilitator has made it easier, cheaper, or less complex to meet its needs by dominating another. After all, although I am a keen advocate of empowering systems, I wouldn't say that they are always easier to establish and run. In a world characterized by control and hierarchy, the chances are that it will actually be harder work to ignore all the services and supports available for 'power-over' and be rigorously self-reliant. In fact it will be completely impossible to operate on a day-to-day basis without some recourse to domination, as the facilitators for any other way of working simply are not there. We might say that there is a grain to society, as there is to wood, and that to cut across the grain is very hard work indeed. Machiavelli, one of the first theorists on power, describes it like this: "Men nearly always follow the tracks made by others and proceed in their affairs by imitation even though they cannot entirely keep to the tracks of others or emulate the prowess of their models. So a prudent man must always follow in the footsteps of great men and imitate those who have been outstanding. If his own prowess fails to compare with theirs, at least it has an air of greatness about it."[19]

Plumwood uses the example of the Tasmanian sealing industry to make a similar point. Convicts were transported to Tasmania, where they were exploited by the seal industry, and in turn exploited the Aborigines. Here, the ships were the facilitator: originally intended to control the poor of Britain, but highly convenient for exploiting the seals and supplying the growing market for fuel oil. The seal trade in turn made the transportation of convicts viable. Within eight years, there were too few seals left to be commercially exploited.[20]

There are also interrupters; ways for power-over to interrupt a self-regulating system, and force it to find an alternative way of getting by. Debt is a good example of this: if someone can be forced into debt, they no longer have the opportunity to opt out of the dominant social structures—the debt has to be repaid, and hard currency has to be earned. The interrupter may trigger new, different interruptions as the effect is passed on down the line, like falling dominoes.

Roderick Martin, in *The Sociology of Power*, describes a way of assessing the amount of power in a given relationship.[21] He is suggesting something rather different—a long causal chain leading to an exercise of power—which I do not fully endorse, since I prefer to see power in terms of sustained process rather than isolated exercise. However, if we take a broader view of power as being present at all points on this chain, and not just the last one, then it is possible to see how the possibilities for meeting needs without power-over are at each step interrupted, leading to a further interruption.

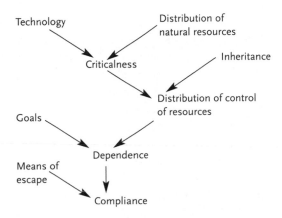

Technology that is designed for resource consumption interrupts a subsistence lifestyle—as does an inequitable distribution of those resources. Once criticalness (the combination of need and scarcity) and inheritance are established, a self-provisioning lifestyle is interrupted, which in turn interrupts self-reliance when combined with materialist goals, which in turn interrupts resistance to authority when means of escape are closed. This compliance might be with the development of further unsustainable technologies, or with the promotion of more materialist goals, and so the cycle is continued. In Plumwood's example, the communities of the poor in Britain, driven to thieve to survive, were deprived of their most active members. This provided compliant labour both at home and abroad. The knock-on effect hit the Aborigines, who were dispossessed, abducted, raped and enslaved. Today, the sustainable culture of the Tasmanian aboriginal has all but disappeared; their descendants are consumers in the global market as much as any of us.[22]

Finally, there is internal dissonance. How long can you sustain a double identity, on the one hand using the techniques of power-over, while on the other hand trying to maintain different parts of your life free from hierarchy? The dissonance operates as an internal form of attrition. Shifting between two modes of action, one concerned with co-operation, consensus and self-realization, and the other a checklist of demands and pressures balanced against levers and opportunities, takes a toll mentally and emotionally. The temptation is to fit in with one process, the one that gets results and which you begin to identify with yourself. It is unsurprising that, without the need for intellectual reflection on the inconsistency, people settle down into a preset pattern of behaviour for handling power. They build a mental set of pathways and algorithms which they bring to every situation, which are loaded with certain assumptions about how to make things happen, and how to meet their needs. It is extremely difficult to sustain the split personality involved in different discourses of power.

These are three mechanisms by which a particular species of power can come to reproduce and diversify itself. There is no conspiracy; or if there is, we are all in on it. Whether in the form of ideological or cultural constructs, or through material objects, or systems of knowledge, power-over leads to more power-over in an unending chain. To coin an old phrase, "and the office boy kicked the cat". Each person passes on the abuse down the line to their 'inferiors'. However, unlike the closed environment of the office, in the open and interrelated space of a society, there is no bottom and there is no top. The chain may start with a corporate executive and end with an embittered parent hitting a child to make it stop crying, and it may seem impossible that the child could ever pass that power on to the corporate boss to complete the cycle. But if the child grows up into a burglar who ransacks the executive's home, the cycle can be completed. And it doesn't have to be the same child burgling the same boss; though it may not involve the same people, there is still a complete circuit, and the power is still passed on.

The Unseen Connections

Of course the connections between different instances of power are often invisible, or obscure. In East London, racist attacks are common: and besides those who carry them out there are a great many willing to justify this persecution. Their discourse is often one of ignorance and prejudice, but there is often a part of it that is grievance: "They steal our jobs", or "They get preferential treatment on the housing waiting list." Invariably these beliefs are proved false, but they continue to arise. I do not believe that they are simply rationalizing a hatred that existed before; I have heard otherwise fair-minded people repeating these lines, albeit in defence of more official racism. When they say "I'm not a racist, but . . ." I think they mean it. They have no problem eating a curry, admiring black sportsmen, or having black friends or colleagues. The few who do cling to a notion of intrinsic evil in those of other race are meaningless without this much larger group whose racism begins with a perceived struggle for allocation—allocation of jobs, allocation of housing.

WHO IS POWERFUL IN THE CORPORATE WORLD?

So if business is a pyramid, who is at the top? In the early days, the answer was perfectly straightforward. The shareholder was clearly in charge, and would play an active part in checking the progress of business. The main shareholder would very often also be the General Manager. However, the nature of shareholders has changed in two important ways. The first is that they are more concerned today with short term financial return, and less inclined to interfere with day-to-day running. If they do not like the way the business is run, they do not object, but simply move their investment elsewhere. This is partly a result of the growing ease of such transactions, and partly reflects the simple fact that capital invested purely for maximum return, without other considerations, will grow faster and hence come to dominate the economy. A second important change is that the investors are now more likely to be corporate than individual. Pension funds and insurance companies between them accounted for 48% of stock market share in 1981, compared to 16.5% in 1963; their gain has largely been at the expense of private shareholders.[23] The fund managers are under intense pressure to detect and follow trends in order to maximize profitability, thus making the markets highly volatile. In some European countries, banks making direct loans are the main source of finance, and stock markets are less significant. So it is increasingly the case that the Chief Executives have an immense amount of discretion.

Or so it would appear. But in fact, the power of the financiers is considerable. Although they may have no day-to-day involvement in the business, and may even have only the vaguest idea of what the business is, they do know exactly what return they are getting from it. Whether it is a bank, or a pension fund manager, or a stockbroker, they react to the figures—and the companies' fortunes can be severely affected. "Majority shareholders, however, generally exercise their power in informal ways. It is common knowledge that many crucial business decisions are made without any close physical connection to the company in question—at a dinner table, in a meeting room at a bank office, at a board meeting of another company that owns a part of the company concerned."[24]

In the same way, as the size of the corporation has grown, the gap between the different layers of management has widened, and the depth of involvement and understanding lessened. In some 'hollow corporations' there is a chain of companies, each owning the one below. Some businesses have in practice only one customer; this customer determines so much of their operations, that their independence is nominal.

Within a conventional structure, the lines of command are clearly laid out. Although corporate speak may politely suggest who an employee 'reports to', the chain is one of superior and inferior down the line. Even where unions have been able to establish a countervailing force, they often find the same hierarchies recreated in their internal structure. The organization is designed so as to leave no ambiguity as to who has power over whom. Though these hierarchies exist everywhere in our society, nowhere are they more naked.

"There is an inherent need to climb upward on the scale. For each little step we take, we gain something to protect and secure. While jealously guarding what we have obtained, we strive to secure a platform to advance and climb further.

"There is also an inherent fear, a fear of losing what we have obtained and of not being able to climb further. We therefore seek power to secure the best possible control over situations that may expose us to any risk of being stopped, or losing what we have obtained. The more we have obtained, the more we have to lose; the more we have to lose, the greater our fear; the greater our fear, the greater our need for power. It is not only our positions or livelihoods that are at stake; it is our very identities."[25]

Some Greens have suggested that these hierarchies are necessary to save the environment. John Elkington writes, "Any company aiming for environmental excellence will need to identify a 'champion' for health, safety and environment, typically a Main Board Director. . . . But the responsibility for ensuring that individual plants or processes are environmentally acceptable must be pushed down to individual line managers. Their suitability for higher positions in the company should be explicitly assessed, as is now the practice in a growing number of companies, on the basis of their success in meeting health, safety and environmental targets, as well as other job- or task-related criteria."[26]

Might we persuade the corporate executives to do the right thing, even if it is for the wrong reason? If we look closely at what Elkington's remedy requires the managers to achieve, it is not necessarily good corporate behaviour. The appearance of good behaviour will do just as well. And if the less scrupulous practice will help meet 'job or task related criteria', then it is that practice that will be followed. The reason why co-operative and community-based businesses (what Robertson and others refer to as 'third sector' organizations—see Chapter 10) are consistently more socially and environmentally benign is that they are able to respond to the full range of human motivations and needs, and can coexist with biological power structures rather than having to compete with them. Power-over opens up artificial chains of command in which information and value is stripped out at every level, leaving only the bottom line—the profit or loss in their currencies of power.

So who is at the top of these pyramids of power? When we try to pin down responsibility for some abuse or crime—whether it is discriminatory practices, a pollution incident, or irresponsible marketing—the employee will always be able to say "I was only obeying orders." Even if those orders were not explicit, the pressure and fear had to be relieved by getting someone, or something else, to carry the burden. Anyone acting responsibly, and taking it all on themselves, cannot outperform someone who is systematically offloading difficult problems on to an 'externality'—something that does not appear in the ledger. Surely, then, responsibility lies with the management to control their staff.

However, the managers—even up to the board of directors—will soon explain they too are under pressure from the company's owners. Even if the shareholders have little contact most of the time, one disappointing dividend could trigger a run that would ruin the business. The drive for market share, for quarterly results, and for higher returns, is unending. The investors must carry the can.

But even they can pass the buck. The mighty pension funds can point to legislation that requires them to deliver the best possible performance to their clients—if they fail, it is not merely slack but actionable. The banks are operating in a competitive market too, in which customers demand the very best service. In all these customer/trader relationships, finer preferences are diluted in the sea of prices. The customer is always right.

And the customers are under pressure because they are the same employees that we heard from earlier. It is a closed circle of pressure and control, in which no one is genuinely in charge. There is no one to whom we can make our demands for sustainability, because there is no one who is totally free to act. It is true that those at the top may have more discretion, and more comfort; but they are there because they delivered the results, and proved themselves to have certain values and preferences. If they had been open to our appeals for justice and compassion, they would likely not have risen so far.

Their sense of being permanently under threat of deprivation leads them to identify and resist anyone who appears to be in competition. In other words the 'power-over' process whereby bureaucrats control whether one is housed or homeless, in work or unemployed, continues into the seemingly unrelated racism. Racism is not just persisting; it is continually erupting as a solution to a problem of powerlessness.

A useful way to understand these interchanges between different power relationships has been suggested by Ian Wingrove. He suggests that we can think of the different forms of systematic aggression as 'currencies of power', analogous to the different currencies in global finance. Just like currencies, these power advantages are a way to meet needs on a daily basis—not just material needs, but emotional needs, needs for meaning, needs for community and identity. Currencies of power may come to us as inheritances (to be born white in a racist state for example) or can be gained deliberately (for instance, by accumulating a lot of money). Although neither Ian Wingrove or I would say that the 'rates of exchange' can be quantified or are in any way fixed, it is true that we can use our status in one hierarchy to offset weakness in another. Further, I would argue that this is not merely a possible use of power, but commonplace in the world of generalized insecurity that power-over produces. A rich woman will experience sexism much less than a poor woman, because she can use the power-over that money provides to offset the discrimination based on sex. These exchanges may take a variety of forms, and these have different dimensions just as Lukes describes. She may use the currency of money to offset the currency of sex by winning conflicts, or by avoiding or selecting conflicts, or by reassuring herself or others that the outcome of a conflict was desirable all along. The latter case is particularly interesting: even where the attempt to avoid hierarchy has failed, and she is clearly reduced to a passive object of men's interest, money can put other people to work to make the subjection comfortable. This use of power does not cure the oppression, and it does not even temporarily neutralize or balance it. It simply passes the psychological pain of it on to someone else.

Racists attacking black people so that 'they don't get houses meant for white folk' have not succeeded in gaining control of their housing from the bureaucrats. They are as helpless as ever they were—in fact more so, having broken the solidarity that they might have gained strength from. And yet their need has been met in one sense: they have regained their identity as being active rather than helpless, and they may even have driven some of their 'rivals' away. When Margaret Thatcher became Prime Minister, that did not necessarily liberate women, or even one woman (herself); she simply surrounded herself with the accoutrements of power to offset the discrimination she would experience as a woman.

This is the true nature of the 'backforce' that Odum realized must be necessary to explain the extended chains of control in modern human society (see Chapter 4). The bottomless hierarchy of power-over could not be sustained without some return at each stage. Why would someone tolerate this control, and pass it on to others, if they don't actually benefit? And yet Odum's suggestion that money was the backforce cannot explain non-financial hierarchies and the accumulation of capital. The backforce is made up of many different currencies of power, exchanged and passed on in the unending struggle for material, social and emotional survival.

Power and Psychosis

There is a distinctive mindset that is associated with continual exchanges of these currencies of power. This is what Derek Wall describes as the 'psychopathology' of power. He says, "Before we can bring about political change, we have to tackle the personal in politics. Individuals cannot repress their egos, insecurities or need for false certainties . . . but they need to be constantly aware of the risks and motives."[27] It doesn't just arise in those struggling to preserve their identity under the weight of oppression: it is also characteristic of those seemingly awash with power. This is because in the dynamic of

BOUGHT OUT

Corporate power is clearly based on turning the world into objects; making commodities out of raw materials and selling them. The principal currency of power on which they are based is money—unusually, you can actually see the exchange taking place. In one direction goes the product, in the other comes money. Those with money have 'demand', and their needs can be met, those without have no demand and must remain unfulfilled. Money is effective as a currency of power because it accumulates, because it is abstracted from what it claims to represent (necessary for control at a distance) and because its power lies not in how much you have, but in how much more of it you have than others. (See also the discussion on LETS in Chapter 12.)

This is seen as a legitimate power, and it is not regarded as any more iniquitous than political power exercised by, say, an elected government. But we can also see other currencies of power taking place alongside that of money. Transnational companies account for most of the flows of energy and resources carried out by humans. As these vast operations take place, they involve other uses of power that are less acceptable. It is only the ability of the corporations to portray them as coincidental that keeps up the veneer of respectability.

The sex industry is one example. As commodities become symbols to boost self-esteem, so women become a means to an end. As the free market entered Eastern Europe, one of the first sunrise industries there was pornography. That is not to say that women were liberated before—rather that as access to the economy was privatized, so was access to women. They became commodities. In a sense, this is not different to anyone else in the labour market—but the terms of trade were far from equal. Maria Mies describes the effect on women of reunification in East Germany: "They lost their crèches, they became the first to be fired when factories were wound up, offices closed or the universities 'de-developed' . . . They are being sent home to 'Kinder und Kuche'. . . The proportion of women unemployed rose from 50% to 62%."

Business also brings with it a division of labour. You are employed not to be yourself, but to do a job—and the definition of the job can come to define the person. This is a relation of power in itself, but it is also a powerful facilitator of other power relations. In South-East Asia, electronics companies employ young women to do delicate and repetitive tasks on the production line, on the basis that they have 'nimble fingers'. The effect of this is to make women the breadwinners in many households, and an expectation among men that their wives will financially support them. Elsewhere in the world, the same arguments about women's physical differences are used to exclude women from the workplace, and from independent earning. The point is that the division of labour by business establishes, or strengthens, the hold that patriarchy has over women. One currency of power creates the conditions in which another can flourish. Women have been turned into a resource, or commodity, leaving them open to colonization and control.

It would be easy to conclude, as many have done, that business is to blame, that finance is the prime mover in the growth of power and instrumental reason. But the cycle can be viewed from another direction. Patriarchy itself has provided the preconditions for capital accumulation by reproducing a mobile and 'free' workforce, and by mobilizing the cost-free household labour that is the precondition for the formal economy. I would even argue that by controlling and desacralizing natural reproduction, the status and worth of commodity production has been elevated and made into the human mission. Would business exist in any recognizable form if we considered household, reproductive work as the basis of our lives, and insisted that commodity production subsidized it as it is presently subsidized?

Any attempt to make economic currencies of power the centre of our study will fail—as will any theory based on the uniqueness of any one currency of power. All forms of oppression have their own logic and internal stability, but as forms of oppression they have an essential compatibility. Whatever their ancient roots and history, they are with us now as autonomous beings. Like all power, they cannot be wholly understood in isolation, nor as functions of a greater whole. They operate for themselves, but without boundaries.

---

power-over, only power itself is truly powerful. Everyone else is permanently insecure, watching their back or struggling to reconcile their actions with their values.

Dick Morris was a political consultant in America. He helped an Arkansas politician to win the Governorship of the state—a man called Bill Clinton. In 1994, President Clinton saw his supporters in Congress routed by a resurgent Republican Party, and realized his chances of winning a second term were in jeopardy and called Dick Morris to rescue him. A series of astute analyses and predictions gave Morris a position of considerable trust and influence with Clinton. "A turning point was Clinton's hugely successful Balancing the Budget speech on June 13, 1995. For me, it was a moment of personal satisfaction. The newsmagazines [provided] evidence that I had 'won' this intra-White House battle. I had crossed a threshold and affected a major policy decision. I was proud, of course, but also felt inadequate. Was I right? Did I know what I was talking about? To convince the President, I had shown great confidence in my political wisdom, but did I really know? I had to pocket these doubts." But this didn't work—currencies of power burn a hole in your pocket. "I overcompensated. I became more and more arrogant. As my predictions came true, I began to believe in my perspicacity as it was reported in the press

. . . I found myself becoming more brusque and sharp with people, more dictatorial where once I had tried to be persuasive. Now I was impatient and often unkind. My sense of triumph manifested itself in other, more self-destructive ways. . . . I began the relationship with the prostitute that led to the President's embarrassment and my fall. I could get away with anything, I felt. I wanted Clinton to win. To do that, I had to help change his course, as he had directed me to do. To do that, I needed power. But power corrupted me and became an addiction."[28]

Power-over depends on a particular way of relating to the world; it has a distinctive culture associated with it. This ideology arises out of the need to rationalize our lives and find a way of thinking consistent with our way of life that I described earlier. It requires us to relate to the world around us as if it were a collection of inanimate objects—things that you hope to control, or influence, or command. It is, in fact particularly compatible with the individualist and collectivist worldviews described in chapter 2, since it implies a separation between these objects, rather than seeing them as interrelated. For instance, a large part of the problems that we have had with protecting endangered species is the public's failure to realize that you cannot save the tiger without saving the forests that it lives in, including all the plants, insects, and animals that make them up. It especially requires a separation between the dominator and the dominated, because otherwise one would believe that what one did to the object one was in some sense doing to oneself. This is largely true (since we live in a highly interconnected world), and many people refrain from excessive use of power-over because they are aware that it is true, but the use of currencies of power is about evading responsibility, and evading consequences. So the culture of power-over tends to deny interconnectedness. This is not to say there is no camaraderie or co-operation—just that such group bonding tends to be strongest when the group can define itself as a superior élite in opposition to someone else. Because the group can be split at any time by difference, it is not inclusive, but a group where you must continually establish your credentials for membership.

The object of power-over is the 'other', the different. Difference fits in with separation, and so becomes an important source of currencies of power. Wherever there is an identifiable difference, a separation between the subject and the different object can be justified. This process is called 'objectification', and it is present wherever power-over operates. It is a process of denial: denial of history, denial of value, denial of rationality or order, denial of agency. Contrast these two views of black Africans. The Arabian traveller Ibn Battuta wrote in 1352, "The Negroes have some admirable qualities. They are hardly found to be unjust, because they abhor injustice more than any other people . . . In their land there is perfect security. Neither travellers nor inhabitants have to be afraid of thieves or violent men." But by 1830, Hegel (the

German philosopher) was writing, "The Negro represents natural man in all his savagery and unruliness; if one wants to understand him correctly, one has to abstract from him all human respect and morality. In this character there is nothing that reminds one of the human. This is perfectly corroborated by the extensive reports of the missionaries. Therefore the Negroes get the total contempt of human beings. . . ." Here is the process of objectification laid out step by step.

Objectification assumes the passivity and valuelessness necessary to justify the use of the object as a means to end, rather than relating to the object as an end in itself. This has been described by many writers as the subtext in justifications for the subjection of women, black people, gays and others. They are lacking in rationality, they are controlled by their animal nature—indeed, non-human nature itself is objectified in this way. It is not only the identifiably oppressed groups who are dealing with power-over—it is the poor confronting capital, it is the citizen confronting government, it is the operator confronting hard technology, it is the entire living planet confronting colonization. Central to the process, as in the above quote, is the idea of what a real human is: pure reason, detached from 'nature' (which is itself defined as not-human), detached from other humans, and in control.

Objectification in Critical Theory

The way in which the world is reduced by modern industrial society to objects for our use, rather than interrelated communities with their own ends, has been noted by many theorists. One analysis coming from the Marxist tradition is that of Critical Theory, and the numerous points of correspondence make it worth closer examination. The phrases used vary—'instrumental reason' is the best established—but they concern the reduction of human thought into a project to control. "What men want to learn from nature is how to use it in order to dominate it and other men."[29] Horkheimer and Adorno use the word 'nature' here in a broad sense, as in 'natural science'. They argue that instrumental reason, by denying any other source of value in the world, chokes off any line of thought that might question it.

As Marxists, the Critical Theorists saw a material cause of this worldview—the development of means of production that demanded an unprecedented concentration of labour and raw materials. I would note that the worldview and the scientific revolution that accompanied it were to some extent the source of the new factories. 'Cultural Marxism' does recognize that historical development is not purely material—ideas do have some part to play. The culture generated by material forces stabilizes the system, containing and suppressing change. Although they still argue that material reality drives history, culture and ideology have an important role also—as the brakes (I will consider the problems of hegemony and the dominant culture further in

QUESTIONING KEN

A few weeks ago, I was standing in the office of the Chief Executive of a fairly typical national corporation in the North of England. The company was called Morrisons, and the man whose office I was in was called Ken Morrison; it was quite a young company—one that was still driven by a human vision, rather than by its own internal logic. This vision was one of supermarkets.

One particular vision was to build a supermarket in the middle of a community in Leeds. The local community were opposed to the idea; they did not want the extra traffic generated by what would be the largest supermarket for miles around, they did not want the loss of local shops, they did not want the loss of green space. They had the support of the local Councillors, and indeed the Council, but Morrisons had a great deal of money at their disposal and this was proving decisive (I shan't go into the details).

So I and a dozen others went to put these points to Ken and see what he said. We didn't have an appointment—it was sheer luck that he was working in the office when we walked in. He was wearing a shirt and tie. We were in casual, or frankly scruffy clothes. He was middle aged, paunchy and male. We were young, and a mixture of types. It was just before Christmas, and the office was festooned with Christmas cards. On closer examination, it turned out that they weren't from people so much as other companies—Nestlé, Procter and Gamble and others.

We had a long talk with Ken Morrison. He was not pleased to see us—this was probably his first experience of direct action, and he was at a bit of a loss. He could not buy us off, because we weren't particularly interested in money. He could not rely on the men to side with him against the women, because there was an understanding among us that men and women should co-operate on equal terms. He could not disparage the community in question as urban peasants, because we identified with them more than we aspired to his executive lifestyle. He could not convince us that this glorious development was part of the progress of civilization, because we saw more civilization in a mud hut than in a skyscraper.

He needed that site, and none of his usual arguments seemed to affect us. We wanted him to take the community's concerns seriously, but if he did it would call into question most of his life's work. He could not understand how we could fail to be swayed by him. "It's legal," he kept insisting. "It's wrong," we kept replying. He looked baffled.

What he could do was use force. His chief of security stood nervously by the door as we smiled at him. The police were on their way. He had the legal right to use 'minimum reasonable force' to remove us, and I made it very clear that we would be wholly passive as we were carried out. The job would have been no more arduous than carrying a few dozen sacks of potatoes. And yet nothing seemed to scare them more. They almost begged us to leave of their own accord. The policeman in attendance was equally thrown. Why would we prefer to be carried out than to leave of our own accord?

They could not do it because it would have been too naked a display of power. Power—even power-over—relies on consent. It is a game, not a war. There must be a trade, an exchange of currencies, to conceal the reality of domination.

In desperation, Ken offered to meet with the representatives of the community. We set a few conditions, and then agreed and left of our own accord. At the time of writing, the supermarket is still due to go ahead. But I suspect Ken has more to learn about the power of direct action.

Chapter 9; and for a discussion of whether material or cultural explanations are preferable, see Chapter 5).

Horkheimer shares with more recent Green theorists an awareness that the growth of power-over is also the growth of powerlessness. "The more devices we invent for dominating nature, the more we must serve them if we are to survive." He sees instrumental reason as the only way one can survive: "Self-preservation . . . presupposes adjustment to the requirements for the preservation of the system."[30] In this way, the only way we can survive control and domination is to control and dominate others. Any perceived difference can be a justification for systematic control.

Is this the reason for the interlocking of the very different processes of power—that the demands of modern life force us to treat the whole world around us as means to the end of survival? Less materialist analyses would argue that the idea of nobility and godliness being located somehow 'above' the natural, vernacular world, is a better model. After all, it is not only the desperate and oppressed who resort to power-over, but those in relatively secure positions too. Or did they only achieve those positions because they had so successfully internalized the practice of instrumental reason?

Here, as elsewhere, I want to resist the temptation to locate the driving force of power in any one place. Instrumental reason, transcendence, and even psychoanalytic concepts like the rejection of the mother will all provide insights into different aspects of power-over. What matters is the process running through them, and how we can escape from it. Critical Theorists remind us that history is a one way street, and that the material conditions of insecurity are closely connected to power-over. However, they disagree over whether that means an expansion in productive capacity—which I would argue would involve an intensification of power-over—or, as Marcuse suggests, a reduction of 'overdevelopment' in favour of post-materialist lifestyles. We cannot go back, it is true; but there is more than one way forward.[31]

Resistance without Revenge

It is not enough to speak of resistance. As Foucault says, there is no power without resistance, and everywhere that people face power-over, they are also to be found establishing identity, security and their material needs. But the strength of the power system is that the easiest and most tempting ways to purchase these needs are with further currencies of power (the fourth dimension of power, as described in chapter 1). Deferring the problem is always easier than solving it, and the pathways of power-over are so well trodden as to invite further use. In our minds, in our tools, in our communities and in our geography, power is the only universally accepted currency. And so we find patriarchy even among those who have suffered so much under racism; we find the poor stealing from each other; we find environmentalists building hierarchical organizations; we find oppressed nations oppressing other nations. This is no way forward.

In a situation where we feel out of control, it is a predictable response to try and gain more control over events using power-over. It is important to remember that not only is such an approach wrong and destructive of power-to, but that it is also ineffective. It does not deliver the control that it promises. For an example, consider the international 'war on drugs'—an attempt to stamp out what is now the fourth largest trade in the world after arms, cars and oil. In Britain, 20% of the population has tried illegal drugs; the number of people addicted to so-called hard drugs is continuing to rise; and the purity and safety of drugs continues to decline. As power-over attempts to control, it raises the symbolic stakes. Profits in the illegal trade are growing precisely because it is illegal; addiction increases because it cannot legally be managed; the aura of 'forbidden fruit' only makes the banned substances more tempting; and the diversion of resources away from social provision into policing and punishment increases people's need for an escape route from boredom and despair. Power-over generates more power-over; control leads inexorably to chaos.

If we treat others as objects, we will find ourselves the losers in the power game. We traumatize each other, carving the patterns of master and slave on our brains. We break up ecological communities, imposing grinding hierarchy in their place. Things do not have to get worse before they can get better. Worse means worse, and there is no limit to how bad things can get for us poor human animals. The stakes encompass everything from our viability on this earth, through to our capacity to feel love and respect for each other. All the struggles against power are our struggle, and the movements that form around a particular issue must recognize the common truth of self-determination that they share with others.

The movements need to co-operate in a single struggle because the system of power-over does. In Chapter 8, I will go on to outline the shape of this system:

CONTAINMENT AND SURVIVAL

If one were deciding how to run an economy in an abstract, idealized utopia, it is unlikely that the modern hierarchical corporation is the model one would choose. In Chapter 7, I hope the outlines of an alternative will emerge. However it is equally true that the consequences of this ongoing colonization need to be addressed on a day-to-day basis. Before we can defeat power-over, we have to contain it.

This is because the spread of power-over closes off any opportunity to develop an alternative. The destruction of the Earth's biological systems leave us dependent on technological substitutes and the power that sustains them. The spread of the values and rationality of power blinds people to the possibility of change—survival demands total acceptance of the competitive ethos. Every new pathway facilitates power-over, just like roads through the rainforest lead to the destruction of the forest by people for whom the road may never have been intended.

The protest movement is the fire brigade of social change. They must respond rapidly to the spread of domination and obstruct its progress. Although in themselves they cannot prevent it altogether, they can hold it back and protect the space from which an alternative can come.

As an example of an effective exercise in containment, let us look at the protests against mahogany and other tropical timbers carried out in the UK in the 90s. Britain was a major source of demand for tropical hardwoods, and the native forests of Brazil and Indonesia were being devastated to meet that need. The protesters identified a chain of processes—the felling of the trees, the shipping into Britain, the storage at wholesale timber yards and the retail through DIY stores. At each stage, the processes could be blocked.

Protesters travelled to Indonesia and met up with the native people of the forests. They had been resisting the destruction of their lifestyle and the annexation of their lands—for them, there was no distinction between defending themselves and defending the forest. A series of blockades of the forest roads forced the Indonesian government into an embarrassing display of force to fell the trees.

As the ships carrying the trees arrived at ports in Britain, protesters occupied the ports. They D-locked themselves to the gigantic lock gates, and climbed into the port cranes. Preliminary discussions with the dockers' unions ensured that work on unloading the ships stopped immediately the protesters arrived. Ships were forced to totally change their times of arrival or even destination.

At the timber yards where the hardwood was stored, mass invasions brought trade to a standstill for days at a time. Overwhelmed by the numbers and at a loss as to how to deal with determined but peaceful resistance, the police gave up trying to exclude us. The companies involved found themselves having to justify their trade to a hostile and inquisitive press. Some companies were caught with wood taken from trees listed as endangered species, and had to explain themselves to Customs Officers.

At the retail parks, the protesters used street theatre and literature to communicate to an increasingly sympathetic public. Demand for mahogany fell, and retail companies found themselves competing to see how quickly they could distance themselves from the trade. 'Ethical shoplifting' invited the companies to prove their ownership of the timber in the courts. They were unwilling to do so, in the face of evidence that the logging was carried out illegally. They could only watch as protesters picked up mahogany products and left without paying.

It would be tempting to argue that the protesters should have concentrated their efforts not at the periphery, but at the 'centres' of power, and should have organized themselves so that their leaders could establish relationships with the corporate bosses. Mongoven, Biscoe and Duchin is a public relations firm that advises businesses to encourage just this.[32] These 'professional' protesters are described as 'realists' and are considered "the best candidates for constructive dialogue" because they accept trade-offs and partial solutions and don't want to lose access to the corporate hierarchy. "Radicals" on the other hand are "difficult to deal with", and idealists "are easily believed by both media and the public". The direct action protests are effective because they provide no support for power-over and grant it no legitimacy.

No one would claim that the forests are safe now, but the companies involved have seen crucial sources of power cut off: access to forests, access to customers, control over labour, control over information. The eco-war has not been won yet, but the battles are nonetheless significant.

---

its connections can be mapped and its physiology understood. Plumwood suggests one way to understand the relationship between the many different, seemingly separate, instances of power and domination. ". . . these forms of oppression are seen as very closely, perhaps essentially, related and working together to form a single system without losing a degree of distinctness and differentiation. One working model which enables such an escape from the one/many dilemma pictures oppressions as forming a network or web"[33] (see Chapter 8).

This doesn't mean that difference should be forgotten or denied. The 'colour-blindness' of treating everyone the same can even reproduce the old hierarchies, since those for whom our society was built will always have an easier ride. Difference is real and means different knowledge, different needs and different ways of being. Tolerance and respect are the key in leaving autonomy at every level: to say that the black woman's struggle is my struggle is not to claim equal knowledge or experience to black people or to women. But we can know that any use of power-over will drive a wedge between us and someone else, even if we cannot yet see who they are.

Our organizations must not mimic those we oppose, or they will mimic their effects too. I share the concerns of those who want professionalism and efficiency. They argue that we can compromise our principles in our organization since 'the brush is not the painting'. However, I don't agree that professionalism and efficiency are the monopoly of hierarchies, and I do believe that the party is the politics. 'The master's tools will never dismantle the master's house.'[34] Living in empowering communities does not start tomorrow, it starts today.

In a survey of 900 executives in 16 industrialized countries:

27% had been involved in questionable business practices ranging from bribery and dishonesty to law-breaking.

53% had experienced a conflict between the demands of their company and what they personally believed to be right.

50% of the Europeans and 40% of Latin Americans said that in the course of their work they had been asked to conceal or falsify information.

33% of managers who acted according to their consciences rather than to company dictates suffered penalties ranging from lack of promotion to job loss.[35]

Chapter 7

No one's Slave,
no one's Master

Empowerment, or power-to, can describe the experiences and practices of Greens in political action, and explain their ability to achieve their goals without using coercive power. It is also an increasingly widespread concept in mainstream society, as a number of social changes make participatory organization more common. However, this 'power-to' takes many forms and is implemented to greater and lesser degrees. Token instances are better understood as simply a repackaging of power-over. Although empowerment is a hot issue in the workplace, it is only rarely being delivered—and then only by changing the whole relationship between employer and employed.

Power-to must involve participation, but not any kind of participation: it is only when it is active and constructive that it meets needs effectively. Empowerment is a process of self-organization and self-realization—a process, because it is passed on through co-operation between different empowered agents. Through co-operation, we can build whole empowered societies.

We can identify a number of sources of power-to—preconditions for the emergence of self-organization. The relationship with the land is crucial, because so many of these power resources depend on a healthy and life-sustaining environment.

Power-to is not a panacea. Within co-operative organizations there are problems and conflicts, many of them recurrent or chronic. But they are problems of negotiation and inertia, and those are preferable to the potentially catastrophic consequences of unbridled power-over.

"In Islam, during the holy month of Ramadan, it is said that one night is holiest of all: al Qadr, the Night of Power. According to Islamic belief, it was on this night that the Qu'ran was delivered to the Prophet Mohammed, and it is thus the holiest of all nights. On this night, prayers are granted 'for everything that matters'. . . .

"I will never forget the Night of Power that shook me, not during the holy month of Ramadan, but in the hot, humid summer of 1995, when I sat on death row's Phase II with a date to die.

"The sun had set behind the hills of West Virginia amid ominous thunderheads, and now the forces of nature struck like a divine assault team.

"Lightning stabbed the earth as if in the throes of celestial passion, and so powerful were the bolts that the lights in the block—indeed, in the whole jail—flickered out. . . .

"I sat there in the first real darkness since my arrival to Phase II, transfixed by the display of such raw, primeval power.

"Watching the veins of nature pulse through the night sea of air, making—if only for milliseconds—daylight over the hills, I felt renewed. How puny man seemed before this divine dance!

"I saw, then, that though human powers sought to strangle and poison me and those around me, they were powerless. I saw that there is a Power that makes man's power pale. It is the power of Love; the power of God; the power of life. I felt it surging through every pore.

"Nature's power prevailed over the man-made, and I felt, that night, that I would prevail. I would overcome the State's efforts to silence and kill me."

—Mumia Abu Jamal, Night of Power, from *Death Blossoms*

It is hard to sum up in a single phrase what I mean by this power of self-management, of co-operation. It is paradoxical to combine the inner strengths of independence and self-discipline with the co-operative, collective work that brings us together; Starhawk, for example, considers them quite distinct.[1] It is also an idea that goes beyond the more general term of 'empowerment' (commonly used in political writing to mean simply delegated power, or individual power) or the more specific words like participation, self-determination, or autonomy (which captures the idea of independence, but not the sense of community). For the sake of readability, I nonetheless use the word empowerment to mean 'power-to'.

Perhaps experience is the best guide to what it means, but even here our lives in a hierarchical society leave us short of real, day-to-day experience of what I call power-to. My experiences of this real empowerment are varied, and may seem to have little in common. However, certain themes recur.

Non-violent direct action has often created situations in which we, who have deliberately made ourselves vulnerable and exposed, have been able to effectively incapacitate the power structures around us. We are not exactly powerful ourselves—we have none of the 'powers over' that those we confront have at their disposal—no guns, no diggers, no chainsaws, no employees, no police—and yet we can make ourselves virtually immovable, we can bring businesses grinding to a halt, we can build entire villages and dismantle destructive technologies. We seem able, some of the time, to protect ourselves: it is almost as though an invisible barrier comes between us and the 'authorities'. On one occasion I was threatened with arrest unless I obeyed an order. I simply held out my wrists for the policeman to put on the handcuffs. He stared back at me in astonishment, and after struggling to find words said, "And don't think I'm going to give you the satisfaction of being arrested—that's just what you want!", and stomped off. Now, I'm not saying that the countless non-violent activists who have been arrested, beaten and even killed somehow got it wrong. The task that we have taken on is so difficult that the best of our power can be overwhelmed. But I remain of the opinion that non-violent defence of just causes can generate a power matching that of the state in effectiveness, and yet qualitatively different in effect.

I have purchased three large houses, with over thirty acres of land, while my income was so low as to classify me as one of the poorest in society. Somehow, the connections I made with others to form a housing co-operative, and by extension with the ethical investors in the Ecology Building Society and Radical Routes, allowed all of us to suddenly and dramatically bypass the economic barriers that should have faced us. We had made choices that would appear on the face of it to consign us to powerlessness—rejecting conventional careers, campaigning for radical, minority political positions, living low-consumption lifestyles—and yet we seemed to have the power to build a home, to bring our gardens bursting into life, and to have at least as much fun as anyone else.

What I am trying to say is that power-to is a process as much as power-over, and in the same way achieves results that are more than the sum of its parts. The term empowerment is often misused to refer to an individual's drive, or ambition, or confidence, that leads them to succeed and out-compete others in the world of power. In my view, this is missing the point of empowerment, and what they are describing is either a situation in which they think they are more powerful than they really are (in that, for instance, they merely happen to conform to the agenda of someone else) or that they are merely exercising a lot of power-over. Just as the 'holders' of power-over do not hold it but are merely part of its pathway, so power-to is participation in a process. However, it is a process of local self-management through the co-operation or symbiosis of equals.

Why Now?

The politics of participation and empowerment have a particular resonance at this time. I would argue that the rise of the Green movement, with its logic of organic, vernacular communities, has much to do with this. However, there are a number of historical movements and forces at work that make many societies unusually receptive to power-to.

Postmodernism is often summed up as the collapse of grand narratives; a state in which monolithic sources of authority fragment. It is both a cultural movement, a belief system, and a set of real changes in the economy and in people's lifestyles. In itself, it is neither liberating nor oppressive—it is the battlefield, not the struggle. However, the interaction of postmodern sensibilities with radical political forces has removed a number of barriers. Radical politics had been tied closely to modernist conceptions of the state and collective liberation, which implied a top-down coordination—replacing the power of the oppressor with the same power dynamic run by those previously oppressed.

Talk of a decentred, self-managing utopia was threatening: it endangered the unity of the collective project. With the rise of the new left, of radical liberalism in Britain, and a revival of anarchist ideas (not to mention the Situationists throughout Europe), alternative models of social change which recognized the role of empowerment began to gain ground. The collapse of a series of East European governments at this time may have been principally of symbolic importance, but it certainly reinforced this trend.

Changes in the economic structures of society have also opened new lines of thought. The changing division of labour has created communities of almost permanent unemployment alongside the relative affluence of those in employment. The rise of the 'hollow corporation' has encouraged a growth in small businesses—at the same time as an increase in their rate of failure. And new technology has enabled more independent, local working units. Power-over continues to be exercised savagely through the network of contracts and competition, where previously it was exercised through control and direction. However, a number of effects resulting from these changes are of interest.

The small businesses and self-employed subcontractors experienced a number of new pressures and insecurities from their situation. However, there is no shortage of people willing to confirm the sense of relief at being 'their own boss', and the benefits of this autonomy. Having experienced this empowering lifestyle at work, many now come to expect it in other fields.

The 'New International Division of Labour' refers to the growing mobility of capital and technology that have led to manufacturing relocating to areas with cheap and flexible labour markets. It has cut into revenue that Western powers used to take for granted, putting pressure on public services at exactly the same time as a more entrepreneurial society demands lower taxation. This means a growing number of groups self-organizing to protect services, and a move to getting more out of the service provision by involving volunteers and the community. Of course, there is much in these two trends that is about quality of the service rather than the quantity, and user involvement has risen on the basis of a confluence of interests.[2]

The underclass of forgotten people has experienced an almost catastrophic level of neglect, and efforts to develop depressed communities have necessarily sought participatory strategies (see Chapter 5), though there is still a heavy focus on 'attracting inward investment'.

None of these factors make empowering institutions and structures inevitable—this is part of a history of discussion of empowerment that has been part of discussions of democracy as long as the concept of democracy has been understood. However, they do give rise to a better range and depth of experience for us to draw on in trying to visualize a social dynamic of power-to. A 1995 survey by the Industrial Society showed that over two to three years, employers expect a trend towards empowerment in business practice. And yet

WHAT IS WORK?

Work is a concept that eludes definition; it covers too wide a range of possibilities. It can be the thing that gives meaning to our lives or that we hope we will be remembered by. It can be an act of love that binds a family together, as parents support their children and prepare them for their place in the world. It can be the means of subsistence, and it can be the drudgery that ties us down.

There has always been power-over in work: for instance, sailors will always want to have a skipper who will give orders in a crisis. But it is a measure of the dominance of power-over in our society today how many people—particularly in industrialized countries—have no work beyond directing, co-ordinating and administering other people. As the scale and scope of organizations increase, more and more work is required to service the hierarchy. Entire industries have grown up concerned with manipulating people. The advertising industry may argue that it is a vehicle of information, and this is certainly true; but the information is linked to a desired action, and sometimes the pressure applied to people's deepest concerns (providing for their children, asserting their masculinity, attracting a partner) is frankly coercive.

Work has become an issue in modern society in a way that it was not before. When I talk to people about their aspirations for work, ideas recur like independence, craft, small scale, convivial workplaces and work that is close to nature. In a world capable of such spectacular achievements and such affluent lifestyles, why is it not possible to do work that we enjoy? Part of the answer is that subsistence or craft work cannot compete with the energy subsidies and the level of capital accumulation in industrialized commodity production. Although one could pass up the affluence of high earnings, this choice of relative poverty carries a high social price. And access to scarce resources, such as land and capital tools, is regulated solely on the basis of money. So a subsistence lifestyle is not easy to achieve—the pressure to achieve employment in the mainstream marketplace is intense.

At the same time, the substitution of flexible, mobile capital for rebellious, expensive labour has reduced the need for full-time workers. As a result, unemployment—enforced idleness—is now a long-term, entrenched problem, not only in industrialized countries but in many developing countries where the poor have been forced off the land. For those in work, job insecurity means that they are in many cases overworked, with long hours, high demands and overtime contributing to stress and exhaustion.

When we ask how many people's working lives are consistent with their most idealistic aspirations, we must conclude that the work required by the dynamic of power-over is simply not what we were born to do.

of the same managers, only one in five thought their organization was empowering at present. My feeling is that few if any understood, or were willing to accept, what they had to give up in terms of control and regulation if they were to achieve this goal of empowerment. The world of work seems to be where all these pressures are coming together to force discussion of empowerment into the mainstream.

Forms and Degrees of Empowerment

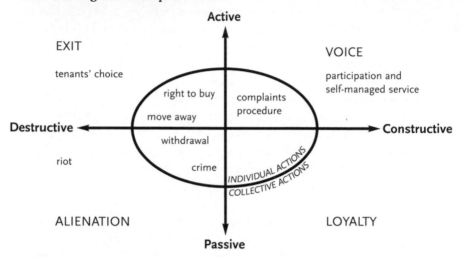

This diagram[3] illustrates effectively the different strategies adopted by people seeking participation or control in our society. The horizontal axis shows whether the action is constructive or destructive, and the vertical whether it is active or passive. This gives rise to four categories—exit, voice, alienation and loyalty. Some of these do not seem particularly empowering. The examples of crime and riot in particular seem more like uses of power-over, although there is a case for arguing that the collective experience of a riot is a process of building identity. A better example of alienated empowerment might be the negativistic and nihilistic subcultures that have emerged as a reaction to the affluent Western lifestyle. I also think that the category of loyalty might be better described as solidarity, or commitment—in an empowering setting, it is not an obligation or expectation, but a choice.

Are the passive and destructive expressions of empowerment ever dysfunctional? They certainly are—those with experience of consensus-building processes are well aware of the destructive potential of someone blocking consensus, and co-operatives are very familiar with the problems of 'free riders' who take more than they give. I will return to this later. It is important to recognise that the actual effects of a process of power are largely dependent on the context—on the other forms of power in operation at the same time. As well as the type of empowerment, we have to be aware how far the logic of self-regulation has been carried.

Croft and Beresford show that over the latter half of the twentieth century, participation was being used in a number of fields—but only hesitantly. In land use planning, there was a growing sense that consultation was important—but that the expert's decision was final. Secondly, there were models of community development work growing out of a colonial history, but adapted to application in industrialized (and de-industrializing) societies. The idea of social change plus user involvement brought results—but often the reality of small, under-resourced groups outran the rhetoric of collective action. Finally, disenchantment with officious public services led to demands for user-led services, rather than provider-led. However, this concept tended to regard the users more as consumers than citizens.[4]

These hesitant steps towards genuine empowerment are reflected in Arnstein's well known analogy, the ladder of participation. The bottom rungs are manipulation and therapy—the involvement of the citizen is simply a way of using them, or correcting them. Next there are informing, consulting and placating, which are progressively more helpful attempts to gain people's support for an agenda decided elsewhere. Then come partnership, delegate power and citizen control: increasingly immediate involvement. Only near the top of this ladder do we find anything really worth calling empowerment. Of course, there is more to empowerment than the amount of nominal control—for instance, access and support.

8 Citizen Control	
7 Delegated Power	Degrees of citizen power
6 Partnerships	
5 Placation	
4 Consultation	Degrees of token participation
3 Informing	
2 Therapy	
1 Manipulation	Non-participation

Participatory development strategies ask people to be active and constructive. It is not simply asking for loyalty, as most authorities do; participation fails if the provider is unwilling to tolerate criticism. And it is not merely allowing the 'service consumer' to 'take their business elsewhere', as the consumerist marketplace does.[5]

This is an important remainder that within an overall dynamic of power-over, token instances of power-to are dead ends. How many of us have experienced our complaints being treated as our problem, to be treated and cured, rather than that of our society? Consultation rarely leads to a product that we genuinely feel a part of. Instead, it is more often a process of building legitimacy and preparing public opinion. By furious protest we get some concessions (step 5 on the ladder), but even here we cannot really claim to be driving the process.

Even in the case of the higher levels of participation, we have to ask: is the question already decided? If a citizen body has decision-making powers, but the environment in which they have to operate is largely controlled by outside forces, the decisions they take will not be in a vacuum, motivated by abstract principle. Their effective options are limited to those that will work, and those are limited by the economic, cultural, political and social structures of power-over. We cannot assess the degree of empowerment for an enterprise on the basis of its actions and achievements alone, but rather on the wider dynamic that it is part of, or that it contributes to.

The phrase 'citizen's control' also fails to capture what I understand to be the spirit of power-to. It suggests democratized, or decentralized control—a fairer or more legitimate control, but still control. That is not to say that true empowerment cannot be orderly or led, but that it should not imply static roles of controller and controlled—especially when the controller is some body claiming to speak for 'the citizens'. As Foucault says, "It is not through recourse to sovereignty against discipline that the effects of disciplinary power can be limited, because sovereignty and discipline are two absolutely integral constituents of the general mechanism of power in our society." If we are to conceive of empowerment in its purest sense (admittedly somewhat artificial, but nonetheless useful to clarify our concepts), then structures of control, however democratic, cannot form a part of it. Consent, or negotiation, is a crucial concept in empowerment. No settlement is final, no outcome predetermined. Those concerned that power-over leaves them out of control will not find power-to delivering the goods: the idea of control is an illusion.

So what is the essence of power-to? It is the process of self-realization, or self-organization. A unit (whether it is an individual, community or network) finds its direction from within and regulates itself; and units combine in co-operative or negotiated local structures to form larger scale communities. Using the energy flow diagrams introduced in Chapter 4, a self-regulating unit can be represented as follows:

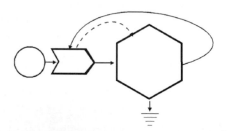

Note that the backforce of symbolic power, which in power-over created 'currencies of power' (see previous chapter), can operate in this dynamic too; however, they feed back to their own source. This could take the form of a LETS currency in which you regulate your own credit; or a cultural ritual that regulates consumption. Imposed discipline is replaced by self-discipline. Empowerment, then, in the sense that I want to use the word, refers to a practice that is self-reliant and self-directed, and that negotiates boundaries with its environment. This in itself seems to describe a rather insular, or introverted form of behaviour—hardly powerful at all. To understand power-to as a dynamic, it is important to describe the relationships between these units.

Power-with

Starhawk says of power-with that it is social power: "The power not to command, but to suggest and be listened to, to begin something and see it happen. The source of power-with is the willingness of others to listen to our ideas. . . power-with is double bladed. It can be the seedbed of empowerment, but it can also spawn oppression." However, she also says, "Systems of domination destroy power-with, for it can only truly exist among those who are equal and who recognize they are equal."[6] There seems to be a contradiction here, since Starhawk tries to say at the same time that power with can be an amplifier of both power-over and power-to (indeed, that neither can achieve much without it) and yet at the same time that it does not combine effectively with power-over. Part of what she is doing here is to stress that just because things like leadership and drive and organization have been associated with power-over, they are not necessarily oppressive: this is certainly a point worth making. However, I feel that it is important to recognize that a dynamic of power is meaningless when described as the property of one individual; the forms of power we are trying to describe are forms of relationship. For this reason, I do not think the social aspect of power is best treated as separate from its dynamic. Power-to, just as much as power-over, operates through a society.

Within an ecosystem, we can see different species interacting to create, in effect, another self-regulating unit on a larger scale. This achieves equilibrium not through plan or control but through feedback, trial and error, or negotiation—however you want to think of it. We can see the same process operating in human communities, with the additional mechanism of language. Language provides the symbolic backforce to bind individuals in co-operative arrangements—just as, in societies dominated by power-over, they are bound together in hierarchies.

What is happening here as a group is not fundamentally different from the self-reliant individual. The process is the distinctive part: the flow of energy into self-regulation, the being as an end in itself rather than a means to an end. Humans are no less capable of such organization than any other species, indeed they have more facilities for co-operation at their disposal. However, these

THE DEATH OF WORK AND THE WORK OF DEATH

The big issue in work, and yet the one that is hardly ever addressed, is that of alienation. Both unemployment and overemployment are symptoms of the loss of control over work and livelihood, but the root problem applies to almost everyone: our work is no longer our own. It is to someone else's specification, or someone else's design, or someone else's profit, or someone else's use. It is no longer part of community but apart from community. In this sense, work has died; the life has gone out of it, as we have lost faith in it. We may believe that what we are doing is useful, but even that is a long way from believing that it is ours. In many cases, such a belief is a justification after the fact.

Such justifications are present even in the unjustifiable. Companies selling arms to oppressive regimes, companies selling torture equipment, companies selling tobacco; all can generate elaborate belief systems about how they are only meeting a need, or behaving more responsibly than others might. These are all ways in which people reconcile an intuitive sense of right and wrong with an everyday reality that is in stark contradiction with it.

Work is even killing the workers. In Japan, there is a recognized cause of death that translates as 'death through overwork'. Although much is made of the compact between firm and employee in Japan, the reality is the ever-present threat of unemployment. Short term contracts and intense pressure to maintain productivity take their toll—a high level of suicide and injury and death at work.

Power-over demands a level of self-deception and denial, as we struggle to find self-esteem and self-worth in tasks that we have not chosen and that are set by forces beyond us. This is not merely a problem of powerlessness as part of an organization or institution, but powerlessness in an economy that rewards work on some tasks but not others. This is not to say that an economy based on power-to would not have its own dictates and direction; but that the work it requires is determined at a more local level and with a higher degree of participation. The criteria by which it judges are human, intuitive ones rather than the abstract calculations of competitive power. The dynamics are towards access and co-operation rather than exclusion and competition.

Work in power-to is driven by our creativity and our needs, and stops when we have achieved sufficiency. The skills of leadership are rewarded, but so are those of critical and selective consent. Co-operation begins with someone setting a lead, but proceeds on the basis of others developing the idea, and supporting or withholding support at every stage as it progresses. For this reason, it favours those with a certain degree of confidence in their views, but not such certainty that they are hard to work with. This quality, often summed up as assertiveness, is a crucial ingredient of effectiveness in empowered work—at least as much as the ability to adopt the goals and values of others is a crucial ingredient of success in power-over.

The 'work ethic' of the 19th century employee is increasingly failing to describe the common attitude to work. It suggested that work—in the sense of earning a wage through commodity production—was an end in itself, and the source of meaning in one's life. To earn a good wage was not a way to achieve affluence or leisure, but simply a measure of one's godliness (or goodness). That this concept is now considered laughable except among older generations is a significant change; but the new ethic is only more cynical. It is the belief that work is a struggle for survival, with the goal of either survival or accumulating enough to rise above the fray. This does have one positive aspect: without the illusion of the nobility of alienated work, there is a real opportunity for people to discover what work might be authentic for them.

But there is also a threat. If work itself is despised, and cynicism limits our goals to those of survival or escape, how can we mobilize our collective energies to the back-breaking efforts that will be needed to build an economy of power-to?

---

powers are equally capable of being used for domination—and although any society, real or utopian, will have a mixture of different types of power, industrialism has almost completely excluded the possibility of sustainable co-operation.

Making Connections

"The truth, the first truth probably, is that we are all connected, watching one another. Even the trees."[7]

The power-to in one person seems a very small thing before the might of armies, corporations or the law. It seems almost inappropriate to describe it as power, since its unassuming innocence does not seem capable of creating or changing anything. And of power-to in isolation, this is largely true. As the last chapter described, the weight of a daily reality in which resources are allocated according to one's rise or fall in the hierarchy can easily crush the spark of power-to that is present in all of us. It is the connections that we make that make it really powerful.

Perhaps the most essential connection is with the Earth itself. Air, water and land (in the sense of living space and growing space, or food) are basic requirements for survival, and they all depend on biological self-management. When human power structures—structures of power-over—come between us and these essentials, we become dependent and vulnerable to control and manipulation. When air and water are tainted or poisoned, we may lack even the power-to to live. In an industrialized country, we may not experience the land as a key asset; but in developing countries it is a crucial demand. The North's lack of interest in issues of land reform is not reflective of our lack of need for it. In fact, our dependence on it is reflected in struggles over housing,

RADICAL ROUTES

"If only I know how to start some kind of business! My dear friend, all theory is dismal and only business flourishes. Unfortunately I have learnt this too late."—Marx in a letter to Engels, 1862, from 'What a way to run a railroad', Comedia 1985.

Co-operation in work has a long history. From the early protests of the Diggers, through the artisans' guilds and friendly societies to the experiments of Robert Owen, then the rise of the Co-operative Wholesale Society and building societies in Britain; in Canada and the Caribbean, credit unions have grown as have (with some setbacks) savings and loans schemes in the USA. They are united by the International Co-operative Principles, agreed as a universal litmus test for mutuality. These require that a true co-op must have open and voluntary membership, must be democratically run, must not sign away all its profits to investors, must reward its members fairly, must be independent and must have educational and social objectives as well as commercial ones.

However, closer examination reveals the ways in which the values of the economy at large, and the dynamics of money and other currencies of power, have co-opted their potential. The mutuals have grown to the degree where the voice of the ordinary member is lost among the other millions. The short term rewards of demutualization have tempted many to sell out, and the need to find a niche in the mainstream marketplace has prompted others to simply ape the consumerism of the private corporations.

It was against this background that in the 1980s a group of co-operators came together to form Radical Routes. They represented different kinds of co-operative—some were in workers' co-operatives, and others were in housing co-operatives, collectively managing their housing. They had all experienced difficulties in getting started—particularly in finance—but were also concerned that accumulating finance would lead to the loss of their principles.

Radical Routes was formed as a secondary co-operative—a co-operative of co-operatives. It used an obscure form of investment—loanstock—to raise a fund for ethical investment in its members that gave the investors no say over the enterprise. Decisions were to be taken, usually by consensus, by delegates representing the member co-ops. A condition of membership was commitment to social change—in the sense of an active challenge to power structures. All new members had to be accepted by existing members, ensuring a durable commitment. To date, Radical Routes has made loans of £300,000 and has enabled the purchase of property worth £1,000,000. Because it only costs £1 to join a co-operative, and because Radical Routes can accept unusual forms of security such as guarantees by other member co-ops, it is accessible to people with little or no money. Because all loans have to be approved by member co-

ops, and because an anti-consumerist lifestyle is a requirement of membership, it aims to support only those with high ethical standards.

I joined Radical Routes with my (then embryonic) housing co-operative.
With the support of the network, our dreams came to fruition—and I set out to
see if I could create some co-operative employment as well as housing. I was
soon involved in a printing and training co-operative. I passed up the rewards
that the conventional economy offers its entrepreneurs, but I have benefited
from the support and solidarity in the mutual sector. Establishing secure livelihoods on this basis is challenging—but it is good work in every sense.

In other words, Radical Routes is practising the same tactic of capital
accumulation, but is then adopting a totally different attitude to this accumulated resource. Instead of using it for private gain, it is directed into a process
of empowerment and co-operative development. These co-ops are then linked
together for mutual support, and they begin to form self-sustaining co-operative economies—indeed, co-operative communities.

---

transport and food—access in a more general sense. Many of these struggles
are conducted at the bottom of the ladder of participation. True empowerment
is impossible while the ground that we live on is under the control of others.

Beyond these basic issues of survival are the connections we make with each
other that enable production (in the wider sense of building our resources) and
reproduction (from day to day and from generation to generation). Friedman
suggests eight bases of social power necessary to improve the condition of life.[8]

1. Defensible life space. Friedman is referring here not just to the home but
to the neighbourhood and the supportive relations within it. It is a base of
security from which other activities become possible. Establishing this space
requires gaining local control of land, buildings and planning, and establishing a convivial technological environment. 'Planning for real' is a practical
example of this—a participatory method for building consensus on land use
in an area, and for collective design of developments. It has been applied in a
number of British cities.[9] Defensible life space also requires a level of social
consensus and institutions of conflict resolution that eliminate violence; crime
and unresolved conflict can effectively destroy the security of this life space.

2. Surplus time. For a great many people in developing countries, particularly women, subsistence takes up every waking hour. Without a respite, life
becomes a meaningless daily grind, with no opportunity for escape or progress.
Causes of the spiral into overwork include exclusion from fertile land, an
oppressive division of labour, intensifying relative deprivation, climatic change
and loss of biological capital, increasing rates of illness, and worsening terms
of trade. This cycle is present in the industrialized world too, as consumerism
sets more and more unachievable aspirations. Power-to processes can enable

the evaluation of more authentic needs, can equalize divisions of labour, establish more efficient co-operative work patterns and develop empowering technologies. A fertile, productive ecosystem is a power-to process in itself.

3. *Knowledge and skills.* The difficulty here is establishing which forms of knowledge contribute to self-reliance and which provide only a guide to managing dependency. Each different dynamic of power has a body of knowledge that legitimizes and supports it (see Chapter 9). Knowledge and skills which maintain the defensible life space and enable the creation of surplus time are clearly crucial; but knowledge of power-over and an understanding of its functioning are also tools of survival in a society dominated by regulation.

4. *Appropriate information.* To some extent I feel this overlaps with the previous category—it might be more appropriate to stress access to information, as openness and transparency of institutions is essential to empowerment. Friedman stresses relevance: as the floodgates of information technology open, the tools for sifting useful information from the deluge are vital to avoid information overload.

5. *Social organization.* This is the source of collective action, and a bulwark against the hierarchies of power-over. Credit unions, tenants' and residents' groups, women's groups, co-ops and buying clubs all enable collective resources to be effectively mobilized, shared, and hence multiplied. Affinity groups, such as women's and men's groups and black caucuses, are vital in identifying systematic processes of oppression and generating emotional support and a secure identity. The need for identity is no less pressing and powerful than that for food and shelter (see Chapter 3).

6. *Social networks.* Although membership of a social organization encourages membership of social networks, this is a wider point about lines of communication and support. Social networks in a dynamic of power-to are typically horizontal (family, friends, neighbours—non-instrumental relationships), compared with power-over's vertical networks (running through the layers of hierarchy, connecting customers, suppliers, employers, political representatives). Social networks are a source of identity and emotional support, but also a resource from which social organizations may arise.

7. *Instruments of work and livelihood.* Friedman begins with healthy bodies, and then the technologies of household and small scale production and maintenance. I would go further to include the technologies of empowering public utilities (from drainage to solar energy) and of co-operative production (permaculture systems, workshops and machine tools). For a discussion of convivial and non-convivial technology, see Chapter 2.

8. *Financial resources.* Access to credit, mechanisms of trade and institutions of ownership are present in any functioning economy. In an empowering economy, they take specific forms. Credit is low interest and not tied to collateral (as in credit unions, LETS schemes, and the 'social collateral' banks

like Grameen). Trade is facilitated through accessible, low-overhead street markets, and through currencies that are local, non-accumulating and not scarce (such as LETS, labour notes, and local currencies). Ownership is a right rather than a commodity, belonging to all stakeholders in the enterprise.

As Friedman points out, each one is a means to another means, in an interlocking cycle. For instance, a LETS scheme can provide a way of rewarding volunteers working in credit unions. The credit union can make loans that allow the investment to develop a productive permaculture plot. This provides food that can be traded in the LETS scheme, which increases its breadth and range. Not only does the process continue flowing, but it becomes a closed loop; a positive feedback loop. Until some external limit is encountered (such as the number of people eligible for the credit union, or the land available for permaculture), it will keep growing and developing of its own accord. Of course, it is not strictly speaking 'of its own accord'—in reality the people involved will have to work very hard. But insofar as they experience a direct reward for their efforts, and there is a continuing incentive to develop each scheme further, it may well come to feel like the community has gained a life of its own.

In practice, we find that the 'glass ceilings' that bring these processes of growth to an abrupt halt are less to do with the limitations of the system itself and more to do with disruption and obstruction from the hierarchies of power-over. The promising experiments with local currencies in Austria were stamped out by government action. The growth of housing co-operatives in Britain was cut short by a change of government policy. Local food production all over the world is wrecked by the promotion of global free trade. Friedman also reminds us that this description of local processes says nothing about structural forces—the legal, economic and cultural effects of many tiny similar power plays that become the causes of their reproduction. Power-to is being kept on the margins by the spread and ceaseless consumption of power-over.

Problems with Power-to

It would be tempting to say that in a society ordered around power-to, there would be no problems and no conflict. I don't believe this is the case. Power-to is certainly a way of getting things done that is free from the oppression and violence of power-over, but it has its own potential for harm.

I have described the typical decision-making progress of power-to as negotiation, which contrasts with the power-over practice of authority. This has limitations: it isn't fast, and it doesn't allow for the inspired vision of an individual. It also lacks certainty and security—boundaries are indistinct and inconsistent.

Based on this, and on the actual experience of people in co-operative organizations, we can make some predictions. There will be conflicts over space and freedom, as a clash of interests cannot simply be resolved by one person giving way to another. There will be frustration for anyone seeking order or

THE MONDRAGON EXPERIENCE

An example of where Radical Routes and other co-operative projects could be leading is the Mondragon group of co-ops. Mondragon is a district in the Basque country between France and Spain. In the late 50s, recovering from the privation of the Civil War, a small group of workers, trained and inspired by the ideas of a radical priest, set up Ulgor. Today, Ulgor is the largest of a network of co-operatives—mostly industrial, but also providing housing, agricultural products, retail, computing, services and education.

Perhaps the secret of their success lies in the second degree and support co-ops. These are co-ops whose members are co-operatives—established to provide a set of services to the growing community of co-ops. Where the capitalist firms compete among themselves, the Mondragon co-ops can provide training, social security, research and development, and above all low interest capital to their members. The surplus generated by the workers is reinvested in the further development of the co-operative community.

But what is it actually like to work in? Does it really feel different to working in a profit-led, employer owned enterprise? There are good reasons to think it does. Firstly, any co-op member is likely to have trained in Mondragon's colleges, where the skills of consensus and co-operation are considered as important as any tool. They are trained not only to be a worker, but to understand the businesses accounts, marketing and managing. Though many workers are recruited by existing co-ops, others will begin work by starting a new co-op. This is enabled through the 'Empresarial division' of the People's Bank; a service co-op which exists to develop a business plan till it is ready for funding. The proposal must be viable, as for any other business; but it must also pass an environmental impact assessment, and the co-operators must demonstrate their ability to work together as a group. The co-op must abide by Mondragon practice of limiting income differentials, and donating 10% of profits to social ends.

Even within larger co-operatives, there is a clear structure for democratic participation. A General Council, meeting annually, elects two bodies. The Governing Council appoints managers, and works with them on long term policy. A Watchdog Council examines their work, and can call in experts to check the details. In addition to this, a third Social Council, elected from the members, provides continual feedback and communication. Finally, representatives to the Co-operative Congress and other Co-op service groups are elected by and from the members. This is a clear and disciplined structure—managers can implement the agreed direction with a considerable level of autonomy.

At every stage, members are aware that they are part of a team, and that that team does not end at the workplace gates but extends throughout the social system. From cradle to grave, the 25,000 people involved in the co-operatives have a say in their destiny. One co-op is named Ederlan, which means 'good work'.

But there is more than this to it: "What surprises other entrepreneurs is the poetic-philosophical vein that we have as entrepreneurs. . . . We could not be pure technocrats who know perfectly the process of chemistry or physics or semi conductors but nothing more. We see the development of these firms as a social struggle, a duty." This is the pursuit not of power or riches but of 'equilibrio': a state of harmonious balance, or peace—the freedom that comes from community.[10]

Mondragon today is struggling to retain its character in the face of an increasingly global marketplace with little respect for local production at fair wages. It has had to relax its incomes policy to attract highly qualified professionals; it has approached the stock market for finance; and people wishing to join the established co-ops now have to find or borrow many thousands of pounds to match the stakes of the existing employees. The principle of mutual aid remains, but under constant threat from an economic environment that has no respect for it.

---

accountability, or rapid decisive action. There will be envy as those more dynamic individuals race ahead of the more hesitant. There will be anger as ambitious individuals are held back by the group, or burdened by 'free riders'. There may also be a great deal of horse trading and even prejudice; cases cannot be considered objectively or on their merits, since there is little abstract law and past history cannot be excluded from consideration.

This sounds like an uninspiring vision, but the goal of an unproblematic flow of power is probably a false one. It is hard to imagine how the flow of energy through our planet can ever be free from conflict, since everything depends on it to live and there will never be enough for every creature's ambitions. The great advantage to power-to is not that it is painless or simple—it isn't—but that it is sustainable. The problems it raises are organic, localized, petty: it does not have the systematic oppression, denial and destruction that power-over implies.

That is not to say that we must resign ourselves to a miserable life whatever. Skills of conflict resolution and consensus building can ease many of the potential hazards, and are important for anyone intended to work co-operatively. Structures that maximize autonomy and maintain a good balance between public need and private space will also reduce conflict. And judicious use of power-over also has a role. Different dynamics of power have always been mixed together, and the human capacity to defer to authority, act decisively and harness aggression is not to be denied or repressed. Within an overall framework of empowerment, specific applications of law and control may relieve tensions that would otherwise explode with catastrophic results. A preference for co-operative and empowering lifestyles should never be turned into a dogma.

Prospects for Empowerment

But is it even realistic to speak of an empowered society? After all it is a long way from describing a few housing co-operatives, LETS schemes and wood-lands, to saying that government, international relations and the economy could be reorganized along similar lines. What are the real prospects for using these organic, ecological forms of power-to to meet our daily needs?

The question of whether such a transformation is possible is a matter for the remaining chapters. Here, I want to argue that it is possible. Perhaps the strongest argument in its favour is that we have done it before—that complex, cultured and enduring societies have been based on co-operative and empow-ering social structures. Even in Yorkshire, the archaeological evidence is that in the 10,000 years it has been inhabited (about a tenth of the time that humans have roamed the earth), for half that time there was no patriarchy (bodies were buried in graves of equal status) and for two-thirds of that time, no war or mass conflict (as evidenced by the absence of fortifications). Indeed, the lifestyle we practice now, constantly supervised by authority and privilege, is anomalous.

Another example is that we do it every day, all of us: these values of respect, mutuality and sharing dominate in many important aspects of our lives—family, friendships, hobbies, crafts, unpaid work. We all of us have some experiences to fall back on. Even though power-over colonizes more and more of our lives, and brings values of competition and control into almost every aspect of our existence, there is a core inside us that will always be self-reliant, because our bodies would fail if it weren't. For all the barriers that go up between us, these is still something there to be reached. Indeed, when you see retired generals and respectable well-to-do ladies joining protesters and resisting the state, you have to wonder if the veneer of authority isn't very thin, and the well of compassion very deep.

But most important is surely the example of co-operation beyond the household level that is a growing force in economics and politics. In the last three decades particularly, there has been a growth in initiatives that empower. Whether they are community-based or participatory forms of democracy, large scale co-operatives, or the self-organization of the poor, there are now too many examples of power-to in action to deny its capacity. It is not a special case, or a primitive, pre-cultural phenomenon: it is an alternative and equally effective way of directing resource flows to meet needs.

Even if it is theoretically possible, how can we believe that it can possibly replace the massive edifice of power-over? We must remember that only a short time ago in terms of the span of human history, capital accumulation (for example) was an obscure practice of a tiny subculture of risk-taking mer-chants. None of the guilds, peasants and landowners for a moment expected that it would affect them, let alone replace their ways of working and trading. Similarly, centralised bureaucracies were an arcane practice in some branches of the state which were never intended or expected to dominate public life. And yet they grew, interconnected, and colonized more and more of our lives. Power-to can also grow in this way, even though it may take generations to achieve maturity.

The rise of power-over was driven partly by inspired innovators, and by their belief in what they were doing. But it was also driven by systemic factors—it was a logical progression within that society. Do the same systemic factors now favour power-to? From our present standpoint, it may be impossible to answer. But the next chapter will try to clarify the question.

No one's slave, I am no one's master
No one's slave, I am no one's master
On my grave they will write this after I am gone
I will be gone
And then my flesh will go to the Earth it lived on
Breath will go to the air it lived from
I am through with the shame of my lying
I've had my fill of the cruelty and crying
Earned my keep in the land where the dying deserts grow
And now I know
And I am looking out with a new perspective
Listening out for a new directive
I am strong like a tree on a mountain
Full and fresh as a free flowing fountain
Bright and clear as the stars beyond counting in the night
I am their light
I am the light that shines in a thousand people
In my eyes every life is equal
No one's slave, I am no one's master
No one's slave, I am no one's master

—Theo Simon / Seize the Day

Chapter 8

Maps and Networks

Systems theory is a tool that we can use to map the connections between different forms of power. Every system is made up of subsystems, so by starting with discrete processes of power and mapping the connections between them, we can build up a picture of power in the global system. This kind of systemic thinking allows us to understand the stability of power structures, and see them as self-regulating rather than planned.

Cycles of violence are a useful example of how local experiences form part of a global pattern. But systems theory can obscure as much as it illuminates, and it is important to look at the many justifiable criticisms that have been made of it. In particular, we have to account for change as well as stability.

Power-over and power-to have similar structures, based around the interactions of five forms of activity. This pattern not only allows us to analyse the present operation of power-over, but also suggests how a society based on power-to might function. They exist side by side, and it is power-to's continual challenges to power-over, coupled with power-over's need for power-to to function, that explain change and conflict in the system.

A strategy for social change will not succeed by seeking to focus on some 'weak link'; the logic of the system will eventually reinstate it. Change comes by identifying entire cycles that can be overturned; then the new order will have the internal stability to survive.

Oh, a sleeping drunkard
Up in Central Park
And a lion-hunter
In the jungle dark,
And a Chinese dentist,
And a British Queen—
All fit together
In the same machine.
Nice, nice, very nice;
Nice, nice, very nice;
Nice, nice, very nice—

So many different people
In the same device.
—Kurt Vonnegut, *Cat's Cradle*

"One must rather conduct an ascending analysis of power, starting, that is, from its infinitesimal mechanisms, which each have their own history, their own trajectory, their own techniques and tactics, and then see how these mechanisms of power have been—and continue to be—invested, colonized, utilized, involuted, transformed, displaced, extended, etc., by ever more general mechanisms and by forms of global domination."[1] —Michel Foucault

In other words, local processes of power are incorporated into more general systems. Although we must start with the tangible, local experience, we can't really understand its meaning unless we can see the whole pattern that it is part of. What kind of analysis can help us to do this? If we believe that different processes of power are linking up in this way, we need some way to map the connections. We have to be able to map the reaches and the boundaries of 'power-over', and identify the narrow passes and hidden routes that will connect the scattered domain of 'power-to'.

In Chapter 2 we saw that power takes place as a network, or process, in the connections and relations between actors. A process (or as Foucault described it, a strategy) has its own logic, its own dynamic to follow; each instance of power is a point on a line running through history. For example:

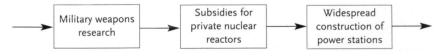

However, as I have tried to show in Chapters 6 and 7, it is also clear that these processes are linking up and reinforcing each other. Two compatible processes of power operating at the same time will reinforce, or cross-fertilize each other.

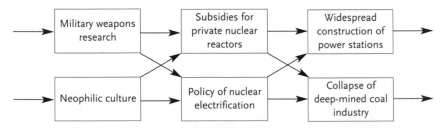

How can we understand these connections? Are they all simply local connections, or do they form processes themselves? And if they are linking up, what patterns emerge from this? The global structures observed by Foucault and many others (indeed, from Marx onwards, politics has gradually become the study of power structures) are the consequence of the creative nature of power.

FIGHTING TALK

After one particularly large and disruptive protest, I found myself faced with a community service order—an alternative to a custodial sentence, doing unpaid work for voluntary groups. I was there for my non-violent protests, but I was working alongside people deemed by the courts to be excessively violent. They weren't evil, or even particularly frightening. Certainly, the violence they had delivered was rarely greater than police officers have used to arrest me, but they lacked the legitimacy that dignifies the physical discipline meted out by the state. Their words tell us a lot about the source of their violence—and perhaps about rationalization of violence, and of power-over, generally.

"If anyone threatens my family, I'll have 'em . . . It's about looking after your own."
"I wouldn't kick him when he was on the ground. I said get up, you bastard, and when he did I laid him out again. There's some pricks just want to put the boot in, but I don't want none of that."
"If I beat someone up, they might come after me with their mates . . . but I'd come after them, go to each of their homes with a baseball bat. All right, I might go down for two years, but I'd come straight out and do the next one. I won't let anyone take the piss out of me, I've got my pride."
"It's traditional, isn't it, you sort it out with your fists. In my community there's always been fighting, my Dad used to beat me up. When people know you'll stand up for yourself, they respect you."
"There's a bad atmosphere round this town. If you keep to yourself, you'll be OK, but anyone who steps out of line gets a beating. When I lived in ——, whenever a gang from another town come into one of the pubs, we'd be going around getting all the lads together to sort them out."
"I went round to one bloke's house with a broken bottle and kicked the door in, and there was this old lady. I said, 'Sorry, does —— live here?' and she said, 'He moved out two months ago'. She was so scared. I just said sorry and left."

Most of us have experienced violence more than once. I can remember fighting the school bully, and being robbed in the street not far from my home. I have been viciously treated by policemen, and almost killed by a dumper truck on a protest. When I was young, I remember fearing a nuclear attack, and thinking that a distant siren might be the three minute warning. At the lower end of the scale, I have faced anger and aggression or been in fear of violence from teachers, friends, strangers . . . I've responded by developing certain tactics, as have we all. Appeasement, retaliation, alliances, pre-emptive violence, deterrence; all of these are common learned habits, and all serve to escalate violence. Less common are negotiation, conflict resolution, solidarity with the weakest, non-violent resistance, and forms of therapy, all of which might reduce the level of violence. They are also learned behaviour, but learned from very different sources.

We know violence by its effects: not so much the physical effects as the psychological effects—this is after all why these episodes stick in our memories. The experience of violence, or a sustained or credible threat of violence, leaves us changed. There is a watchfulness and hesitancy about us that is connected to the pain we have experienced at other people's hands.

To discharge its potential, and realize its entropic logic, it must connect. To understand it, and work with it creatively, we must follow those connections. They can be seen anywhere—even in casual speech. And perhaps the most locally visible form of power we could examine is violence. Our language is peppered with references to 'cycles of violence' and 'escalating violence', which seem to imply that there is some systematic property behind it.

Cybernetic Solutions

Traditional models of structure have sought to build up mechanisms based on cause and effect. This way of thinking goes back to philosophers like Descartes, who said, "I consider the human body as a machine. My thought compares a sick man and an ill-made clock with my idea of a healthy man and a well-made clock."[2] In a clockwork mechanism, the spring drives the cog, the cog drives the lever, the lever drives the ratchet, the ratchet turns the hands—each effect has a cause in a linear chain.

Today, applying this metaphor to living organisms, let alone societies, seems simple-minded. In a complex network of processes, the effect can also be part of its own cause. Processes go in cycles and loops rather than one after the other in a line.

This 'feedback' allows an organism to regulate itself, and recover from destabilization. This new view of nature is systems theory, or cybernetics. Computer models using feedback have been found to closely reproduce the observed behaviour of ecosystems, the climate, evolution and even the stock markets. Derek Wall explains its importance for Greens: "We need to find some way of swinging society into another mode, where it will naturally defend itself against attempts to reintroduce capitalist growth, hierarchy and ecological destruction. . . . Cybernetics describes systems that tend towards stability and resist change. Political, economic and social subsystems can all be modelled in such a way. Greens are not just up against capitalism and power structures or greedy individuals or perhaps 'human nature', but the conservatism of system dynamics as well."[3] Just as mechanistic thinking drew on the way science at the time was looking at the world, so systems thinking derives much of its force and legitimacy from developments in 'new science'—ecology, chaos theory and quantum physics. Renaissance scientists got their results from the mechanical technology available then, whereas today the huge processing power of computers has allowed researchers to model, test and demonstrate system properties they had previously suspected but been unable to prove.

Ecology introduces the idea of 'emergent properties'—phenomena that cannot be explained in terms of the sum of the parts, but arise out of their interaction. For instance, the climate over tropical rainforests cannot be explained as the sum of the climates generated by the individual trees, nor as determined by the global climate, but arises out of the complex ecology of the forest.

Chaos theory shows how seemingly self-contained systems can behave in intrinsically unpredictable ways. The reverse side of this is that highly fluid, seemingly random systems can be 'self-organizing'—rearranging the whole so as to achieve stability. Both of these are to do with feedback in systems. Since positive feedback magnifies tiny events, the beating of a butterfly's wing could in theory 'cause' a hurricane—or give rise to a stable, repeating mode of behaviour. This is the so-called 'butterfly effect'.

Recent advances in physics are paradoxical and baffling—for instance, describing phenomena as being simultaneously discrete particles and waves in an energy field. Modern physics describes the universe as diffuse fluctuations in the energy field, with every point linked to every other point. This is all a far cry from the billiard table model of reality that gave rise to 'classical' analysis, in which atoms were seen as solid objects following predictable paths. They also suggest ultimate limits to our knowledge. Heisenberg's uncertainty principle states that we cannot know both the position and the velocity of an electron, since the act of measuring one affects the other.

Fritjof Capra makes these links most explicitly, in *The Tao of Physics* and *The Turning Point*. "An analysis of cultural imbalance that adopts a broad ecological view . . . could be called a systems view, in the sense of general systems theory. Systems theory looks at the world in terms of the interrelatedness and interdependence of all phenomena, and in this framework an integrated whole whose properties cannot be reduced to those of its parts is called a system. Living organisms, societies, and ecosystems are all systems."[4]

Systems theory can be traced back to Ludwig Von Bertalanffy, Gregory Bateson, Arthur Koestler and René Dubos. One person who has applied it to the study of politics and power is Ervin Laszlo. For him, systems theory can explain four features of society. The wholeness and order of a society suggests that its properties are irreducible, and not just the sum of its parts. Its capacity for 'adaptive self-stabilization' allows it to both maintain stability and undergo progressive differentiation as the society develops. 'Adaptive self-organization' refers to the ability to fundamentally reorganize, by switching from stabilizing negative feedback to self-organizing positive feedback. Finally, intrasystemic hierarchy reminds us that each system is both a component of another, higher system and comprised of lower systems (this is also referred to as a holon-property). Fritjof Capra advises avoiding the word hierarchy because of its top-down connotations—in systems theory, no level is seen as 'superior' even though it may operate over a larger field.[5] Laszlo describes the development of societies as showing a trend towards increased differentiation, as individuals adopt increasingly specialized roles. Periods of self-stabilization alternate with periods of self-organization as a move to a more differentiated state takes place.[6]

So a cybernetic model is a dynamic one, and a systemic one. This means that, unlike much political theory, it has no 'final cause'—no prime mover. It treats society as an ecosystem rather than a conspiracy; interconnected but not planned. Society is a system made from regular interactions between its building blocks. These building blocks will themselves be systems, but more local (in the sense of covering a narrower field of action). Depending on the analysis that we want to take, these building blocks could be communities, people, sectors of the economy or any other relatively self-contained unit. In 'Mapping energy flows' in Chapter 4, I showed how an ecosystem could be depicted as made out of different building blocks, depending how the organisms in it were grouped together; this is the same issue. Connections between the different divisions of the system form cycles, which generates feedback.

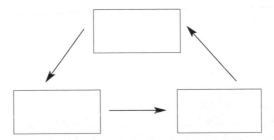

A stable social order is one in which each of these connections is in some way consistent with the others, creating self-stabilizing negative feedback. In other words, the system has some overall character, or direction; the feedback loop has found a point of balance which stabilizes the elements of the system without overloading or starving them. In terms of the last three chapters, we might say that the present dynamic of power is one underpinned by 'power-over'; it stabilizes and reinforces hierarchy, fear of difference, and an instrumental attitude to the natural world. This is not the only form of power possible, but it is the dominant system. 'Power-to' can form closed systems in the same way. These are virtuous circles of self-determination, non-violence and co-operation. They are practices that can be applied systemically—but at this time they are marginal, disconnected and starved of resources.

Can we use a cybernetic system to model networks of power in today's hierarchical society—and in a future ecological society? There are many theorists who have studied political power through systems theory, including David Easton, G. A. Almond and Karl Deutsch. Perhaps the most influential is Talcott Parsons, whose framework is based around the ways in which society meets four essential needs—those of adaptation, goal attainment, pattern maintenance and integration. His model, in its essence, looks like this:[7]

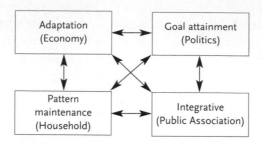

Parsons sees power as the capacity of the system to ensure that these functions are properly carried out 'when the obligations are legitimized with reference to their bearing on collective goals'. In other words, Parsons' view is that power only exists where an obligation is generally accepted as legitimate. This runs counter to intuition; we are most aware of power precisely when it is most controversial. The theory does not seem to accept the existence of disadvantaged or oppressed groups within the system.

Is this a necessary consequence of using systems theory? It is certainly a common one. However, I believe this is primarily to do with a perception that there is only one kind of power. If this is the case then either it has little or nothing to do with the social system, and is therefore unimportant (Deutsch argues, "Power is neither the centre nor the essence of politics."[8]), or it is a force for stability and not conflict, as Parsons concludes. As I have shown in previous chapters, power is not homogeneous but takes radically different forms. Even when, in the 'fourth dimension of power' (see Chapter 1), it shapes people's interests and requires them to adopt certain roles, the presence of alternative processes of power ensures that resistance has an outlet.

I believe systems theory can be a useful tool for understanding 'process power'. However, systems thinking can provide as many wrong answers as right ones. A key question is the building blocks, or subsystems, which we use. Parsons' functionalism is not appropriate, given that I see these systems as controlling society rather than serving it. As I want to look at flows of energy and processes of control, it makes sense to group together similar types of process, particularly where they are in very close interaction or serving similar functions. Economic relationships, for instance, deal systematically with issues of value, access and exclusion; and actors in the economy deal with one another in very similar ways (contract, employment, ownership and so on). Government is another area where a community of people and institutions

VICIOUS CIRCLES

Do we really understand what violence is? Everyone seems to know, but no one finds it easy to define. Is there any difference between a policeman deliberately inflicting pain on me in a protest to gain 'compliance', and a mugger knocking down an old man to steal his wallet? In terms of degree and context, certainly. In terms of power, I would argue very little. Both are physically creating a symbol of power over life to meet their perceived needs. Their needs are a product of power-over, and the effect of their violence is to generate patterns of behaviour that reproduce power-over.

A threat can be almost as violent as its realization. Like most animals, we are able to dominate or coerce with signals or displays. The 'otherness' of violence is important too: distance (whether physical or emotional) is necessary to carry out more serious violence, and the experience of it drives home that sense of separation. Self-inflicted injuries might constitute violence where their root is low self-esteem; typically, though, violence is one against another—an 'other' that is different in some respect, excluded from the circle of compassion. Violence and empathy are fundamentally inconsistent. In the same way, having experienced violence from someone, that person becomes other. We catalogue the differences between us and begin to recognize otherness everywhere around us.

The relationship between violence and power is clouded. They are not simply the same. Violence can be a way of getting something—but equally it might indicate the failure of power, that this is the only way a goal can be achieved. As Arendt puts it, "Violence appears where power is in jeopardy."[9] While this may be true of political violence, well established systems of power also have levels of violence associated with them. A competitive, centralized economy needs markets to be forced open; the military establishment demand opportunities to test their hardware and utilize their strength. By making visible power-over's domination of others, it can even reinforce pride and a sense of identity.

So a set of codes and signs develops to distinguish between legitimate and illegitimate violence. Political opponents may disagree with the boundaries, or may even simply invert them, but often they are just establishing their own idea of more functional violence, rather than actually opposing violence as part of the social structure.

It is not true either that the amount of power one has is equivalent to the violence you can inflict. An army might give a ruler power; but the credibility of the army's threat is underpinned by the level of willing obedience to orders within it.[10] Violence may be a medium through which power can flow. However, it exists not in isolation, but as one among many links in a network. As long as it is consistent with the rest of the network, it is powerful. It belongs only in a culture that can use fear and hatred. It cannot be pressed into the service of a different goal, no matter how it is directed. Arendt says, "The very substance of violent action is ruled by the means-end category, whose chief characteristic has always been that the end is in danger of being overwhelmed by the means."[11] Where violence is compatible with a power dynamic—as is the case with the dominant forms of power today—its language and mechanisms will be used everywhere, from factory farms to schools, from pageantry to policing.

---

dealing with law, legitimacy and sovereignty have a fairly unified identity. Building blocks like these will be the basis of a model of global power.

Change in Systems Theory

These systemic models come across as somewhat deterministic—a fixed order, immune from historical development and governed by iron laws. Yet no process is so straightforward as to be free from impediment or instability. To a large extent, the very point of such a model is to stress negative feedback— the inherent stability of such a system. There is after all an observed fact, the persistence of an oppressive order, to be explained; and only a model based on stability can explain it. But change has to be explained too, unless we want to reject the concept of social progress altogether. Do systems offer any hope?

Systems thinking can certainly account for conflict, provided it remains within the 'rules of the game'. Conflict theory concerns which actors become dominant in economic or political relations, not the nature of those relations. But this tells us little about changes of the system itself. Normally, an equilibrium is preserved, with established roles in each area ensuring that the system functions are carried out. Laszlo suggested that social differentiation tended to increase each time society enters a chaotic period of self-organization. This is typically the result of a crisis that overwhelms the self-stabilizing capacity of the system. This could be an external change (such as climatic change) or an internal disturbance (such as the introduction of a new technology). Equilibrium is lost, and instead of the normal consent to legitimate power in these four areas, force must be used to maintain stability. If this leads to a failure of legitimacy, revolutionary changes of the system are possible. But this hardly explains why some subsystems might take advantage of the stress and seek to push the system further from equilibrium.

There is a different kind of conflict, usually referred to as a contradiction, which arises out of the processes themselves.[12] The best example of this comes from Marx, who could be described as a kind of systems theorist. He argued that the process of capital accumulation assembled its own gravediggers, in the shape of the disgruntled proletariat. The transformation of the system can be predicted because the system contained the cause of this transformation from the outset. The criticism of systems theory as being too conservative applies mainly to over-

simplified models which lack any contradictory tendencies. However, it is no criticism to say a system is described as too stable if that is the observed reality. It is
noticeable that the Marxist proletariat has not played the role he anticipated.

The issue of roles within systems leads to another telling criticism. Roles
are important for systems theorists because they typically constitute the point
of contact between system requirements and individual behaviour. Firstly, one
has to be careful to not treat the system as a real being: to quote Marx, "Avoid
postulating 'society' as an abstraction confronting the individual. The individual is the social being."[13] Roles are presented to us by other people, and this
gives rise to four problems for role theory identified by Roderick Martin:

- the conflict of expectations of a given role held by different significant others,
- the conflict between the expectations associated with different roles in
  the role set, and the unpredictability of modes of resolving them,
- 'deficiencies' in socialization which may result in incomplete
  internalization of expectations, and
- the more or less idiosyncratic interpretations individuals bring to role
  playing.[14]

I don't agree with Martin that these constitute fatal flaws for systems theory.
The first two are real problems for any monolithic theory that only allows for
one source of power determining roles, such as Parsons' functionalist theories. However, I argue that it is the competing and conflicting types of power
in society that give rise to these conflicts. The second two arise from the
system finding a balance between rigid socialization and the systemic need for
innovation and adaptation; overly rigid systems tend to fail under external
stress, so a certain level of confusion over filling roles is in fact self-stabilizing.

The Substance of the System

Systems can be both too materialistic and too idealistic. In Chapter 4, I looked at
the problems with materialism as a worldview; although the desire for concrete,
tangible evidence is understandable, force and economics alone cannot account
for everything. For example, while materialists can show the connection between
the arms trade and the military, they may neglect connections between militarism and, say, racist violence—or domestic violence against women. However,
many feminist researchers have suggested that the threat-identification that
bonds an army together is essentially the same cultural force behind other, seemingly unrelated forms of violence. Cynthia Enloe writes that an explanation of
militarism that focuses on social and economic institutions is inadequate: "It
leaves untouched, unexplained and unchallenged some of the most powerful
ideological and 'private' processes that perpetuate militarization."[15]

However, a purely cultural approach also raises difficulties. By going so deep
into our psyche, it demands too fundamental a transformation. We despair of

being able to bring about such a paradigm shift, and are unable to see any way we could contribute to it. As we try to persuade people to change their way of thinking, they are trying to cope with immediate, material problems. Idealism is also a hazard. We should be wary of the idea that these dynamics and systems that we identify are in any sense real. Korzybski wrote, "The map is not the territory",[16] and this model is not reality, either—reality is our lived experience. If we say that a tribal society somewhere practices some ritual which serves a practical feedback mechanism (say, regulates their impact on the local forest) it does not mean that the same ritual will have the same effect if it is carried out in Leeds or Los Angeles. Any system is embedded in its context—biological, historical, social, economic—and an abstract system taken out of context is there to suggest an approach to perception, not to tell you what you are seeing.

As suggested in Chapter 4, the reality of both types of processes have to be acknowledged. In particular, as Enloe points out, "It is possible to be less fixed on the discovery of 'original causes'. It might be more useful to ask: how do these values and behaviours get repeated generation after generation?"[17] Combining cultural and economic analyses raises problems—for instance, the mathematical certainty that is (theoretically) possible in a materialist explanation is undermined by the more intangible and unpredictable ebb and flow of ideas. It is also the case that the two types of analysis work on different units, and even different scales. Nonetheless, we must recognize that the sharp division between culture and matter is an artificial division we impose for our own mental convenience; our actual experiences blend the two seamlessly.

Morris Berman criticizes systems thinking from another direction altogether. He agrees that mechanistic views of the world are impoverishing our analysis, and shares a wish for a 're-enchantment' of the natural world, seeing it as interconnected and self-organizing at every level. But he is concerned that, "The holistic and cybernetic thinking of the 1980s . . . is purely abstract and formal, capable of being bent to any reality; it often has the appearance of being value free, but in fact projects a *Lebenswelt*, a total vision of reality that circumscribes an entire world."[18] He sees a choice for holists, between "a sensuous, situational, living approach to process [and] an abstract form, a type of process mechanism . . . which really represents the last phase of classical science, not the beginning of a new paradigm at all."[19]

Berman suggests a test to distinguish between benign and harmful applications of systems theory: "Does it take me into the things I fear most, and wish to avoid, or does it make it easy for me to hide, to run away from them? Does it enable me to shut out the environment, ignore politics, remain unaware of my dream life, my sexuality, and my relation with other people, or does it shove them in my face, and teach me how to live with them and through them?"[20] This is challenging for any theorist; but I believe that Berman is raising an important issue. Grand theories that claim to explain everything have a totalizing power regardless

THE VIOLENCE OF PEACE

It is commonplace to say that Western Europe has enjoyed fifty years of peace. This begs the question of what we mean by peace: does this really describe an economy dependent on the arms trade, a cold war based on the threat of total annihilation, a steady increase in racism and violent crime, and massive public expenditure on arms?

In Germany in the 1908s, this tension was palpable. West Germany was then a densely populated country whose people shared their space with military forces from seven countries and 5,000 nuclear weapons.[21] In 1979 Gert Bastian was a General in the West German Army; he renounced his commission when NATO agreed to prepare for the deployment of Pershing and Cruise nuclear missiles if negotiations in Geneva failed. Because Cruise could fly underneath radar, it considerably increased tension, as the Soviet forces contemplated a surprise attack. He had understood that military service was about protecting the people and places that you love—and it was clear to him that nothing could be protected in a nuclear war. Even when (as in the INF treaty) missiles were removed, the treaties said, "Before the missile is destroyed at a site intended for this purpose, the nuclear warhead . . . may be removed." Pershing II is dead; long live Lance, carrying the same warheads.[22]

Siegfried Lenz, a German author, wrote: "We live in peace, but are still at the mercy of force, a privileged kind of force that is condoned by public authorities and is making our world more and more uninhabitable."[23] His point was that 'national security' was being used as an excuse for repression.

It was never going to be possible to site so many soldiers in a country without having an impact. A kind of cultural imperialism was also taking place, as American media began to be more and more ubiquitous. It is hard to complain when everyone says they are there for your protection. The local population find themselves becoming camp followers, servicing the services. Military culture has always been based around a very specific form of masculinity. When British soldiers left Portsmouth for the Falkland Islands, they were shown pornographic films to replace the officially tolerated prostitution on shore.[24] Military wives, too, are subject to repressed violence in military bases. A 1979 US Inspector General's report on domestic violence said, "Social workers . . . agree that military service is probably more conducive to violence at home than at any other occupation." In addition, those civilian men most likely to assault women are men with prior military service.[25]

The connection between militarism and ecological damage is absolutely clear; the US military is the largest single source of greenhouse gases (those causing climate change) in the world. The British Army has huge stockpiles of CFCs, hazardous to the ozone layer, for tank fire extinguishers. Aviation fuel does not carry the same taxes as petrol, and is burnt in huge quantities in jet flights. However, these processes are absolutely crucial to the industrial economy. West Germany was in the 1980s the fifth largest producer of weapons, despite the constitutional limitations on its army. Rudolf Bahro was a dissident in East Germany who remained critical when he reached the West. He argued that the direction of industry was inextricably linked with the growth of militarism: "You cannot get rid of the tanks until you are ready to get rid of the cars."

Although Germany's constitution prevented involvement in military action outside its borders, it is nonetheless dependent on military force to secure resources and markets in developing countries—the South. Many of these countries were governed by undemocratic and oppressive regimes installed and maintained by Western powers. President Suharto of Indonesia invaded East Timor in 1975—the same time that George Bush was head of the CIA. Because Indonesia was a US ally, no action was taken. In return for siting US bases in Indonesia—a crucial position for 'containing communism' in SE Asia—and letting US companies operate in Indonesia, Suharto's looting of the country was condoned. Other countries had economic levers used against them. The threat of sanctions was invariably backed up by support for 'covert operations' like the funding of the Contras in Nicaragua.

Was this really peace? Clausewitz said that war is the continuation of politics by other means. Today one might agree more with Hannah Arendt, who argues that peace is the continuation of war by other means—since full-scale war would not permit the continuation of anything, but would be an abrupt halt to history.[26]

---

of the methods used. I will try to develop models that involve us personally, rather than depicting us as particles caught up in some super-organism.

How complicated should we make a model? Let us consider how we will actually use this device. It is there to help us make sense of the persistence of social forms. What we are interested in, then, is the closed loops—the complete dynamics. Equally, at any time we should be clear which process we are following, or which system we are concerned with, and seek only the connections and relations relevant to that. This is a different way of seeing the world to that used by most political analysis: we must be sensitive to symbiosis and co-operation in self-regulating dynamics, rather than the clash and competition of isolated forces. Of any system of power, we should ask: how do the actors and forces involved contribute to stabilizing and regulating it?

Models like this one stand or fall on whether they help us to understand and interpret our own lives and experiences. They are a way of guiding our awareness beyond the immediate, the object, and towards a sense of connection with a global network. With this awareness we become more compassionate—in the sense of lowering our ego boundaries, empathizing and sharing responsbility.[27] We also see potential connections—the chance to complete dynamic loops, and to initiate strategies of power. Being powerful, in the sense of controlling one's own destiny, is very much a matter of perceiving one's location and choosing a way forward from it. Although Foucault speaks of "more global forms of domination", it doesn't mean that the connections can't be seen at a local level. The process is not a statistical effect: it is the real actions of individuals impacting on those around them, forming repeated patterns.

The Green Analysis

So what systems and global structures have Greens identified as stabilizing and developing power-over? It is certainly the case that new social movements—peace, environment, women, gay rights, community rights—have focussed on the state as the source of change. This has something to do with naïvety, perhaps (the development of Green economics has lagged somewhat behind Green politics), but it is also clear that it is difficult for the state to deny responsibility for the demands being made by the Green movement. Issues of environmental regulation, of alternative lifestyles, or of discrimination by authorities, are issues that can only be laid at the door of the state. James O'Connor argues that this is because new social movements are concerned with production conditions—things that are commodities in the sense that capital requires them for production, but which are not commodities in that the market cannot provide them. They are things like land, non-renewable nature, and people. Although they are often 'purchased' with rent, wages or rates, we intuitively know them not to be commodities. It is in practice the state which controls access to land, nature and people—indeed by creating infrastructure, schools and hospitals, it ensures that that access is as favourable as possible.

"The typical struggle to defend or redefine conditions of production as conditions of life takes the movement right into the state—the police department, the zoning authority, the Board of Forestry, the City Manager's Office, and so on. At this point in the life cycle of the struggle, those engaged in social movements are heard to say more or less the same thing, namely that the state is unresponsive, oppressive, and too bureaucratic; relies too much on experts; conceals vital statistics; lies; and cannot get anything done." [28] So O'Connor's view is that the state determines and maintains rules and institutions that commodify nature; these rules and institutions deliver resources to economic actors; and the economy delivers crucial resources to the state. There is a stable feedback loop.

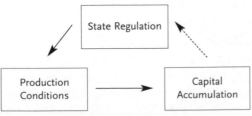

Alan Carter does something similar in his essay 'Towards a Green Political Theory'. He begins with a concern that political theorists should "start taking the state seriously". But by 'the state', he is not simply referring to government, or any single entity, but the 'supra-institution' made up of the relations and forces in both the political and economic spheres. This provides a fourfold distinction between relations of political control, relations of economic control, forces of defence and forces of production.[29]

A traditional Marxist analysis is based on economic relations determining the 'superstructure' of politics; pluralist theories, by contrast, argue that 'civil society' (the aggregation of interest groups and non-governmental organizations) directs the state. Carter argues that both of these fail to recognize the capacity of government for autonomous action, and the extent that its self-interest is served by the relations around it.[30]

The idea that economics—the meeting of people's material needs—should be the driving force behind human affairs has a powerful intuitive appeal. After all, there is no government without money, surely? However, when you look at the actual practice of economic transactions, they take place in a highly structured setting—regulated by institutions, conventions and assumptions. The concept of the commodity—things produced for exchange—is not a natural or obvious concept, but a culturally specific phenomenon. Property, exchange and incorporation are all legal, cultural, and political creations—and they determine economic relations.[31] If it is true that there is no government without money (and the state needs revenue indirectly—for the military which protect it, and the services it delivers, rather than for its own existence), it is also true that there is no money without government.

Relations of production are difficult to identify; they are so much a part of our everyday environment that we take them for granted, not perceiving them as chosen by anyone, let alone the state. However, when an effort is made to challenge them, the situation becomes clearer. "In 1932-33, at a time of very high unemployment and depression, the Austrian town of Wurgl created its own interest-free currency which was distributed in return for public works. The notes were date stamped, and decreased in value by one cent each month, which encouraged rapid circulation. Taxes were paid, unemployment greatly reduced and local shopkeepers flourished. There was great interest, but the Austrian National Bank took legal action against it and closed it down."[32] A currency that did not accumulate represented a challenge to the state's role in determining relations of production. So they stabilized them by outlawing the experiment. Similar hostility from the state may now threaten or limit the development of LETS schemes (see Chapter 12).

However, government is still not a 'prime mover' in Carter's model. The economic actors are not simply passive recipients of the state's instructions; they are themselves pursuing their interests. Carter sees two main concerns for them: selecting technology which will enable the forms of production they need, and supporting forces of defence that will secure the legal and physical environment that they need to operate in. And finally those forces of defence need both legitimacy and resources—so they select the relations of government and economics that will provide them (although I feel that Carter does not fully make the case that forces of defence are directly involved in establishing economic relations. Colonialism and neo-colonialism, for example, are primarily about establishing government structure, which then go on to establish capitalist economic relationships).

Technology may appear to be the odd one out here. How can inanimate objects have autonomy as a system, and play a determining role? Many of us would prefer to see technological artifacts as neutral, capable of being used well or badly. As the example of nuclear energy in Chapter 2 suggested, technology really can 'structure the field of possible actions' (exercising power in Foucault's sense). We make our choices: Ivan Illich points out that where cars have been introduced as a technology of transport, other forms of transport have been eliminated. "[Cars] can shape a city in their image—practically ruling out locomotion on foot or by bicycle in Los Angeles. They can eliminate river traffic in Thailand. That motor traffic curtails the right to walk, not that more people drive Chevies than Fords, constitutes radical monopoly."[33]

It would be easy to assume that technology is simply the outcome of discoveries about the natural world—as our knowledge increases, new tools logically emerge. This view of a rational, linear progress allows only two possibilities: going forwards and going backwards. But the critics of industrial technology have long argued that research and development is focused on some areas and not on others, leading to a distinctive and restricted path of technological development with a powerful momentum of its own.

In Carter's view, the main consequence of this is to empower a particular set of forces of defence. I feel that it goes further than this, as will become clear further on. In any case, this is how Carter's dynamic model of human societies appears as a completed circuit:

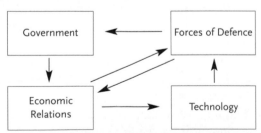

What is it that these arrows represent? It is not simply flows of resources—if anything, they flow round the system in the opposite direction. In each case, the arrow is suggesting that there is a 'backforce', a flow of control or regulation which has a determining effect. For example, he is suggesting that although our technologies provide wealth and resources for the economy, the actual power relationship is the other way around: it is the economic relations which determine the type of technology, where is is distributed, how it is used. In some cases, the relationship is one of determining; in other cases, selecting, stabilizing or legitimizing. The common feature is that it is a sustained flow of influence and interdependence. In many ways, it is these connections that are the real substance of the system, and not the units that they link up. These processes are the carriers of information and the actual practices of power.

Carter does have to justify his assertion that the relationships between these relations and forces must always exist as he suggests, even in very different societies. Both his analysis of the existing, 'environmentally hazardous dynamic' (broadly corresponding to my conception of power-over), and his preferred, potential 'environmentally benign dynamic' (corresponding to power-to) have the same overall shape. This has at least the advantage that we can see clearly how an alternative society can be constructed within this one— a theme I return to in Chapters 11 and 12.

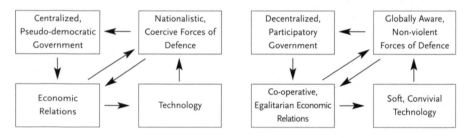

Carter argues that the reason that the state regulates the conditions of production and the relations of production in this way is to secure its own self-interest. This seems to me to imply too much of a conscious, conspiratorial role; I would rather simply say that the state establishes economic relations that are consistent with its political relations. Each block 'gives' something to another block—a mixture of resources, direction, and favourable conditions. Only sometimes is a direct return shown. Is Carter saying that the actors in each area are consciously aware of the system's requirements? Or that it is some kind of act of altruism? Both these explanations are unsatisfactory. There must be an immediate benefit of some sort, and my view is that it is one of economy of means. If you are an actor in competitive economic relations (for example), you will simply find it more straightforward and easier to develop hard technologies. No conscious plan is required; the activities in each area support other areas as a byproduct.

We might also question the four 'units' in the dynamic. Are they the only relevant factors? And do they have the relative autonomy that allows us to describe them as indentifiably separate? I would argue for one addition. Illich, Gorz and others have identified the growth of the public sector as the institutionalization of care. This is the introduction of a paternalistic and/or authoritarian approach to the functions of nurturing, development and maintenance previously carried out at a community level, using shared knowledge and skills rather than relying on experts. Feminists, too, have noted that these institutions deny long established knowledge held in communities (particularly by women), and instead make them objects of (male) control.

I don't wish to demean the worth of much of the work carried out in schools, or the real commitment of medical professionals to preserving life, or undermine their struggle to achieve the necessary resources to do this well. But there is considerable evidence of the pervasive influence of business interests over public services, of systematic violence maintaining a gender division of labour in the home, of experts abusing their position of trust, of relations of care being geared to providing labour, soldiers and resources. The conflict about community control over and access to these services surely reflects the different discourses of power behind them.

In short, relations of care in this society are dominated by the cult of the expert, and by conformity, impersonality and standardization. By providing a large part of the 'conditions of production' (a healthy, educated workforce for instance), they are supporting/enabling economic relations—much as O'Connor suggests above. The dominant forms of technology and the political structures in turn determine the forms that these public services will take.

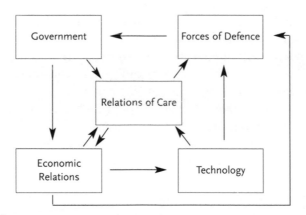

There is a danger that if we play this game too far, we will create a diagram of such magnificent complexity that it accounts for everything and actually tells us nothing. However, I believe that this is a worthwhile addition to the model. If we consider the human experience to be about the interactions between our human environment (other people), our non-human environment and social structures (which we experience as memory, language and other acquired knowledge and practices), then these five blocks cover all the interrelations between them:

Politics	human environment —→ social structures
Economics	social structures —→ non-human environment
Conflict	social structures —→ human environment
Technology	human environment —→ non-human environment
Care	human environment —→ human environment

Since our knowledge and memories don't relate to each other independently, and the non-human environment's interactions aren't part of human experience, these five categories more or less exhaust the possible power structures we encounter. Of course, any categorization is an oversimplification and an arbitrary division of a seamless world; but an exercise like this helps to establish whether we've omitted anything. Not to categorize at all creates 'a night in which all cows are black'. As long as we remember that this model is just a model, it may be a useful guide to action.

Systematic Change

Social change is about breaking these loops, redirecting flows, and creating new circuits and dynamics to take their place. Returning to Carter's dynamic, we can see that certain approaches will find the 'environmentally hazardous dynamic' very resilient. For instance, Carter examines 'single issue' challenges to each of the four features he identifies. The state could be democratized; technology could be made convivial; the forces of defence could be pacified; economics could be reformed along co-operative lines. However, any of these by themselves would be at odds with the prevailing flows of power. Competitive economics simply does not favour convivial technology; centralized government is incapable of stabilizing local economies; mass NVDA (non-violent direct action) is not reassuring for a pseudo-democratic, centralized regime. If this is the case, then there is no 'weak link'; the dominant dynamic presents an impenetrable wall against attack.[34]

Carter argues that there is an alternative approach: "The various elements of radical Green political thought consist in the systematic negation of every element of this dynamic."[35] In other words, the four elements of an 'environmentally benign dynamic' are themselves a self-regulating system, capable of stabilizing itself and providing a solid base for resistance to the industrial order.

Of course, this system already exists. It is not as dominant in the public sphere as the dynamic of power-over, but it is impossible to eradicate. Without power-to, there is no life at all; the earth depends on it, and human society depends on it in its most basic nurturing and reproductive activity.

So there is an ongoing tension between the two systems, competing for

THE PATTERN IN THE PAIN

There is a body of thought that sees much violence as resulting from diet. Certain biochemical types (the theory suggests) are prone to certain nutritional deficiencies. If the diet fails to meet these needs, the part of the brain that channels anger and helps resolve conflicts doesn't work effectively; violence is the outcome.

Certainly, much violence emerges from an inability to negotiate. And it is equally clear that a range of environmental causes exacerbate violence—overcrowding is only the most obvious.

But improving the nutrition of the Western armed forces would not have prevented hundreds of thousands dying in the 1991 Gulf War and its aftermath. Against carpet bombing of the sewage treatment plants, dietary supplements seem somewhat inadequate. We need to map the cycles that drive violence, and to understand the stability and persistence of local and international insecurity.

Violence has certain inputs that drive it, shape it and stabilize it. Economic relations contribute in two ways: firstly in the provision of personnel, men and women, in combat and in support; and secondly in competition for scarce and unequally held resources. The dominant technologies are an input, also in two ways: the destructive tools of violence, and a technological environment that induces psychosis (as noted above). Its outputs are economic relations (opening markets, maintaining access to resources, and building an arms trade) and political structures (nation building, securing legitimacy for a monopoly on force, and international organization).

However, social violence is both part of a system and a self-regulating system in itself. The dynamic of aggression, identity and coercion is self-stabilizing. We can identify a number of closed loops in the system, where negative feedback maintains a stable structure.

Cynthia Enloe describes one such pattern. "Militaries need women—but they need women to behave as the gender 'women'. This always requires the exercise of control. Military officials and allies in civilian élites have wielded their power to perpetuate those gendered processes that guarantee the military its manpower. This is what is so strikingly revealed in the experiences of women who have been used as the military's prostitutes, rape victims, wives, widows, social workers, nurses, soldiers, defence workers and mothers." In other words, militarism and patriarchy combine in a process of military reproduction—ensuring the next generation of soldiers are nurtured, trained and supported. Part of the process is the definition of women as the 'home front'—the idea that male armies are fighting to defend their wives, girlfriends and families. Essential to any violent act is the idea of friend and foe, us and them, national and foreigner, self and 'other'. Myths of home front and national identity are the cultural justification for the continual reproduction of male violence.

This takes place alongside a dynamic of relations concerning relations between different military groupings. As soon as an identity is established—typically, but not necessarily, a national identity—it becomes possible to identify allies and common enemies, and structured relationships emerge. This also becomes an issue of control and reproduction—on an international scale, as the establishment of a 'world order', and on a local level as trading and cultural connections. The phenomenon of Americanization—essentially a violent attack on identity—is an example of this. It is cyclical, because the relationship generates further needs for control and coercion, and that reinforces the nation building process and hence the polarization of friend and foe.

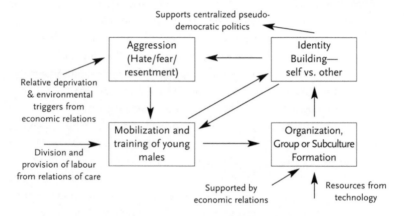

Nationalistic, Coercive Forces of Defence Subsystem

I don't claim that this explains all violence; but I do suggest that an awareness of these cycles puts in context a range of experiences from seeing toy shops selling toy tanks to racist assaults and domestic violence. With that understanding, we can understand our own collusion in these processes and build stable and uncompromised alternatives.

---

resources and control over our behaviour. This explains the presence of change in seemingly self-regulating systems; power-over is constantly exceeding the capacity of the system that supports it, and has to give ground. This is the dynamic tension that we experience in the repeated clashes between movements for empowerment, communal self-determination and sustainability on the one hand, and commerce, progress and central authority on the other. These conflicts have been endemic for over a century now, from the Green socialism of William Morris and Thoreau in the nineteenth century to the eco-warriors of today. Although there is constant conflict and movement, a kind of balance has been maintained. Power-over has always been strong enough to contain power-to; but power-to has always grown in response to the excesses of power-over. The question is: will the cycle of overshoot followed by concession end with concessions that make power-over unsustainable, or an overshoot that cannot be recovered from?

It is conceivable that the tension can be maintained indefinitely—but only at the cost of a steady loss of biodiversity, leaving a more and more unstable ecosystem, more at risk of overshoot. It is even possible that power-over will attempt to become independent of ecological limitations through technological development: if this happens, will we truly be human any more? More likely, I think, that sooner or later power-over will have to give up so much ground that power-to can overtake it. My fear is that by then, the new society will inherit a ruined earth.

The Big Issues

We can break down the model on page 177 to show the main cycles of feedback within the dynamics of power-over and power-to. There are three main cycles, each involving three of the subsystems, which correspond closely to processes identified and resisted by the new social movements:

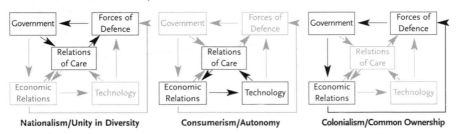

Nationalism/Unity in Diversity   Consumerism/Autonomy   Colonialism/Common Ownership

Then there are three more extended cycles involving four of the subsystems each. Again, there are some clear correspondences with the actual experiences of Green activists.

Military Industrial complex/   Patriarchy/Community   Gendered/élitist division of
Radical Technology   labour/Work and skill sharing

Each of these cycles has an internal stability—not only under power-over, but also under power-to. I agree with Carter that a key strategic objective is to negate not just one subsystem in the dynamic of power-over, but entire cyclical processes. His word 'negate' does not for me capture the essence of building a

DIE GRÜNEN: UNPICKING THE NETWORKS OF VIOLENCE

Through the 1970s, a peace movement was growing in Germany as protesters gathered to blockade and bear witness at both nuclear missile and nuclear power sites. Some of these protesters introduced a radical new set of tactics, generally known as 'non-violence'. In contrast to the traditional Marxist left of campus politics, they did not attempt to take on police and army in pitched battles, but instead sought to gain the trust and sympathy of the public by resisting passively and protesting peacefully. At the same time, they sought to increase their effectiveness by bringing a wider range of activists to the front-line (non-violence does not exclude the elderly, or physically weaker protesters), and by organizing in small, autonomous groups so as to outmanoeuvre the more rigidly organized authorities.

At one such protest in 1975 at Whyl in the Black Forest, an important meeting took place between Roland Vogt and Petra Kelly. Both held the view that concerns about the environment and peace were inextricably linked—one could not be adequately addressed without the other. Single issue politics was powerless to make real changes, because the issue was actually driven by other issues. Society was not a set of discrete, separate activities, but a complex, interrelated organism. Roland Vogt recalls, "The original focus was ecology, then we joined peace, and then we realized that neither had a chance without restructuring the economy. Once we realized that Green thinking can inform every area of politics and life and that our central issue is survival, I created the term 'vitalism' as a contra-term to exterminism."[36]

In 1978, Vogt and Kelly were both on the executive committee of the BBU—an umbrella group for ecological groups. They were contacted by two organizations interested in trying to build a political programme out of Green ideas—the Action Committee of Independent Germans and Green Action Future (formed by Herbert Gruhl, a CDU parliamentarian). Two other groups interested in alternative politics became interested—Action Third Way (followers of Rudolf Steiner's teachings) and the Free International University (made up of independent-minded leftists). They agreed that the 'new politics' needed a new party to oppose the exterminism of all the other parties.

Representatives of all the participating groups met in Offenbach in November 1979 to attempt to agree a set of principles for the new party. It soon became clear that it was not going to be easy. August Haussleiter said, "I myself had been almost desperate with the situation because there were 3,000 people screaming their own positions in the convention hall. This person kept saying, 'Don't give up. Don't give up. They're getting tired.' Although agreement seemed impossible, I took a piece of paper and wrote four words [in German] on it: ecology, social responsibility, grassroots democracy and non-violence. Then I called together Gruhl and Reents [of the FIU] in the room where the journalists were and said, 'Sign.' We then went back into the convention hall and announced, 'We have a programme!'"[37]

The realization that these four broad areas were interconnected—that none could be effectively tackled without reference to the others—parallels the more recent work of Alan Carter, who argued that a social dynamic that was environmentally benign would combine alternative technology (the 'industrial disarmament' central to the German Green's ecology platform), grassroots democracy, non-violence and co-operative, egalitarian economics. The relationships between them that he describes were similar to the cycles that the German Greens had identified. The military industrial complex is replaced by globally responsible community production; the coercive state maintaining private wealth is replaced by a participatory democracy founded on cooperation. The relationships between different sectors of society remains unchanged, but the content is wholly changed; if all these aspects of society are changed at the same time, and the new relationships established, social change becomes possible.

The most difficult period for the Greens comes now, as they start to enter posts in regional and possibly national government. As Petra Kelly said before her untimely death, "How should one deal as a Green minister with the violence inherent in the state? How should one deal as a Green minister with the structural violence often inherent in governmental polices? I do not believe that we have yet found an answer, but we all know that we must try to transform those institutions of violence into non-violent institutions."[38] This proved prescient: within days of taking office as Germany's first Green foreign minister, Joshka Fischer was condoning a massive and largely ineffective bombing campaign in the Balkans. Greens and other political reformers are in grave danger of stepping into positions they believe to hold power, only to find that the only effective sources of that power are irredeemably tainted. The crucial alternative power bases have been so neglected by them that they offer little help now.

---

viable social alternative. It is about opposing, blocking and limiting the current, dominant process; but it is as much if not more about substitution, about finding alternative ways to meet needs within those subsystems and then linking them together.

Single issues alone are not sufficient; they create incoherent and unsustainable programmes that attempt to reconcile the irreconcilable, and ultimately betray their intention. Pressure groups are beginning to realize this. In 1996 in Britain, a formidable alliance of single issue groups representing a total of almost 6 million people united around a programme of reform covering economics, government, technology and public service. Individually they had found that they needed to reach beyond their issue in order to adequately address it. The Child Poverty Action Group found themselves considering the urban environment, just as Friends of the Earth found themselves discussing housing policy. Although their narrow focus had succeeded in uniting broad coalitions and achieving pressure for reforms, their efforts were constantly undermined by the effects of seemingly unrelated issues. The 'Real World' initiative which brought them together may not be sufficient in itself; but it is a necessary recognition of the complex connections at work.

Part Three

Strategy

Chapter 9

The Economy of Truth

Even when it appears at its most banal, power-over is systematically suffocating our ability to live authentically human lives. Its influence is felt everywhere, in every trans-action and interaction, and in particular through the mass media. This endless repeti-tion of 'what is, must be' has the effect of closing off our minds to all other options.

This is hegemony, as defined by Marxist theorists similarly concerned with the difficulty of bringing radical ideas to a mass audience. This 'organized consent' takes place through formal organizations and media, but also through casual social interaction. Wherever someone tries to exercise hegemonic leadership, their effectiveness will paradoxically depend on being both radical enough to make a dif-ference, and close enough to the mainstream for their message to be viable.

This is not to say that what most people believe is false, and only people who read this book will understand the truth. Our consciousness can be organized and shaped, but it is no less a description of reality for all that. Revolutionaries who, instead of insisting on the truth of their ideas, have encouraged people to listen to their own desires for guidance, have had considerable success. But that success has proved to be short-lived, because the desire for change it creates can easily be bought off.

So what is needed is a message that gains the participation of the audience, but which carries real content—a viable alternative set of rules and practices. Again, systems models of how social practices affect social contexts (and vice versa) are helpful in understanding the processes involved. Resistance is about scepticism, challenge and viable alternatives.

"The struggle of people against power is the struggle of memory against for-getting."—Milan Kundera

Foreman: You know what's worst about all this?
Vanek: No, what?
Foreman: I'm damned if I know what to tell 'em every bloody week. What do I know about you . . . you tell me that, next to nothing, right?. . . and as for the tittle tattle I sometimes hear . . . that you've been seen a couple of times with Marge from the bottling plant—I ask you, is that any good?
Vanek: I'm sorry, but I hardly think I can help you there.

Foreman: You're an intellectual aren't you? And you write, don't you? In that warehouse you'll have plenty of time to spare—what harm would it do you to put it down on paper for me once a week. Don't I deserve it? I'll see you don't come to any harm. That Tonda Masek is a decent sort . . . I've known him since we were boys . . . and he really needs it. Didn't we say we'd stick together? That we were going to be pals?

Vanek: Yes, I know, but . . .

Foreman: It's all up to you now Ferdinand. If only you do your bit, everything's going to turn up trumps. You help me, I help him, he'll do me a good turn and I'll do you one—we'll all benefit.

What are you staring at me for?

Vanek: I wasn't staring at you.

Foreman: You'd like to be in that warehouse, wouldn't you? Nice and cosy and warm . . .

Vanek: That would be wonderful.

Foreman: Well, then what's the story?

Vanek: I'm most truly grateful to you for everything you've done for me . . . please don't misunderstand what I am going to say, but I just can't . . . I can't inform on myself.

Foreman: Inform? Who's talking about informing?

Vanek: It wouldn't do me any harm . . . but there's a principle involved. How can I be expected to participate in . . . something I have always found repugnant?

Foreman: Now you're really showing your true colours. A fine pal you've turned out to be. You'd take a nice cushy job in a warm warehouse from me, but a bit of the dirt I've got to wade through every day, that you won't.

—from *Audience* by Vaclav Havel

In the preceding chapters, I have shown that processes of power link up to form self-maintaining networks; and I've shown that these circuits have essential characteristics that make them compatible or incompatible with one another. I believe that systems dominated by 'power-over' have become dominant, in the sense of providing the most accessible mechanisms for meeting our needs. In Chapter 3, I described the way that power-from-within us gave us choices and the ability to exercise moral judgement. In this chapter I want to see how this is suppressed and stifled by the ubiquity of a given worldview and way of life. In particular, I want to look at how our consent to power is enlisted, and our active participation maintained.

The novelist and literary critic David Lodge says, "Narrative is one of the fundamental ways of organizing human experience."[1] We look for stories in the world around us, and we unconsciously help the story to achieve the 'right' ending. Politicians use this by creating stories for themselves; advertisers weave stories around their products. Once Bill Clinton had established his identity as 'the comeback kid', he created an aura of inevitability around recovering popularity after a disgrace. If you held out against it, it would somehow feel wrong; as though you had failed to read the direction of events. And yet nothing in this world is inevitable; for business to carry on as usual requires an immense co-ordinated effort. We believe it to be inevitable because that is how the story goes. It is not that change is impossible; if it is linked to a familiar narrative structure (the wrong that is finally put right, the prodigal son, the lifting of a curse), it can actually become inevitable. But most of the stories currently being played out require continuity; and so the status quo continues.

A phrase that is increasingly being used by social workers and therapists working with survivors of childhood abuse is 'ritual abuse'. While this phrase is also used by fundamentalist Christians to describe their controversial claims of satanic abuse, I prefer its use to describe a total environment of abuse, surrounded by rules and rituals. When abuse becomes the norm for a child, the abuser gains a new level of power because the abused is unable to conceive of social relations other than abusive ones. The survivor is also effectively trained to become an abuser themselves, and given a range of choices in how they should abuse. The participation in their own and others' abuse leads to a sense of complicity. They may leave the situation, and yet continue to deny, defend or continue abuse because they feel guilt at the part they have played—even though their 'choice' was no choice at all.

I would argue that this pattern of internalization is typical of any situation in which a system of power has become dominant; it is the only reality. Life in industrial society today is similar in its circumscribed range of choices which make the abused participants in their own abuse. To many of my readers, a term like 'abuse' will seem unnecessarily loaded, and not reflective of their experience. Certainly it is true that power-over is typically more banal than horrific—although that is seen without the benefit of an alternative standpoint. My point is not that power-over always causes great suffering, but rather that a great deal of suffering, and in particular the global problems of human survival, have power-over at their root. Further, all instances of power-over are interconnected in a mutually supportive network, so even the most routine and unquestioned uses of power have complicity in the bigger picture.

What makes this complicity possible is the distance of the connections, which allows responsibility to be endlessly deferred and a blind eye turned to anything beyond the immediate and the concrete. We can all say 'I'm not to blame', 'I'm only doing my job', 'I'm not the one you should be talking to', and we can all be wrong. A narrow focus on the material, the individual and the tangible is a necessary response to the moral stress power-over places us under. It leads to a paradoxical situation: a shared experience, and a level of communication between people greater than ever before—and yet at the same time, a content more banal and superficial than ever. The mass media is a crucial expression of the rituals of consumerism and the environment of power-over: not through any conspiracy, but simply by repeating and endorsing the same things that are the day-to-day discourse of most of us—particularly those of us furthest from the pain and abuse of power-over.

Defining Hegemony

The word usually used to describe the total dominance of a certain system of belief or morality is hegemony. Although it first appears in early Bolshevik writings,[2] the concept was popularized by Antonio Gramsci, an Italian Communist imprisoned by Mussolini. A great deal of what he was trying to do relates to his situation—he was trying to explain the success of fascism in Italy, and to find a latent idealism in Marx's early writings. Neither of these are particularly relevant here, so I will concentrate on the broader applications of hegemony theory.

Hegemony refers to the moral leadership that exists in societies—Carroll defines it as "a historically specific organization of consent that rests on a material base".[3] Particularly important is the word consent. It is not about total control, but rather about mass participation. It is the 'material base' (the connection to people's everyday lives) that ensures this participation takes place. Equally, it is not about political participation so much as participation in the propagation of the values that underpin a political regime. Bocock writes, "At any given stage of historical development a particular philosophical worldview may provide the major way of grasping what is going on in the world and of living creatively in it."[4] The Catholic Church has held hegemonic power in the past; but typically it is not an organization or even a group in society, but rather a system of thought and action (or, I would argue, a system of power).

Hegemony is generally held to take place crucially through 'civil society'— a catch-all term referring to religion, arts, pressure groups, media, voluntary associations, local forums and interest groups. However, Gramsci was less than clear about the relationship between civil society and the state. Are schools an arm of the state, indoctrinating their pupils? Seen in this light, the state is educating as far as is necessary to train the population for a certain level of productive technology. Or are they a part of an autonomous civil society, collectively socializing their members? Are elections a process for establishing consent and building legitimacy, or are they only possible once consent has been gained through cultural leadership?

I think a large part of the confusion here stems from the assumption of state sovereignty. Since Foucault, there has been a growing awareness that top-down models of social control miss out a massive part of the story. Although the state undoubtedly has powers of coercion, most social order cannot be attributed to them. Relationships in civil society, and between individuals in everyday life, are just as much relations of power. If they seem to have less impact, then we must bear in mind just how numerous they are. We interact with each other as people far more often than we interact with the coercive powers of the state. What is more, when we do encounter the legal power of the sovereign, we invariably experience it through the medium of another person, with his or her own interests, desires, language and history. When we speak of 'thought control' (as well we might) we should remember that there is not controlled and controller, but rather a shifting, evolving (but self-maintaining) discourse within which we all have to speak, and which we reproduce when we do so. Media moguls like Rupert Murdoch and political leaders like Bill Clinton are all subject to the same limitation of thought, experience and action. Their actions may be more prominent, but they are replicated and reinforced every day by the millions of people we think of as 'less powerful' than them. It is the propaganda that is powerful, not the propagandist, because the propagandist can only choose from the limited range of propaganda that is viable in that setting.

This is important, because it reminds us that the problem of social consent to the destruction of the Earth and its people is not a question of 'them' against 'us'—although certain groups may play critical roles at certain times. We have to be aware that we are potentially part of the problem if our everyday lives reproduce the values, knowledge and organization of power-over, and that we cannot hope to counter those values simply by gaining access to some position or role. If we replace a propagandist for power-over with a propagandist for power-to, we certainly impair the maintenance of consent for power-over, but we do not spontaneously create consent for power-to. The message needs a source in 'reality', and it needs a receptive audience.

So, the 'organization of consent' takes place through both formal and informal channels. The question is, what is the relationship between the two? Do informal social transactions set the limits within which civil society can operate, or does civil society provide the leadership which is then amplified through repetition? We can look at many examples of cultural shifts and social change, and trace the causal links back without end. The only conclusion we can come to is that any individual, or group of individuals, can exercise leadership and contribute to hegemonic formation (or, as we shall see further on, counter-hegemonic formation): the key is the crucial balance between viability and radicalism. What they are saying or doing must be radical and new (otherwise, it won't make any real difference) and at the same time close enough to what is already understood and practised to be easily integrated into people's lives. By this, I mean that the base resources must be available to draw upon (these could be economic, political or cultural resources) but they must be directed along new pathways.

Hegemonic leadership is the building of new linkages and processes of power. Like completing an electrical circuit, there must be a potential difference—an accumulated charge of new ideas, which finds a pathway through

SELL IT TO ME

Advertisers are constantly innovating. Countless studies have shown that children are able to discern between advertising and non-commercial programming, and respond with appropriate scepticism—and this is even more true of adults. Advertisers have responded to this by increasingly being knowing, self-referential and ironic, or simply entertaining. They engage the audience as accomplices by giving them something that they want (a good laugh, or respect for their intelligence) in the hope that they will accept the commercial message at the same time. An advertisement becomes powerful when the audience willingly participates in picking up the message.

Most advertisers are looking for the TV channels watched by people with high disposable incomes—and that means the channels which say what such people want to hear. How can a station criticize a lifestyle or a culture when it depends for its existence on that lifestyle? How can it speak in a language that is incomprehensible to the audience it needs to attract? This has consistently been a problem with media produced with the specific intention of criticizing the status quo. The only chance they have is when there is a significant number of businesses trading with that audience—and indeed, where alternative therapies, fair trade, wholefoods and ethical investment have been turned into profitable businesses, then counter-hegemonic publications have been supported.

If the broadcasters forget that the advertisers are in charge, the advertisers will remind them. David Edwards cites the example of WNET, who lost their advertising from Gulf & Western after a programme criticizing corporate activities in the third world. It wasn't that the programme criticized Gulf & Western, but simply that its message was "virulently anti-business". Procter and Gamble instructed their advertising agency to boycott any programme that might "further the concept of business as cold, ruthless and lacking in sentiment or spiritual motivation". General Electric (who own NBC) insist on "a programme environment that reinforces our corporate message".[5] In 1998, Chris Patten was writing a book about his experiences as the last British Governor of Hong Kong. He was astonished when his publishers unceremoniously dropped the book at the last minute—until he realized that the publishers were owned by Rupert Murdoch's News International, which was trying to secure investment in China, and did not want anything that might cause the Chinese offence.

Edwards draws on the work of Chomsky and Herman, who identify five 'filters' that ensure that mass communications present a message consistent with the dominant power system. The sheer size and commercial ruthlessness required of media companies to reach large audiences means that they are run by the people that benefit from the status quo and identify closely with it. Another filter is the symbiotic relationship between media and sources of information. In

a society dominated by power-over, the key nodes of power-over are indispens-
able as sources of information; so the spin doctors of the White House, for
instance, are in a sellers' market. 'Flak' is Chomsky and Herman's term for
aggressive action taken against non-conformist media. The recent McLibel trial
showed how McDonalds could use the law to censor critics (and also how those
critics could turn that against them). Finally, the external enemy—until recently,
communism—provides a useful label to denigrate any critical voice with.[6]

Chomsky's propaganda model is a real set of processes that are conditioning mass media. Marcuse, too, has written about the way that mass communication suppresses discourse that involves critical judgement and leaves us
unable to challenge the false choices it presents. These are important reminders
that the media is neither as neutral nor as inconsequential as it may appear.

---

people's needs, concepts and experience. When this happens, the new idea will
be reproduced and amplified (and quite possibly substantially modified). Plenty
of very worthy ideas will fall on deaf ears because they do not make that connection. Finally, in order to survive in the long term, the new practice must find a
role in a system of power, like those described in the last chapter. This is true of
anyone innovating in power-over (just because it is hegemonic, does not mean it
is unchanging—quite the reverse), just as it is true of anyone seeking to resist it.

Semi Consciousness

Distinctions between civil society, the state and the economy suffer from their
arbitrary and artificial nature. The linkages that bind people—not just cultural,
but economic and political—cut across these boundaries at the local level.
Since the local level is the one at which most interaction takes place, its importance should not be underrated. Hegemonic formation ultimately takes place
at this level, although formal institutions may be important sources of
resources and opportunity.

This begs the question of the apparent consistency and uniformity of
hegemonic culture. Later in the 20th century, as 'cultural Marxists' continued
to work on Gramsci's question ("How can cultural inertia prevent a proletar-
ian revolution?"), this kind of analysis became more and more important.
Social change activists were now up against a rapidly diversifying range of
media, broadcasting a seductive message of comfort and convenience for all.
'Hegemony' came to refer to the culture—particularly the American culture—
being promoted through this. For the most part, they concluded that mass
culture was playing a kind of vast confidence trick, deluding people into believing that their needs were being met. 'False consciousness' theories argued that
the workers' perceptions of their real interests were being obscured, distorted
or deceived by the endless reinforcement of capitalist values in the media.

There is an obvious flaw with this view. Who decides what is false and what is true? By defining Marxism as a science, Marxists were calling their own opinions facts, and other people's opinions delusions. It seemed clear that the sheer power of consumerist culture was putting down deeper and deeper roots into people's minds, but equally clear that traditional revolutionary Marxism was not what they were ever going to want.

May 1968 in Paris brought all of this to a head. A remarkable group called the Situationist International finally succeeded in engaging thousands in active resistance to government and corporations. They described modern society as the society of the spectacle—a 'big lie' that paralysed culture and ossified social relations. "When the real world changes into simple images, simple images become real beings and effective motivations of a hypnotic behaviour."[7] But they were not interested in the traditional tactics of opposition. They abandoned the goal of a mass party; the SI only ever had a hundred members (bizarrely, almost all were at one time or another purged for ideological error). They abandoned the goal of a 'dictatorship of the proletariat', and instead called for self-managing workers' councils. They ignored the usual tactics of revolutionaries, and instead mounted cultural guerrilla warfare through defaced adverts, spontaneous occupations and cryptic slogans—"Be realistic: demand the impossible." In fact, their propaganda was not primarily aimed at gaining support for a programme, but rather worked to expose the overblown pomposity of the ruling powers. By making the images of business, state and industry seem immoral, fatuous, laughable or unreal, they succeeded in creating a sense of empowerment and infinite possibility in those who had long held suppressed feelings of resentment.

Two things are immediately apparent from the results. Firstly, against all the odds, it worked. Massive protests, running battles, occupations and strikes overtook a previously orderly, modern, industrial society. Secondly, it failed. Not only were almost all the protesters bought off with the offer of a pay rise from the government, but it was almost obvious from the outset that this was what they wanted and was what they would settle for—hence the failure of the communist party to get involved. The Situationist International had clearly solved part of the problem—but only part. Their strategy of 'cracking the spectacle' and introducing the thrill of real life into a banal succession of alienating images did succeed in triggering a revolt, but it was a dead end. On one level, the hegemony broke in an orgy of disobedience. But at another level, a more fundamental level of desire, aspiration and imagination, it held firm. Even within a turbulent and disrupted state, people could not conceive of any more desirable good than a pay rise. As the Situationists understood, and Gramsci had not, "The Spectacle is sustained not by the images produced by the media, but by us when we reproduce these images in our daily life— which, in turn, are represented by the media as examples of 'reality'."[8] But as

HOSTILE WITNESS

In the early 80s in Britain, the growing peace movement attempted a new and radical tactic. They did not gather to voice their opposition to the American Cruise Missiles in the places of conventional political appeal—the Houses of Parliament, or Whitehall—but outside the bases themselves. Further, they did not meet, protest and disperse; they arrived in relatively small numbers and they stayed. In benders, tents, caravans and lean-tos, they established a 'peace camp'. Faslane and Greenham were two of the most long-lasting; Molesworth perhaps the largest and most confrontational.

The strategy had its roots in a Christian pacifism that stressed the importance of 'bearing witness'. The protesters weren't principally interested in winning an argument with authority, because such arguments were being conducted on the basis of a value system they did not share. Instead, they believed that those who actually implemented the policy should be asked to consider the morality of their action every single day—that being true to one's beliefs meant conducting a sustained vigil at the place where those beliefs were being violated.

This is a strong moral position, but it also gained power from some of its other effects. The smooth, professional, dignity of the bases was ruined by banners that spoke of blood, murder and death. The camp broke up the image of peacekeeping by focusing attention on warfighting. Also the meeting point—permanently maintained—meant an increase in the number of direct actions taking place. Local courts had to hear the political arguments, local newspapers excitedly reported the developments and employees at the base increasingly came into contact with people who silently accused them of genocide. The camps were also a way for any local opponents of the base who were reluctant to protest to find a role for themselves as camp supporters. Donations and visits deepened their commitment to the resistance. The authorities could not tolerate them as they had tolerated other protests; the largest peacetime military operation in British history was mounted to clear the Molesworth camp.

Through the next decade, the tactic was refined and extended to other locations. There were camps outside nuclear power stations, such as Sellafield; outside the Hazleton Animal Testing Laboratories; outside US Spy Bases like Menwith Hill; and in 1991, at Twyford Down in the path of a motorway extension. With the road protest camps, a new dimension emerged: they could not be ignored, as they had to be moved forcibly in order to build the road. This tactic has itself been extended to the second runway at Manchester Airport, where it took seventeen days to dig out the last tunneller.

I am typical of thousands who have visited, but not lived at, a protest camp. Like others, I found a community, built on a sense of precious values. I found a seriousness and a clarity from being so close to the frontline; I did not have to wait for media to tell me about it, or imagine it—I was there, I could see it. From that vantage point, I could see past the façade of normality to the reality of war and destruction: there was a crack in the hegemony.

In fact, it felt like I had stepped out of normality into a zone where different rules applied. Molesworth was perhaps the first to create a microcosm of a different society, a protest village; but Claremont Road in the path of the M11 brought it home. As I walked down this otherwise typical Victorian terrace in East London, I saw a functioning community, with a café, an art gallery, an information point, a workshop and meetings in the open where decisions were taken. It felt in many ways like an open air art gallery, as many local artists had treated the street like a canvas where playful, angry and startling images could be created. The combination of local residents and dedicated protesters was both well grounded and audacious, and the excitement of feeling the dead hand of conformity lifted as you walked into the street was tangible.

When the protesters were evicted, it became more than a protest. People cried as the houses and the trees came down and were swept away: hundreds came to defend it. The scaffolding tower that rose above the houses was visible for miles, sending the message, "There is another truth, another reality. It doesn't have to be like this." Those who saw it will not quickly forget.

---

well as breaking this pattern, something had to be put in its place. If the establishment was immoral and greedy, that did not necessarily mean that we should be anything other than hedonistic ourselves. If the establishment was overblown and pompous, that did not necessarily that any other big idea would be more authentic. If the establishment offered only banal and tedious activity, it did not necessarily mean that anyone knew of a viable, sustainable, non-banal way of life—only that tedium should be better paid.

Since then, activists have tried to develop forms of resistance which undermine the façade, but at the same time convey something extra; a moral purpose, a more authentic culture, an alternative way of life. The results may not have been so dramatic, but they rest on more solid foundations.

Our Silence is our Collusion

Hegemony is not, in fact, simply a cultural phenomenon—something that happens in our minds, or in the mass media. It is our co-operation with and reproduction of structures of power, and this takes place in physical forms. Consider our geography: pavements interrupted by roads, houses cut off from each other, dormitory towns and shopping centres. And yet we willingly and without coercion walk on the pavements and not the streets, live in our houses and abandon the common spaces between them, and leave our community to do our shopping. As I described in Chapter 2, processes of power operate through the technologies we build as well as through the words we speak. Processes of power are not 'material' or 'cultural': they are systematic, endlessly diversifying, growing and extending into every corner of our lives without respect for the artificial boundaries we erect. "The basic tautological character of the spectacle flows from the simple fact that its means are at the same time its goal. It is the sun which never sets over the empire of modern passivity. It covers the entire surface of the world and bathes endlessly in its own glory."[9]

Time, also, is structured so as to reproduce social relations. Conventions and expectations, from church on Sunday to working 9 till 5, provide a framework to structure our lifestyle. We can only meet our vital needs by being in the right place at the right time, and the more of our time that is accounted for in this way, the less that can be done with the time remaining. As social beings, we need these shared rituals, and we would have to invent them if they did not exist. There does not need to be any kind of conspiracy here—it is simply that the complexity of power relations intrudes into so much of our lives that it limits our space for developing alternative ways of being.

The difficulty for the Situationists—and for other cultural Marxists, such as the 'Critical Theorists' referred to in Chapter 6—is that they were, despite their best efforts, reproducing the spectacle themselves. Coming from a materialist background, their arguments for change depended on offering material satisfaction to 'the workers'—exactly the same reward that the industrial hegemony advertised. They could not grasp that the spectacle did not deceive people. It isn't a 'false consciousness' or a 'third dimension of power'. It is what people want, what they really, really want.[10] Power-over has defined our interests as being that which only power-over can deliver.

There is no way out of this paradox unless we accept that interests are not absolute—that in fact they are linked to the dominant processes of power. If that is the case, then a different dynamic of power can establish different interests—ones which are unmoved by the images of the mass media. We have to do more than expose the stupidity or banality of consumerism; we have to offer an alternative. It is that which will enable people to laugh in the face of power, and will split the hegemony we face.

Michel Foucault takes the argument a step further. In his studies of power, he concluded that the 'discourse' in a society was not merely concealing power structures—that in some deeper sense it was the power structure. He speaks of power/knowledge—the way that a body of knowledge validates certain social relations rather than others, and the way that social relations have a creative ability and generate a body of knowledge. This is an unnerving line of thought—it suggests that we cannot even talk about power, since our frame of reference is itself constructed from power. It suggests that we cannot escape from power, or be able to speak of objective knowledge, since all knowledge is what is 'true' for those particular relations of power.

"The working hypothesis will be this: power relations (with the struggles that traverse them or the institutions that maintain them) do not only play with respect to knowledge a facilitating or obstructive role; they are not content merely to encourage or stimulate it, to distort or limit it; power and knowledge are not linked together solely by the play of interests or ideologies; the problem is not therefore that of determining how power subjugates knowledge and makes it serve its ends, or how it imprints its mark on knowledge, imposes on it ideological contents and limits. No body of knowledge can be formed without a system of communications, records, accumulation and displacement which is in itself a form of power and which is linked, in its existence and functioning, to the other forms of power. Conversely, no power can be exercised without the extraction, appropriation, distribution or retention of knowledge. On this level, there is not knowledge on the one side and society on the other, or science and the state, but only the fundamental forms of knowledge/power . . ."[11]

For Foucault, the nature of hegemony is that power cannot exist without constituting the body of knowledge that is true under that power relation. Our thoughts, our culture, our behaviour, our lifestyle—all these are constituted by the apparatus of power. We cannot survive without true knowledge, and we cannot establish something as true without a process of normalization. This does not take place at the level of the state, or even through the agencies of civil society, but is exercised by individuals, unconsciously, in every transaction. He does not regard the process as one of general consent: he stresses that all power carries with it resistance, and that the unceasing struggle may lead to reversals and shifts as one process gathers pace at the expense of another. However, he does deny the possibility of an escape from power.

In this book, I have picked up on the one glimmer of hope Foucault offered. He suggests at least the possibility of a different dominant discourse, and a different knowledge, with a network of power relations distinctively different from what he calls 'discipline' and 'sovereignty'. I believe that this distinction is emerging, from the knowledge of ecology, the practice of non-violence and co-operation, and the economics of mutual aid. What is true, and correct, under the relations of power-over, may be as fictitious and irrelevant in an empowering political culture as co-operation is considered now.

The Powers that are Being
One difficulty that Foucault presents us with is relating this network of microscopic struggles to the formal power of organizations and states, or to the systematic domination of one group by another. Perhaps the key lies in the nature of organization: it is something that we treat as though it were real, but in fact is a shared body of knowledge. In organizations we can see power/knowledge more clearly in operation than elsewhere. A theorist who has based his study of power on organization is Clegg, who uses a model he describes as 'circuits

SHARED DREAMS

Protest camps are a powerful challenge to the dominant hegemony, but they are transient. They are anti-hegemonic rather than counter-hegemonic, in the sense that they disrupt the dominant culture rather than establishing a different one. 'Reclaim the Streets' is another example of this. The street parties that have taken place in many European cities (sometimes in combination with Critical Mass cycle rides) have been more than simply an interruption of traffic. They have been genuine festivals of resistance, where space has been reclaimed, transformed and subverted. By setting the cultural parameters to those of freedom, empowerment, and harmony with nature, the physical and material environment is changed. One cannot experience the same place again without remembering the excitement of its recolonization. It creates a powerful opposition between its normal use and the joy of the street party. If the atmosphere could be maintained (the shared experience in the local community, the sense of freedom and empowerment, the assumption of a different set of values) and combined with a viable economic base, it could make an enterprise with radical potential.

One example might be the 1 in 12 Club in Bradford. Owned by an anarchist collective, it provides a venue for punk bands and raves (important elements of the British counter culture) and a vegan café. It has kept going for over a decade, and it is no coincidence that many political groups use it as their mailing address and venue for meetings. Cooltan, a long term squat in Brixton, London, had the same function as a meeting place of dissidents. However, both lack a broad base: if you are over thirty, or in full-time employment, or don't go for either punk or rave music, it can feel exclusive and even intimidating. A lot of centres for the counterculture are not orientated around people with jobs, or children, or are simply so messy and unkempt that they discourage the faint hearted.

There is no reason why this should be the case. Just as Working Men's Clubs [sic], Liberal Clubs and Conservative Clubs brought together people who shared a political culture in the last century, so today's new social movements need spaces in which the emergent values of empowerment can be assumed and enjoyed. This works on any number of levels: as before, many will use the convivial atmosphere to make business connections, and develop the interconnectedness of the alternative economy. It is also a socialization process for those on the fringes of the movement, encouraging them to develop a sense of countercultural identity.

Munching my way through a veggie burger in the 1 in 12, I felt a deep sense of being at home. Perhaps I would have liked a more polished presentation, and a more cosmopolitan atmosphere; but at some very basic level I felt I gelled with my surroundings. I no longer felt like a weirdo, or a crank; I felt normal and at ease. The same thing was true of living in a housing co-operative—a home, and a community, that embodied my values and provided a bulwark against the consumer culture of the outside world. Being an eco-activist shouldn't imply a sense of isolation or marginalization; it certainly shouldn't be a youthful indulgence. In a supportive setting, it doesn't feel like that at all; and when you spend time in more conventional settings, the knowledge that you have a secure base frees you from defensiveness, insecurity and lack of confidence.

of power' (see diagram on page 200). He argues that 'rules of practice' are the obligatory passage points for all power structures—in Foucault's terms, we might say that only what is 'true' for a given society carries any power. Social relations—the building blocks of organization and social structure—are established, fixed or undermined by this common sense of society.[12]

At the level of agency, causal power relations are 'real'; we can see contests over resources, policy and control. From the outset, I have argued in this book that this is not where real power lies, even though it feels very real to those who are engaged in these struggles. In Clegg's diagram, the left and right arrows at the top represent resistance and authority, and show these struggles taking place. But the context of the contest, and the rules that it follows, are set elsewhere. Social structure, Clegg argues, is not directly a result of these episodic, causal power plays: it comes from deeper levels, and he identifies two such 'cultural' motors. The first is the 'rules that fix meaning and membership', and the second 'production and discipline' (this is culture in the sense of technique or behaviour—not just ideas). Clegg says that he is to some extent following Mann's 'four sources' of power—ideological, political, military and economic (hopefully the correspondence is clear).[13] This distinction is quite common— C. Wright Mills suggests that the government, the economy and the military are the three main power bases,[14] Russell and Galbraith both categorize power as either force (military), reward (economic) or conditioning (ideology).[15] However, what Clegg is suggesting is quite different.

Rather than take these as the main organizations which affect outcomes (power at the level of the agency) Clegg suggests that they are fundamental in a different way: outcomes of any sort which affect or change common practices in these fields will shape social relations not causally (i.e. one thing clearly leading to another) but normatively (by changing common practice, they make new relations possible). Meaning is about values and aspirations, tastes and preferences, and it is dispositional—it works at the level of influence or inclination. Membership, similarly, causes ripples of influence. If there is a change in the inclusion or exclusion of certain groups, then besides any causal changes in the balance of power in the organization it affects there will also be wider shifts in people's expectations and assumptions. For instance, winning the vote for women may have led to legislation in Parliament that women had expressly voted for: but the real social change that resulted was the dramatic improvement in status for women.

With production and discipline, Clegg takes us to a deeper level still, the level of system integration. He describes this as both 'domination' and 'facilitation'. This is apparently a contradiction, but I take it to describe the broad application of law and consumption in industrial society. The use of the word 'discipline', rather than 'military' or 'force', is a clear debt to Foucault, and makes the link with production: both are about the ordering and direction of bodies. Clearly, a given regime of production and discipline will permit some social relations and will destroy others. It is facilitative in that it opens spaces for a certain range of social interaction without requiring or causing them; it is dominating in the sense that it covers our lives absolutely. The system that is formed, overall, has some similarities to Carter's dynamics (see Chapter 8) but with a clearer representation of the different levels at which change takes place.

Circuits of Power (edited version of diagram by Stewart Clegg)

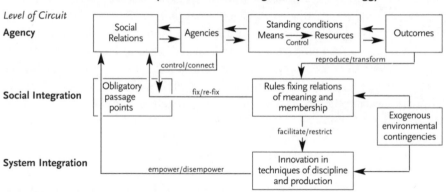

I find Clegg's model useful, but there are some points I would raise. Firstly, like all systems models, it is strongest in explaining continuity, and weakest in explaining change. He includes the impact of factors external to the system (environmental contingencies) but as we have seen (in Chapter 4) there is little that remains external to the global power networks. He stresses the way that the unintended outcomes of power struggles between agencies lead to deep shifts due to changing cultural or productive regimes; but the impact of social change movements (like the suffragettes mentioned earlier) is very much an intended consequence, coming from an agency following a completely different set of rules of practice. There is also an ecofeminist critique that a category of production tends to omit reproduction—and the effectiveness or otherwise of reproduction goes directly to the availability of resources in episodic conflicts, a potential motor of change that short-circuits rules of practice. If—as environmentalists continue to warn—soil fertility, or ecosystem maintenance, or human genetic material undergo sudden or catastrophic change, it can dramatically change the balance of power. Claims that such a process will force the public to recognize the importance of Green social relations may be well founded. But it is equally possible that the competition for survival will produce outcomes leading to exclusive rules of membership and brutal discipline. This in turn creates the conditions for further ecological collapse as dynamics of power-over intrude even more into the power-to of natural systems.

I would also stress that knowledge, technique and their infrastructure are reproduced daily. The nodes in Clegg's model are not merely points of decision or confluence, they are dynamic systems in themselves. Rules of meaning, for example, are rehearsed, repeated and reaffirmed continually in conversation, broadcasts and publication. Discipline and production is an engine that ticks over and regulates itself, whether or not rules of meaning and membership alter. All these are themselves generative processes, capable of creative innovation regardless of outside forces. It may be unusual for significant change to arise this way, but it is far from impossible. In such a case, their output may empower or fix the flow of power in a completely different dynamic.

In short, the multi-level approach of Clegg needs to be combined with an understanding of the different dynamics of power that operate alongside one another. The tendency of power-over processes to combine, reinforce and reproduce each other, operates as much at the level of belief and culture as at any other, and there is clear evidence of persistent opposition—today, from a dynamic of power-to. The next chapter will consider how these competing, mutually antagonistic systems operate side by side in modern society.

Nurturing a Counterculture

There is a hegemony in place—a belief system that states what is true, possible and realistic. However, there is no conspiracy at work. The hegemony is the body of knowledge, the accumulated environmental changes, and the techniques that must inevitably accompany any process of power. Power is not a discrete part of our lives, a clear decision; it is an ongoing experience, a visceral act of being. There is no point at which we can view power 'from the outside', and there is no discourse we can use to examine power that does not itself carry power (even this one).

However, although hegemony refers to this totalizing effect of power in its dominant form, there are alternative forms of power and alternative discourses associated with them. There are, then, two levels on which we can oppose hegemony. First, there is the anti-hegemonic activity pioneered by the Situationists—cracking the illusion, by exposing its dishonesty, or its arbitrariness, or simply by ridiculing it. By attacking the rules of practice, we can interfere with the reproduction of social relations. However, to actually bring about social change, we require a different level—that of counter-hegemonic work.

This is, in Theodore Roszak's phrase, "the making of a counterculture".[16]

First, the breaking of hegemony. R. D. Laing describes the experience of rising above 'reality' as a transcendental experience—possibly even a religious one—and a form of madness. "[In order to cope with a changeable world] we scurry into roles, statuses, identities, interpersonal relations. We attempt to live in castles that can only be in the air, because there is no firm ground in the social cosmos on which to build. . . . Psychotic experience goes beyond the horizons of our common, that is, our communal sense. What regions of experience does this lead to? It entails a loss of the usual foundations of the 'sense' of the world that we share with one another. Old purposes no longer seem viable: old meanings are senseless: the distinctions between imagination, dreams and external perceptions often seem no longer to apply in the old way. . . . No one who has not experienced how insubstantial the pageant of external reality can be, how it may fade, can fully realize the sublime and grotesque presences that can replace it."[17] Few political activists would claim to be able to drive people mad, or that it would be desirable if they could. But an act that calls into question the roles and rules that we have internalized, and can make us see them as flimsy and insubstantial, might move us into a position from which we are open to a new moral leadership.

Yet trying to live outside all norms and conventions is no joke. Without an alternative moral frame, and a set of social relations to accompany it, you are very alone. Indeed, it becomes hard to function in society, and this is where madness takes many people—to the stage of being unable to cope, unable to feed, clothe or look after themselves. Within the Green movement, and particularly in protest camps, many have had experience of people who have lost track of society to the extent that they can barely get by. In other cases, it is mainstream society that cannot cope with non-conformism: in at least one case in Denmark, a radical Green protester came close to being classified as mad and forcibly placed in an institution.

Anti-hegemonic action is fragmented and episodic—unable, or unwilling, to build viable social alternatives. This position of extreme criticism is to a large extent what makes it effective in puncturing over-inflated symbols and exposing absurdity. Its advocates include Paul Patton, who calls for a "nomadic, de-territorialized social theory"—an opportunist resistance of local and highly specific protests.[18] He does not suggest any kind of coalition, but nonetheless believes that a diverse range of unconnected attacks will lead to gathering momentum. I am certain of the necessity for such autonomous action, but I don't believe it is sufficient. I don't see hegemony as a restriction on our natural freedom, but as a body of knowledge that enables us to function socially. Anti-hegemonic revolts may destroy that knowledge temporarily, and sow valuable confusion in the networks of power-over, but it leaves a void that can only be filled by the reassertion of the dominant power systems—much as in Paris in 1968.

Another kind of local resistance is that advocated by Chomsky—acquiring the 'tools of intellectual self-defence'.[19] This consists of a state of alertness to a betrayal or absurdity slipping past us under cover of common sense. It is a demanding state, since one must mistrust one's own belief system. Nonetheless, in times of extreme oppression it has been the mainspring of principled resistance.

So we come to counter-hegemony—the creation of power/knowledge systems that are total, rather than partial, experiences of empowerment. I have described the process of hegemony as a circuit, and so I do not believe that there is any one starting point. Opportunities will arise spontaneously: out of fragmented resistance, in the outcomes of power-over, in environmental changes, in contested rules of practice, in innovations of production. The important point is to take their logic as far as possible, and connect these different social movements so as to complete the circuits and create an empowering culture.

The model I have arrived at, then (see below), owes much to Lukes' 'three dimensions of power', but with the additional level of domination and facilitation

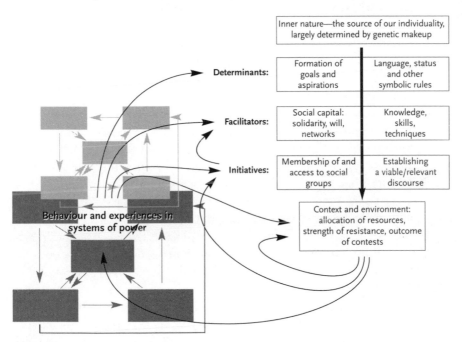

This diagram illustrates how power shapes our ways of thinking and acting, and how they in turn can affect systems of power. Although we all have our own individual character, this is very soon shaped by our experiences in social systems.

Although we can directly affect the context in which others operate, and possibly build up social resources and influence, the unconscious determinants of behaviour are almost always the result of hegemonic (whole-system) power.

However, local actions can weaken or strengthen systems by making or breaking linkages, or by affecting the outcome of contests between competing systems.

(my 'fourth dimension'). Like Clegg, I see these four dimensions not as a hierarchy, but as nodes in a circuit, or system. Unlike Clegg, I argue that (at least) two systems are in operation—both going through the same processes, but competing for very different outcomes.

On the left of the diagram, we can see the actual work and activity that is the essence of power, taking place in two competing systems (as I have said elsewhere, there are almost certainly more than two distinct power systems; but it is the dominant power-over and the sustainable power-to that I am most interested in here). These behaviours and experiences give rise to three levels of hegemony: the first is that of initiatives, in which access to the means of social interaction is limited by our lived experience. The second level is that of facilitators—the way in which our lifestyles inform us, or equip us with the social, mental and spiritual resources, so that we can see certain possibilities. The third, deepest level is that of determinants: the essential tools of understanding and thought which are established and maintained by the history of power.

Below them on the diagram are the standing conditions under which any power contest must take place. These are also set by the systems of power in operation, but they are not strictly speaking hegemonic, in that they are tangible and locally determined rather than being emergent properties of the whole system. These four levels have some correspondence with the four dimensions of power described in chapter 1; at the first level, power is the ability to win contests, at the second it is the power to prevent contests being staged, at the third it is the power to prevent anyone seeing a contest as being in their interest, and at the fourth it is the power to actually shape those interests.

At the top I have indicated that an important factor that governs even the determinants is the pull that we all feel towards the authentic. Whether you see this as spiritual, genetic, cultural, or a combination of such factors, it is clear that there are some inner drives that exist prior to power, and set limits on our malleability (this is discussed more in Chapter 3). To some extent, these can be shaped: genetic modification of future generations is a real and frightening possibility. Our genetic make-up also changes over longer periods of time: for example, Europeans are descended from people who survived terrible famines, which implies that certain genetic traits which favour survival are more prevalent in our society. There is also growing suspicion that environmental factors may affect the development of embryos in the womb, exacerbating some personality traits: but for the time being I think we can assume that most of this inheritance comes from millions of years of human evolution. For this reason I think it is a reservoir of support for power-to, moderating the excesses of power-over through our conscience and compassion.

The arrows indicate how one factor (and each of them is itself a dynamic, self-maintaining system) influences or changes another. So the main process is one of deeper levels determining the more visible ones: our goals determine the skills we acquire, which give us access to certain agencies and organizations, which give us more or less power in overcoming resistance. However, it is also the case that the outcome of such a contest may then change those standing conditions, or the rules governing initiatives; and a change in what initiatives are possible may alter facilitators. However, the main way that individual outcomes can break hegemony is through changing our actual lived experience, by making or breaking connections in the systems of power. This is something we return to in the next chapter.

If we understand these processes, we can see our efforts in a wider context, and piece together individual struggles for mutual benefit. Effective action in imagery and awareness need not founder for lack of a solid base; pioneering campaigners need not feel like outcasts from society.

Under these conditions, anti-hegemonic work becomes much easier, since the clear existence of a viable alternative, and a group in society who have renounced complicity with the abuse of power, stand in open contradiction to the ruling knowledge. One possible example of an effective counter-hegemony is what is scathingly referred to as political correctness. This term itself demonstrates the fierce resistance being mounted to the increasingly effective rules of practice referring to inclusion and membership of oppressed groups. 'Political correctness' is criticized as a restriction of freedom; in a sense it is, but this is missing the point of power. Any dynamic of power makes some things possible and not others. 'Political correctness' has succeeded in 'outlawing' certain forms of discrimination in a limited number of settings (primarily universities and media) and has opened valuable possibilities as a result. However, it is fragile and under sustained attack—its position is at odds with most processes of power, and the growth of a consumerist conception of education and the commercialization of media both threaten it. Its bases of support are very narrow.

Any divide between culture and economy is artificial—the word culture originally referred to both thought and action. It may well be the case that a different worldview requires different productive relations to maintain it. Roger Hallam has worked in building economically viable social alternatives for many years. "Most of us need personal support from others to sustain an isolating radical lifestyle in this society. There are many people . . . who are profoundly alienated by capitalist society, and if there were viable alternative opportunities, would choose to live and work in a co-operative, non-consumerist and supportive environment. . . . Social alternatives also help to actually create activists through the support they can offer. It's a common belief that people become radical through argument or through experience, but in my experience the critical factor is whether the opportunities exist to become radical.

"By taking over economic resources they are able to make money to support struggles and purchase space—like the role of the Quakers in the peace movement, whose willingness to use their property to hold meetings was vital. Other successful political movements of the past have relied upon an economic power base.

"This is not to forget that co-ops are in themselves changing the power relations in society themselves. Every time money is made or property bought which is co-operatively controlled and used for the community rather than for private gain, society has been changed in a small but concrete and tangible way. Just as feudalism was undermined by a gradual change in the ownership of the economy from the landed aristocracy to the capitalist class, so the capitalist class is vulnerable to losing their power to co-operatives if the latter are able to be more successful in the marketplace. There is also the power of example. The existence of concrete alternatives may not bring the edifice crumbling down, but it will certainly help to take the wind out of the sails of the moral argument of capitalism."[20]

While I share Hallam's concern for economic viability, I want to stress the alternative (political) culture existing in these enterprises. The requirements of co-operative working and living create a knowledge, and hence a power, that are extended to social relations generally. The association of radical values and ecological statements with a durable and accessible milieu, meeting people's needs, makes those claims 'true' in a way they were not true before. "The workers, and others, hold the values and political ideas that they do as a consequence of both trying to survive and of attempting to enjoy themselves within capitalism."[21] Perhaps it is when the need not just for protest and resistance, but also the need for enjoyment and fun can be met in a different context, that a real counter-hegemony can be said to be established.

Chapter 10

On the Edge

Power-to and power-over exist side by side, but they are closely interconnected.
Each depends on the other to function; and many people experience both equally.
If we recognize the difference, there is great potential for change in making connec-
tions between them.

Although the dominant system of power-over is capable of co-opting us into
maintaining it, we have to use its resources and mechanisms to build an alterna-
tive. If we are aware of the potential hazards, we can set up processes of positive
feedback that further destabilize the dominant powers.

Making an accurate assessment depends on recognizing both the positive and
negative aspects of any interaction, and identifying the 'neutral' positions in the
power structure. Strategies for economics, campaigning and politics that do this
can form a particularly effective combination.

> "We've got to find a different way of living—something spiritual, without all this
> greed. But that doesn't mean we can't eat Sugar Puffs."—Glen, Exodus Collective

This chapter is about dealing with the hard reality of the world we live in. We
can perhaps visualize a different way of living, a dynamic of power that is co-
operative: but it cannot help but appear as a utopian dream in the face of our
daily experience. The interconnectedness of power systems is such that we
cannot step outside them. We cannot because it would isolate us and cut us off
from social contact. We cannot because it would cut us off from the ability to
buy and sell and hence live from day to day. We cannot because there is no
physical space outside the power system—no corner of the planet untouched
by power.

I have described power-to as a system, with the potential of being self-sustaining and autonomous. This would, on first sight, seem to suggest a strategy
of separation and withdrawal; creating perfect havens of ecological wisdom.
Anything else, surely, would be compromise—a surrender to the rule of
power-over. However, the record of such model communities is that they rarely
succeed in cutting themselves off. Either they were founded on the earnings
of the mainstream economy, or they depend on the welfare state for support.

Even when this is not the case, such model communities tend not to have a dramatic impact on wider society, but rather become insular and cut off.

I have known people who have deliberately set out to live completely apart from straight society. They have refused benefits and conventional work, even money itself. Some have rejected all petrol-driven vehicles, or even all transport other than feet and bikes. Few have lasted long: either the stress and struggle of day-to-day existence has ground them down, or they have fallen into contradiction and disillusionment. Rarely do they inspire significant numbers to join them. And, more to the point, they have not succeeded—they have relied on charity (ultimately derived from the industrial economy), or if not that they have eaten food grown by capitalist businesses. They use the same roads as everyone else. Even if they could overcome all those hurdles, they think using a language loaded with assumptions they did not share. We cannot separate ourselves from the powers that destroy our planet, and our attempts to do so can cut us off from the people whose participation we need, as we appear increasingly alien, cranky or judgmental.

Complicity

We cannot, because in reality there are not two systems. Human society is a single system: one species on one world, interconnected and self-contained. What I have argued is that there are two (or more) characters, or modes, of power—but that is not to say they lurk self-contained behind their barricades, each regarding the other as alien. They are closely linked—intimately linked—and everyone's lives, from the dreadlocked protester to the corporate executive, contain elements of both.

In fact, they are dependent on each other. The factories of power-over depend on the production and reproduction of 'natural resources'. The subsistence farmers of agrarian nations are an important pool of reserve labour, and reproduce the next generation of factory workers. Evidently the structures of power-over are parasitic on those of power-to. However, the reverse is also true. Those same subsistence farmers are trading for hard currency to buy televisions and other consumer goods. Tribal forest dwellers choose to buy metal tools and mass-manufactured clothing. Even self-styled radical protesters in industrialized nations will buy their beer from a multinational brewer and share a mass culture. Who can blame them? There is no place where a line can be drawn—everything is connected to everything else.

So the two networks exist to some extent in worlds of their own, but with a large number of points of contact. When one is living a lifestyle dominated by a particular form of relationship, it is easy to believe that is all there is. We adapt to our surroundings, and if the ubiquitous experience is one of hierarchical regulation, it is easy to forget that there are other ways of relating to the world around us. Similarly, those people who have chosen to live a simple

STATE OF DEPENDENCE

Much of our present day political theory has its roots in the 19th century, when the institutions of the modern state were in their infancy. The concept of the nation does not go back far beyond the French revolution, and without that the state is little more than the agents of the monarch—a rule of law, a standing army and a power of taxation. So in the nineteenth century it was this conception that dominated political debate. Whether you were an anarchist calling for its abolition, a liberal seeking to make it rational and representative, or a Marxist seeking to place it under the control of the proletariat, it was 'other'—external and separate from society.

We still have laws, and armies and taxes. But throughout the 20th century, the state was spreading and dissolving. It was being given an increasing number of tasks to do by its demanding democratic bodies, and increasing its taxation revenue to match it. The repetitive process of a social problem being identified, the state being called upon to solve it, and the increase in taxation being found to pay for it, was proceeding throughout the West (and in the more artificial nation states) regardless of the parties and ideologies involved. At the same time a corresponding process of privatization—seeking to maintain accumulation and competition in as large a sector of the economy as possible—was injecting economic values into supposedly altruistic work.

Today, the state is a sprawling and loosely connected edifice which involves so many people and so much of our economic activity that we can no longer relate to it as an external object. Our lives are inextricably bound up with the state, and its bureaucracy is the social relation that exemplifies our times. The sovereignty of power-over has operated through the state to colonize vast swathes of our lives.

We cannot be for or against the state under these circumstances, because we cannot get outside it. Our health, our education, our built environment, our wastes and our society are all administered, monitored and maintained through it. We depend on it, and it depends on us. We don't merely support the state or oppose it, we live it every day, acting out our role in its grand drama.

Those working in social change know that to refuse to deal with the state would make them meaningless and marginal, with no relevance to the lives of the people they wish to work with. But equally they know that to co-operate with the state will lead them into reproducing and managing a set of power relations they have to overcome. Working in society has become a choice between irrelevance and complicity.

lifestyle, close to the earth, have often found themselves at a loss when return-ing to industrial society. Assumptions and habits that they thought they could take for granted—from urinating in hedgerows to conserving woodland—are not shared by mainstream society, and the realization of this can be shocking.

Perhaps the areas of greatest interest to the student of power are not these extreme cases, but those individuals living and working at the interface between the two worlds. If we consider being powerful as having the opportunity to see choices and to alter outcomes, it is these people we might expect to be power-ful. Having access to two different dynamics of power, the possible connections and combinations, and the potential for creating relationships that lead to change, are greatest for them. Perhaps the largest numbers of people having to deal with hierarchical power at the same time as trying to heal, enable and empower, are to be found working in the modern welfare state.

Working at the Interface

The potential of hybrid life may not always be apparent. A great many people who find themselves on this frontline are unaware that they are on the edge of their social system. This gives rise to feelings of confusion, and sometimes even impotence. When police officers confront non-violent protesters, it is very hard for them to understand the complex network of very different beliefs, economic relations, practices and culture that the protesters are tied into. Passive resistance, which could be taken as an opportunity for negotia-tion not usually present in a public order situation, may appear instead as dumb insolence, or bloody-minded stubbornness. The police officers are liable to miss the possibilities raised by communication and building a relationship, and instead use force—try to make the dissident conform to their expectations.

The error can equally be made in the other direction. A conservationist is invited to co-operate with corporate sponsors—on the condition that he or she severs any links with more radical environmentalists. The conservationist agrees, and makes the connection, unaware that the motivation of the sponsor is far more to do with marginalizing radical opposition and creating an image of respectability than about a genuine commitment to change. The relation-ship between systems is again unusually powerful—but one party in it is unaware of what they are conceding to.

Although the option of communication is sometimes less obvious, it is potentially highly effective. Where two social actors have needs and resources, there is the opportunity for a process of power, or a relationship—even though the types of power that gave rise to those needs and resources may be incon-sistent. Such relationships will always be fewer in number than in the fertile and homogeneous cycles of a power dynamic, but they will be more significant.

Entropy tells us that energy can only do so much work—that there can only be so many processes of power—before it is too dispersed and degraded to be of any use. That means that there is only a limited quantity of power available to be shared between different systems. Within a system, there will always be opportunities to further refine the organization and regulation processes in order to gain greater returns (though as noted in Chapter 4, power-over squanders energy where power-to conserves and recycles it). But between systems it is practically a zero sum game; if one system of power 'leaks' energy, the other will gain from it. For example there is a certain amount of money, almost all generated though the use of capital as power-over, available for investment. If conditions of ethical investment are placed on it, it will 'leak' out of the cycle of reinvestment into ethical investment in the alternative economy. Similarly, if Green politicians are dependent on the support of voters addicted to unsustainable lifestyles, they must either risk 'leaking' support to the power politicians or 'leaking' political effectiveness by compromising on their principles. Either way, they face a thankless choice.

So working at the interface between systems of power is effectively opening up a conduit between the two. You are allowing a flow of energy or resources from one to the other (or more often, a combination of both). In any encounter, it will often be far from obvious where the gains and losses are. But it is this information which is crucial in understanding your role, and the power that it carries. It is the connections between different systems of power that determine what resources are available to them, the rate at which they can expand or contract, and indeed their long-term viability as social systems. Anyone seeking to work for empowerment, equality or social change will have relationships with many bodies shaped and governed by power-over. Even when the flow appears very clear—providing a grant, making a donation—we must always be aware that strings may be attached.

Avoiding Co-option

Most connections are made quite unconsciously, and without any awareness that a boundary is being crossed and a decision with far-reaching consequences is being taken. When building societies were first established in Britain, they were fully mutual, democratic organizations: people in a community pooled their resources so that, one at a time, they would be able to build or buy homes for themselves. Their success and growth led them to seek recognition in law so that they could continue to grow and offer their financial services to a wider range of people. The decisions that were taken at that time, about their aspirations, their legal status and their powers, were a profound decision about whether they would remain mutual, empowering organizations, or whether the capital they had accumulated would become more and more profit-driven. Today, there is a wave of demutualization taking place. Although many building societies are committed to remaining co-operative and offering the lowest interest rates, many more are converting into banks

LOTTOCRACY

Voluntary organizations are an anomaly in many ways. They are formed not out of the drive to accumulate, as commercial businesses are, nor by the order of the state, but out of an altruistic desire to mobilize resources to meet some perceived need. However, they immediately come into contact with the realm of power-over—in the form of law, as they adopt a legal structure, of money, and particularly in the paternal relationship with their beneficiaries. The role of trustees, the requirements of charitable status (which in Britain explicitly exclude enquiring into the causes of social problems, or projects managed by the intended beneficiaries) and the relations between volunteers, employees and clients, create an uncomfortable mixture of shared, community support on the one hand and the authoritarian control of resources on the other. Few, if any, can claim that their organization is so pure that no element of hierarchy has crept in; and those that do might well admit to being small and unambitious.

As the reach and grip of power has intensified, so the pressure to work with commercial and state powers has grown. In Britain, government grants have become a massive source of revenue as private charitable giving has fallen off (particularly since the introduction of the National Lottery). The Millenium Commission, the Single Regeneration Budget, the Lottery, English Partnerships . . . even more remarkable, charities are earning almost 15% of their income by tendering for commercial contracts from government.[1]

The growth of the state as an employer peaked in the 70s—a national will-to-power propelling it to take responsibility for more and more of our lives. Power-over is not only about a ruler mentality, but also about a child mentality. The state became a 'super-parent' for us all, as communities devastated by oppression failed to cope. The attempt to contain this impossible aspiration in a monolithic structure crumbled, and the private sector was invited to fight over the disintegrating body of the nanny state. Voluntary organizations realized that they had many of the skills and resources needed to take on these contracts and could implement them more effectively than private sector counterparts and direct the surplus into their charitable aims. But at what cost? The modern voluntary organization, seeking to involve those it intends to aid, should be about mutuality and shared responsibility—not about extending the relation of consumer/provider into more and more aspects of care.

and handing out millions in windfalls to members (as they become customers or shareholders) and more to their executives. Even some of the more principled Societies are facing takeovers by groups of greedy members. The rubicon was not crossed with the decision to demutualize, but many years before in the decision to abandon participation in the search for the mass market. By contrast, Radical Routes (see Chapter 7) has tried to adopt rules that will prevent individuals motivated by greed and power from having any say in the running of the organization in the future.

So does this mean that the safest way to preserve the principles you hold is to have nothing to do with conflicting power relationships? There is much potential for those committed to change to live a lifestyle consistent with their beliefs. They can replace money transactions with LETS transactions, work in co-operatives and save in credit unions. I believe this kind of process is natural and will gather its own momentum, building greater and greater independence. Those seeking a pure and uncompromised lifestyle are indeed doing important work. However, it is not the case that every connection with the dynamics of power-over weakens the process of social change. When protesters decide that they badly need a pint of beer, they are not necessarily capitulating to capitalism; they may well be correct in thinking that for the pound they hand over to the corporate world, they will gain the rest and the recovery that they need to go out and inflict five pounds worth of effective resistance. There is a widespread belief that a useful contribution to social change is to buy products that are made by more responsible companies, have a lower environmental impact, or were more fairly traded. These products are typically more expensive than mainstream goods. I am a supporter of ethical consumerism up to a point: if we engage in a hair shirt culture of denial, we may be grinding ourselves down more than we are grinding them down.

My point is this: interaction between two systems of power can take many forms. A flow of power from one system another does not, in itself, tell us much. It may as well be a process of subversion as one of co-option. If a Green politician has been elected to office, it is equally simple-minded to say either that they have been co-opted into the ruling class or that they have gained the power to protect the environment. We have to understand the full process involved. That means a close examination of the structures and mechanisms, and of the precise intentions of the individuals concerned.

Feedback and Change

These are problems of the sort that Derek Wall raised in *Getting There*, when he wrote about 'positive feedback reforms'. "External change (the growth of the Green movement) tends to be met by compensating internal change (reform) aimed at maintaining the basic integrity of the system—a process of negative feedback. . . . Incremental change proposed by 'liberal pragmatists' in

UNHEALTHY RELATIONSHIPS?

The King's Fund in London (which boasts Prince Charles as its patron, and was founded by the wealthiest of Victorian philanthropists) fought for 50 years against plans to nationalize the health service—and yet today it is deeply involved in health service management and training. Observers believe that its acceptance of state authority has led it to support hospital closures and an ethic of management rather than care. However, the Fund points to its work for patients' rights and its efforts to improve health service organization as real benefits that could not have been achieved any other way.[2]

Robert Whelan argues that voluntary work is becoming 'whatever the government will pay for'. The voluntary sector used to stand in contrast with the rights-based welfare state as aid that fostered self-reliance. Can this survive 'contract culture'?[3] When almost two-thirds of equipment in neo-natal units is donated, there is a real concern that charities are supporting core services, while funding in the reverse direction through contracted services can lead to the values and ideals of the volunteers being left out. Judi Clements, the Director of the mental health charity Mind, says, "Some local Mind groups negotiate on terms; others feel they have been bounced. But we are not agents to have terms dictated to us; we are independent bodies." But will that remain the case, when three-quarters of voluntary organizations in an NCVO survey agreed with the statement, "We are increasingly becoming more like a business"? Clements also says, "Sometimes local groups say it is difficult for them to campaign because they might lose their funding. I would be extremely worried if the voice of the voluntary sector was silenced because of being embedded in contract and service delivery."[4]

It is possible for voluntary organizations to gain contracts in such a way as to extend their values and practices into the welfare state rather than the other way round—success stories are not hard to find. But this only happens where those groups are aware that they have different values—that there is a difference between serving and empowering. There is no point in remaining pure if by doing so you are unable to reach those that you exist to help. But there is no point in being a voluntary organization if you only ape the machinations of rulers and profiteers. At the end of the day, the question is not whether or not to sup with the devil, but rather whether the spoon is long enough., the form of new laws and reforms will simply strengthen the system without changing its real nature.

"There is an alternative. Some forms of change can lead to chain reactions that change the nature of a system, whether political, social or biological. Greens must try to create such positive feedback, which causes the system to add to, rather than compensate for, external pressure."[5]

Consider the diagram below. Within the overall social system—a system of systems—we can distinguish a highly interconnected dynamic of power-over, and a subsidiary dynamic of power-to. They are linked by a number of processes. In this simplified model, I have shown just two—the flow of resources into the 'environmentally benign cycle' and a flow in the other direction.

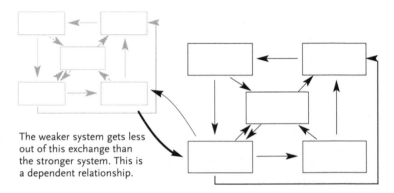

The weaker system gets less out of this exchange than the stronger system. This is a dependent relationship.

The arrows represent the transfers resulting from some local interaction—say taking out a bank loan to finance the purchase of a wind generator. In this example, the benefits to the conventional economy (interest payments, publicity, collateral) outweigh the benefits to the generators (finance for the purchase, and the generation of renewable energy that it allows). If these arrangements continue, wind power generators will be stuck in an increasingly dependent relationship with a financial system more interested in funding high energy, hard technologies. This is just for the sake of example—I'm not claiming that all commercially financed renewable energy schemes are a big mistake—but this kind of approach is needed to establish which projects will actually contribute to social change.

The first important point is that there is a point of dynamic equilibrium that must exist in order for the two systems to exist side by side as they do. If the flow of resources into the subversive system continually exceeded the flow out, it would grow to become dominant. If the reverse were true, it would wither away altogether. So a point of equilibrium must have been established at which if the counter culture grows, it loses resources; and if it shrinks, the drains on its resources also shrink to allow it to recover, or the excesses of power-over create a new surge of support for it. There are good grounds for arguing that the Green movement is growing stronger all round the world, but the overall picture is of a persistent, but minority, movement. In order to go beyond this, more connections on better terms are needed with the system of power-over. A situation where the flow to the system of empowerment is greater than that in the reverse direction, implies that the former is 'feeding' off the latter and growing at its expense. This is unlikely to continue indefinitely: in practice, the dominant system will reorganize so as to improve the terms of this trade, or the weaker system will be unable to sustain the process.

But this is not the only way to gain from connections between systems. The next diagram shows that even if the compromise is giving more to the system of power-over than it provides to that of power-to, what it does give may be crucial in completing a link or a circuit that makes the network of empowerment more self-reliant or stronger. This kind of systemic benefit could actually bring about a long-term shift in the equilibrium between the two.

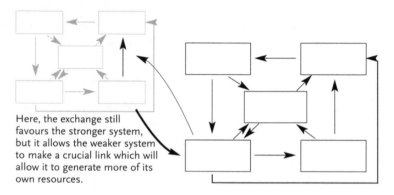

Here, the exchange still favours the stronger system, but it allows the weaker system to make a crucial link which will allow it to generate more of its own resources.

This is an example of an apparently bad deal that has greater strategic importance. Maybe the bank loan to buy the generator is in this case supplying a protest camp with electricity, and so dramatically improving their effectiveness—as well as giving the protesters the skills and the experience that will make them less dependent on inappropriate technological solutions. Another example might be if the loan this time was to set up an organic agriculture system. The strategic issue here is different. By taking the loan, even on bad terms, land and ecosystems are brought under sustainable management—and as I argue in Chapter 4, this is very important for any system of power.

Roger Hallam considers the ethics of such compromises in his 'Anarchist Economics' with an example based on his own work in a co-operative delivering organic food. For ethical reasons, the group wants to use electric vehicles (not necessarily a great improvement—running them on biodiesel might be preferable—but it'll do for an example). Hallam suggests three strategies:

"1. The group cannot abide using diesel vehicles as it is against their principles. An electric vehicle to buy is £12,000. The group can only raise £6,000.

Unwilling to consider another option, the group breaks up and maintains that it is not possible.

"2. The group realizes it cannot afford an electric vehicle but engages in a research and planning process which leads it to the realization that petrol vehicles can be hired for £50 a day. The profit on each bag of vegetables is £2 and the initial market is 100 bags. The group therefore works out that by using a petrol vehicle for 30 weeks it will raise the profit (£2 x 100 bags x 30 weeks) of £6,000 needed to purchase the electric vehicle. The group follows this strategy, hires a petrol vehicle for 30 weeks then buys an electric one. Then the running costs of the electric vehicle cover the remaining profit and the group remains in a steady state.

"3. The group realizes that if it hires a petrol vehicle all the time, every 60 weeks it will have enough profit to buy another electric vehicle. It chooses this option and the co-op continually expands." [6]

The point of this example is that the ethical compromise that the group might feel uncomfortable with what is in fact the precondition for bringing about an effective social change. Rather than trying to detach themselves from the reality of a society based on fossil-fuel transport, which would lead to people eating non-organic food transported by exactly the same petrol vans, Hallam suggests that they embrace it—in order to build up the capital needed to create an alternative. In this way, the power-over of the industrial system is used to subvert it.

A third reason for compromise is illustrated here. Here, the gain to power-over exceeds the gain to power-to, and doesn't particularly enable greater self-reliance. But what it does do is remove some important source of power from the dominant system.

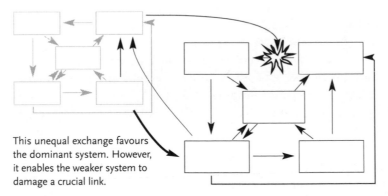

This unequal exchange favours the dominant system. However, it enables the weaker system to damage a crucial link.

Now the imaginary bank loan is being used to fund a direct action which will put the police in a difficult position, and show their public unwillingness to enforce some iniquitous law passed by the government. The deal, even though it is on bad terms, is causing a failure of an important connection in the system of power-over by driving a wedge between the state and the forces defending it. Another example of this kind of approach might be to say that we

BETWEEN PEOPLE AND POWER

Local government has varied roots. In a few small states, it is the sovereign body; in Britain, it has its roots in the local magistracy, appointed by the monarch, and the urban corporations established by the Victorian philanthropists; in America, the states were independent units that chose to federate. Just how local it is varies; although most countries have some kind of 'neighbourhood councils', most of these are advisory or administrative bodies operating at the beck and call of a larger scale, more remote district or county council.

The more local our government becomes, the more its character changes. There is less opportunity for technocrats to claim exclusive knowledge; there is easier access for members of the public keen to have their voice heard; there is more genuine accountability of elected representatives, and they are easier to hold to their mandate. At least, this is the potential. As a largely subservient arm of central government, local authorities all too often demonstrate insularity, special interests, cliquiness and corruption. Any body with little legitimacy or real autonomy is doomed to this fate—as the public see it as less significant, so they participate less in it and hold it accountable less effectively.

And yet truly local government is so obviously part of our need for cooperation in a community that we reinvent it when it is absent. Residents' associations, community businesses and local environment groups are all a reflection of the impulse to collectively manage and protect our local environment. Where they have become effective, and realized their full potential, they have the unstated aspiration to fill this gap. However, they are handicapped by a legal apparatus that still pretends that all power comes from the Crown—always a fiction, now an anachronism.

The crisis of the state that is causing it to fray at the edges means change for local government as much as for national government. Two futures are visible. In one, the pressure to 'hive off' functions to private companies leads to an injection of profit-driven values into local government and sharp business practice among the competing contractors. Voluntary organizations are pressured into providing cheap labour for social services providing 'industrial-scale care'. The element of local government that is about participation is pressed into service as a fig leaf for legitimacy and withers away into cynicism and resentment.

In the other, the same pressures still lead to privatization and contracting out. But the organizations benefiting are community businesses, established through neighbourhood councils to provide both economy and quality of service. Private sector capital is led into joint projects designed and managed by the service recipients. Voluntary organizations bring their understanding of the dignity of client groups into the contracts, and scarce resources are allocated locally, transparently and democratically. The difference is not in the decision to work with the private sector or not; the decision is one of strategy, setting the rules of engagement in such a way as to subvert the seemingly stronger force.

Whether this happens is partly up to the Council, partly up to the local people, partly up to the voluntary organizations, and even partly in the hands of the private sector. But it is also made a lot harder or easier by the statutory framework put in place by national government. Will those at the head of the nation regard such futures as threats or opportunities? For many in that world, community empowerment is a challenge to their identity, their financial security, their technocratic aspirations and their egos. Will they allow it?

---

should elect a Green Councillor not so much because of what they might achieve (maybe accepting that they will be co-opted), but because they will occupy a position that would otherwise have been held by someone actively supporting the growth of power-over. A good example here is where a Green has been elected to a 'hung' Council in which no one grouping has a clear majority, so giving Greens the balance of power. If any other party had won the seat, it would have been business as usual, but by denying either party a majority, the Greens greatly strengthen their position.

Assessing the Necessity of the Evil

So if foul can be fair and fair can be foul, how are we to decide what course of action will lead to the greatest empowerment? Clearly, we cannot reach a conclusion without following through all the possible consequences of a given course of action. One useful tool for doing this is a PNI analysis—standing for positive, negative, and interesting. This is a technique intended to help us think beyond 'good' or 'bad' to see the full complexity inherent in any outcome. Taking the example given above, a PNI analysis might look something like this:

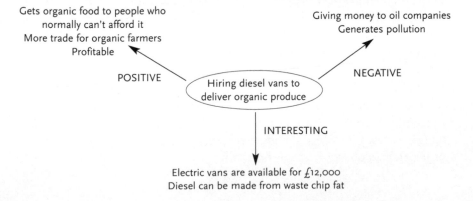

Gets organic food to people who normally can't afford it
More trade for organic farmers
Profitable

POSITIVE

Giving money to oil companies
Generates pollution

NEGATIVE

Hiring diesel vans to deliver organic produce

INTERESTING

Electric vans are available for £12,000
Diesel can be made from waste chip fat

Rather than focusing on one factor that might seem to have overwhelming importance, we can see all the possible connections here. That includes factors that are not clearly good or bad, but might suggest trade-offs and imaginative solutions. By putting together the positive and interesting points, we can see a way to offset the negative points that would otherwise have blocked further consideration of the project. Incidentally, I believe PNI is an anti-hegemonic mental tool: it forces a revaluation of things that appear to be 'obvious' and insists that 'hidden' or 'denied' considerations be included. One example that was related to me was a discussion about crime in which participants—including police officers—were asked to list positive things about crime. They came up with an impressive list, which served as a reminder that knee-jerk, punitive responses failed to understand the complexity of the issue.

Another technique for assessing different courses of action comes from the Quakers' 'Turning the Tide' programme of training for social change activists. It is a graph in four quadrants, where the vertical axis is how hard it is and the horizontal axis the effectiveness for social change.

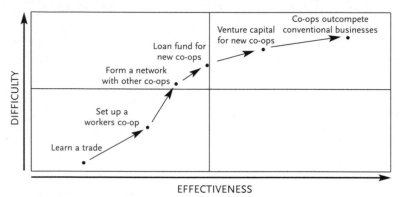

The top left box in the diagram below shows things that are hard to do and have little impact for social change (e.g. going over Niagara Falls in a barrel), and the top right things that would be wonderful but are almost impossible (e.g. abolishing war). Of more interest is the bottom left—things we can do easily but which have little impact on the world (e.g. buy a poster of Che Guevara to put on our wall). But is it worth bothering with them? The bottom right is the important category—both achievable and effective. Of course, there are fewer things falling into this category, but that is all the more reason to pursue them. Some relatively easy projects provide a platform from which more difficult schemes can be reached. Linking these together gives you a strategic pathway to radical change. Start with projects in the easy/low impact area which lead on to more significant things.

WHO WANTS TO BE A GREEN MP?

Interacting with the state, then, poses considerable problems for anyone seeking to build empowering relations. But these issues cannot be ducked. Green Parties (at least, those understanding the range and extent of the changes needed for sustainability) are at the cutting edge of such encounters. They have to find practical ways in which the main form of public political participation—the vote—can be used to create forms of political self-management beyond voting.

Part of the solution is in a new contract with the voter. Many candidates for the UK Green Party published a 'Charter for Local Government' in which it pledged that candidates elected would use referenda, parish meetings, petitions for recall and citizens' initiatives to enable their electors to participate directly in local government. This shows clearly that although the mechanism may be the same, the relationship resulting from it is not. In this way a radical political practice can enter into the mainstream through an utterly conventional channel.

The UK Green Party's campaigning approach in the 1990s, particularly as it has been shaped by Ron Bailey (Campaigns Co-ordinator from 1992 to 1995), has almost succeeded in making a virtue out of the necessity of operating from outside Parliament. The Green Party, denied any seats in Parliament by the electoral system, used its status as 'within politics but outside politics' to advance a series of popular and yet highly subversive reforms. The Energy Conservation Act, for example, gained support from all sides at Westminster, and was endorsed by a sufficiently wide range of groups within civil society to overwhelm the resistance of the government.

How did a Party with so little resources succeed in passing three separate pieces of legislation—more than the Labour Party achieved in the same period? The key was to identify the parts of the Party's programme that fulfilled a number of criteria. They had to stand alone—to be effective without the other components of the programme. They had to make use of the existing structures and institutions to achieve their ends. They had to tap into the 'common sense' of civil society in such a way as to make them seem self-evidently desirable and hard if not impossible to resist. And they had to be very simple—capable for being introduced as a Private Member's Bill (a procedure which almost never succeeds).

The Energy Conservation Act and the Road Traffic Reduction Bill satisfied all these categories. The former in particular gained immense support, from social welfare groups (such as Help the Aged) and environmental organizations, and from the general public. It had the sense of an idea whose time had come, and a simple measure that could only yield benefits. And yet the government of the day, almost alone, fought a desperate rearguard action to keep the measure off the statute books.

The reason for this was that they could see what else would be achieved beyond simply insulating a few houses. With targets set and spending required, it would have a significant effect in cutting down fuel use. The newly privatized generators would see their production outcompeted by conservation. Responsibility for the plans was to be handed to local government, giving the Councils much needed credibility, and the opportunity to be seen to be helping their constituents. And if electricity demand was significantly affected, the last arguments for nuclear power would fall away.

In this way, a seemingly powerless organization with minority support can set in train processes that use the power structures' own strength against them. Such political jujitsu, subtle and elegant, represents the future of revolutionary politics.

Staying Subversive

This is not to suggest that the goal of building a network of empowering relations is mistaken. If the search for effectiveness leads too far into co-operation with the dominant powers, then we will become part of the problem, and not part of the solution. The terms on which these deals are struck are only ever as good as the power system that backs them up. The nature of power-over is that its constant pressure on us invites us to continue the process and practise it against others. This is what we will end up doing if we do not have an alternative ready.

Radicalism and purity are not sufficient; they get no purchase on the slick mechanism of power and are swiftly marginalized. Conformity is equally ineffective; by using the systems uncritically, we are used by it and we strengthen it further—we become part of the problem we set out to solve. I'm not saying anything new here—for centuries, those seeking to realize their compassion in action have faced the same dilemma in a variety of forms. How can we be in the world and yet not of the world? How can we organize effectively without reflecting the environment that we organize in? How can we use money and position to ends that oppose money and position? How can we use the language of the powerful to tell the story of the powerless?

This paradox has often been described as a balancing act, but I do not believe this is an appropriate metaphor. In the end this is not about compromise, or splitting the difference. Such an approach will always result in the worst of both worlds. Rather, it is the search for imaginative solutions—seeing the pattern in the world's affairs that can be a pathway to a different order. Perhaps 'walking on thin ice' would be a better metaphor, conveying the sense of hidden depths and points of strength and weakness. There is no 'middle way' when one side in the contest is so dominant. There is no way to remain above the grubby worlds of politics and commerce when to abstain from power altogether is to cut oneself off from the means of life. Connections have to be made, and the key is to identify the most productive and neutral mechanisms in the established order—those which presently support power-over, but which could be used to serve a different purpose. It is not being in the mainstream which gets results, nor being revolutionary; it is the connection between the two, the ability to have a foot in both camps and your heart in empowerment.

When I say 'neutral mechanisms', I'm talking about things that are functional in more than one system of power. They may be techniques, institutions, technologies or forms of thought or behaviour. If some device which facilitates the flow of power is at work in the system of power-over but is (in part or as a whole) suitable for use in a system of power-to as well, then it is a particularly important point to 'capture' or to have influence over. If we think that a grassroots, participatory democracy might well employ elections and some element of representation, then it is highly appropriate to organize electorally under power-over. If we believe that nuclear power stations can in no way be considered 'soft' or convivial technology, then it is probably not appropriate to work in one. The example of the organic box schemes shows how business planning tools, company law, vans and even a certain entrepreneurial culture can be turned to radical ends; and indeed Birmingham Chamber of Commerce was somewhat disconcerted to discover that the fastest growing business in Birmingham was run by a co-operative group of anarchists. Money (as presently constituted—see Chapter 12) might not be part of a co-operative economy, but trade skills and delivering goods to customers certainly would be. The use of certain techniques of co-operation in order to bring capital under the control of a wider community of interest allow capital accumulation to be 'tamed'.

However, there are conditions on this. Firstly, it is noticeable that the organic produce supplied by Organic Roundabout was filling a demand that did not come as a result of advertising or marketing by corporate grocers, but through grassroots campaigning against industrial agriculture. If the community is to truly control capital, it has to influence demand as well—otherwise the competition with established businesses will lead to imitation of them. It is the way that certain reforms open up business opportunities that can only be met from within the Green movement, or the way that campaigns create a demand for more ethical products, that enable Green business to function. LETS is particularly interesting here, because it can turn need into demand by creating its own liquidity. Meanwhile, successful Green businesses can be the basis for highly effective fundraising for Green campaigning (either by donating part of their surplus, or by creating opportunities for volunteers to earn money), can make the tools and equipment they use available to less well funded activists, and even provide secure and flexible employment for activists unable or unwilling to rely on welfare.

Campaigning and protest, however, are highly conducive to becoming a full-time lifestyle. For many, it becomes a vocation, a full-time activity. Such people are the mainstay of the campaigning side of the Green movement; their commitment builds up contacts, experience, resources. However, it is an inevitable risk of such a lifestyle that they lose touch with mainstream society. With their mission at the forefront of their minds, mass culture seems trivial and can be regarded almost with contempt. They may find that they have become a professional élite cut off from any wider base of support. As anyone who has been involved in campaigning knows, this can be the kiss of death. Professional political activists are widely mistrusted—perhaps simply as a reflection of the contempt they sometimes seem to show for the 'masses'.

Campaigns are powerful when they embody a cross-section of society— certainly including the professional campaigners, but in co-operation with a mix of ages, backgrounds and beliefs. This also provides access to a range of skills, resources and knowledge that would not otherwise be available. Under these circumstances, the mass culture can actually feed a culture of resistance. An article in *Do or Die* magazine describes the difficulties and potential of this co-operation at a site in South Wales being mined by Celtic Energy.

> "[The protest] demonstrated one of eco-protest's perennial problem in attempting to involve those outside of an unemployed (in capitalist terms) sub-culture. Clearly it's difficult to engage in disrupting work during working hours when committed (jobs, family etc) at these times. . . .

> "Celtic Enemy's head offices had already been cased with invasion in mind. . . . on the 2nd day, locals loaded their vehicles full of protesters, driving them to CE's offices. It remains one of the most effective actions. Despite claims from Wales Today (regional evening news) that protesters 'went too far' by going off site and breaking laws, locals ferrying them to the target clearly negated this. Having said this, they still took a back seat role. It was wholehearted involvement. The abilities and levels of commitment, if anything, suiting the respective parties' attributes."[7]

Activists working in the field of Green politics have perhaps the greatest threats and opportunities arising from an institution that exists on the border between power-over and power-to: elections. The combination of democratic potential and the practice of elective dictatorship makes this an obvious target for Green political activity, but one with considerable dangers (see also Chapter 2). Many of the reforms that can be achieved depend on the support built by campaigners at the grassroots level—and they can also create opportunities in the alternative economy.

Mutual Aid

Community economics, campaigning and protest, and political activity have been three of the most productive areas for the Green movement. Although sometimes misunderstanding and mistrusting each other, there is a potentially rewarding connection between them. These three areas of activity can operate close to the edge of the counterculture, using many of the tools, techniques and institutions of power-over and bending them to the service of empowerment.

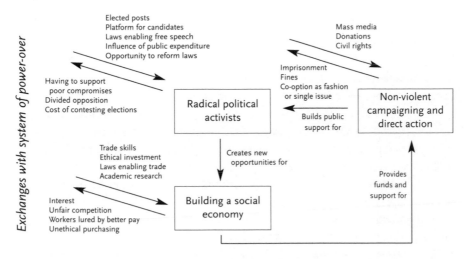

Provided they work closely together and recognize what each can contribute to the others, they can colonize and capture considerable power for the empowering structures. However, all are playing a high risk game. Business and capital accumulation has a dynamic towards unrestrained growth and accumulation of power. Politics is an endless process of deal-making and compromise—a minefield for the unwary. Campaigners are always at risk of co-option and marginalization. It is the leaps of imagination they make in their own fields, and their willingness to co-operate with each other, that are the best hopes for the success of these operations.

Chapter 11

Global Reach

Humans have always succeeded in maintaining an apparent paradox; being concerned with local, immediate realities while at the same time developing practices and structures on a global level. From ancient trading routes to modern internet communications, local behaviour gives rise to world systems.

Today, power-over (which thrives on distance and accumulation) is able to introduce global technologies—and perhaps biotechnology is the most far-reaching in its potential. These global technologies are taking advantage of an increasingly deregulated trade system to shape the very substance of life.

Colonialism was the key process that turned the emerging European power structure into a world system. Today it is less tangible but no less disempowering, as transnational companies take over from colonial powers as the new empire builders. There has always been resistance to the spread of power-over—resistance that has been overcome principally by force. Their new world order is just starting to emerge—and it is stimulating an organized global response, using many of the new information technologies. Power-to can organize effectively on a global scale, but it is only just starting to happen.

The Contracting Parties to this Agreement:

Desiring to strengthen their ties of friendship and to promote greater economic co-operation between them;

Considering that international investment has assumed great importance in the world economy and has considerably contributed to the development of their countries;

Recognizing that agreement upon the treatment to be accorded to investors and their investments will contribute to the efficient utilization of economic resources, the creation of employment opportunities and the improvement of living standards;

Emphasizing that fair, transparent and predictable investment regimes complement and benefit the world trading system;

Wishing to establish a broad multilateral framework for international investment with high standards for the liberalization of investment regimes and investment protection and with effective dispute settlement procedures;

Noting the OECD guidelines for Multinational Enterprises and emphasizing that implementation of the Guidelines, which are non-binding and which are observed on a voluntary basis, will promote mutual confidence between enterprises and host countries and contribute to a favourable climate for investment;

HAVE AGREED AS FOLLOWS:

(Preamble to the OECD draft of the Multilateral Agreement on Investment 1/10/97)

The world is a big place. Even E. F. Schumacher once said, "People ask me how we can decentralize the World Bank. I couldn't decentralize my local corner shop."[1] The staggering scale of trying to take political action that will affect the lives of six billion people leaves many at a loss. It is not just the numbers, or the distance. It is also the apparent diversity. In the tangle of languages and cultures, can we really discern a pattern and an order in human affairs across the planet?

The debate over whether or not we should speak of a 'world system' (as Wallerstein named it) has surely moved on from whether or not it exists, to what form it takes. Although I have stressed throughout this book that I believe that analysis should begin at the level of interpersonal relations and communities, I have to accept that the 'ascending analysis' must lead us to a global theory. In the language of complexity theory, local rules generate global order. This emergent, higher level pattern is not just the sum of the parts: it is real, differentiated, and feeds back to affect those local rules.

In fact, humanity has operated as a global system for a long time. Trading links between far-flung nations have been a significant factor in people's lives for hundreds of years, and few communities can have been untouched by the range of mercantile operations, from the silk routes to China to the slave trade in Africa. Without powered transport or electric communications, stable patterns of exchange between almost all human societies was underway.

Going back even further, Clive Ponting points out the way in which changes in technology have emerged in different parts of the world at the same time. He suggests that the pressure of population is felt globally, like the air pressure in a balloon, and that this pressure drives both technological and institutional change. As migrating communities reach the limits of available living space, or boundaries with other human populations, extra people cannot simply move on. Population density has to increase, and this forces technological change.[2]

The first big change was the emergence of settled agriculture, less than ten thousand years ago (in other words, taking up about 1% of human history). I believe that up to that point technology, culture and social order were earth-centred—dominated by power-to, or similar variations on that theme. As population pressures forced people to work the same land over and over again, a new lifestyle emerged in which the earth was controlled and suppressed, and hopes and fears centred around the sky, and the climate. At the same time, the surpluses generated by settled agriculture supported a more differentiated society, with a warrior and a priesthood. Neighbouring communities, being tied to their land, were ripe for plunder and tribute. This is the basis for the emergence of a system of power I call 'power-from'; a system of rigid stratification and obligation. At the top of the pyramid, a male sky god responsible for the success of the crops; below, a king or warlord whose divine right to rule is endorsed by a priesthood, and whose position is supported by a warrior class. Technology was largely that of extraction and craft rather than manufacture or distribution. As a system, it might have looked something like this.

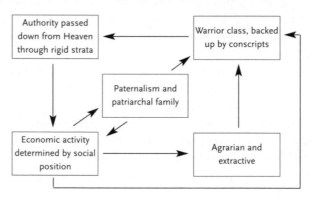

This supported a series of city states and empires. Some exhibited features that we know in power-over, like money, representative government and mechanical production. All had remnants of the earth-centred lifestyle present, particularly when the priests and warriors were absent. China is the exemplar: a sustained social order of ascending roles and duties toward heavenly purity, run by warlords and monks with little technological ambition. For almost six thousand years until the late eighteenth century it was the 'middle kingdom' at the centre of the world system of power-from.

The shift to a new system can be seen in the renaissance, the industrial revolution and growth of mercantilism. Many of the ingredients of power-over were present in the empires of the ancient world, but somehow they did not mesh. The armies were too reliant on plunder to embody a nation; the rulers relied far more on force than on legitimacy; the economic system did not permit enough accumulation or extended reach of ownership; and technologies were predominantly limited to extraction and control of territory. The later stages of this system were marked by terrible famines, as agriculture struggled to support armies, aristocrats and a growing population. Warlords fell before the superior technology of nation states, and the urban masses brought together by concentrating capital demanded representation in government. Power-over had arrived, and the knowledge and beliefs received from above fell before it.

Today, even the most remote communities can be found drinking the same canned drinks and watching the same sporting events as I do. As recently as the 70s, the idea of thinking globally was the preserve of idealists and radicals. It is now the case that global planning is part of corporate culture, and 'global reach' is part of the jargon of power-over. Although a global system may always have been present, there is something qualitatively different about the process of globalization presently underway.

The observable signs of this global system are an immense movement of people and goods. Air transport is growing exponentially, giving the impression of humans swarming to and fro, sometimes seasonally, sometimes routinely. However, permanent migration is largely conducted on foot, as refugee populations flee poverty and war. Migrant labour is also on the move—largely south to north, by rail and sea. But the movement of commodities is vast by comparison—millions of tons of oil in supertankers or through pipelines, vast trucks carrying manufactured goods, and increasingly air transport being used to deliver agricultural goods. The scale on which production and consumption are planned is global, and also highly complex—a single product may have components manufactured in any part of the world, with materials from equally diverse sources.

Global Technologies
If we might say that previously there was a world system based on diversity and sporadic interaction, now the outline is emerging of a global, centrally planned economy. Or to be more accurate: the operation of the particular centres of manufacturing and distribution are relatively autonomous within a monocultural setting—Western values and concepts, global icons and a materialist worldview. Films, advertising campaigns, music and magazines are increasingly designed for a global audience with a shared understanding and acceptance of the broad mechanisms of power-over. This message is willingly received because there is an imperative of survival and meeting needs. To be successful in an economy that is tied into the world system requires an understanding of that global culture: where there is globalized economic activity, there you will also find global culture.

This is only possible because of a range of media technologies that have been adopted globally—TV, CD, PC, VHS and high volume colour printing have provided the commentary for globalization. Just as this explosion in information technology has been selected and driven by the last generation of power-over entrepreneurs, so today we can see vast resources being poured into biotechnology. In 1996, 2% of the world soya bean crop was from a single genetically engineered strain of soya. This bean had been engineered not to adapt to any other living process, but to be resistant to a powerful artificial herbicide. It was, you might say, a power-over dependent plant. In 1997, 17% of the world soya crop used it. In 1998 it was expected to reach 40%. You have probably already eaten some.

This opens a new front in the struggle between our minds and our bodies. I said in Chapter 4 that although power-over is 'natural' in the sense of arising out of life, living organisms depend on power-to; systems based on power-over inevitably come into conflict with ecosystems as a result. Now biotechnology poses a new strategy; modify and colonize the stuff of life itself. DNA that is, in effect, adapted to power-over is being created and substituted for evolved DNA. Genetic modification of human beings is close behind—initially, of course, for purely medical reasons. Later, inevitably, for purposes of standardization and control. If that seems outlandish, you should be aware that just as it is possible to identify genes that predispose us to depression, so it is possible to see correlations between certain genes and a predisposition to crime. What if dissent and radical thinking were 'cured' as a side effect of an attempt to cure us of criminality? The same gene that causes sickle cell anaemia protects us against malaria. The reason that genetic disorders have survived millennia of evolution is that in many cases, without out realizing, the same gene that is causing the 'disorder' is also equipping us with some very necessary resource. If we eradicate mental illness, what else will go with it?

This kind of technological assault is not possible on a local scale. Only the processes and mechanisms of a global system made it possible to mobilize the $200 billion that were invested in it. The entire structure of delivery, marketing and processing, the legal framework of trade, investment and property, and the political-cultural ideas of high-status food, technological benefits and disconnection from the land, have become so widespread that this has become possible. Power-over, in its technologies, economy and hierarchies, can only really operate globally. Or, to put it another way, it will always seek to expand, and to extend itself further. The world system may only recently have become an operational reality, but the aspiration has been inherent in this system of power from the outset.

Colonies of Power

It is important to study the way in which the Western model of power has so successfully spread globally, so that we can see how deep are the foundations on which it rests. Its roots in Europe began with trade, and it might be tempting to see the global system as simply a massive trading system. However, there have been a number of major discontinuities on the way—in particular, an age of empires and colonization and millions of deaths from war. Is there a connection?

EUROPABIO

So let us look at the methods used to insert the new biotechnologies into the European marketplace. EuropaBio describes itself as "The voice of the European biotechnology sector". It is one of a range of industry-specific lobby groups. Competition is undoubtedly a key feature of the power-over economy; but that does not exclude co-operation when the need arises. Corporate power readily organizes itself as cartel or conglomerate, because power-over is the driving force, competition merely one of its effects. Industry lobby groups illustrate this well, as they position themselves for market access and tax breaks, and oppose regulation.

EuropaBio was created in 1996 through the merger of the Senior Advisory Group on Biotechnology (SAGB) and the European Secretariat for National Bioindustry Associations. It is made up of 500 companies of a variety of sizes. "From now on, we will speak with one strong voice when discussing with the EU and national politicians the need for a regulatory environment in which European industry can grow and expand." If it seems strange that a panel of advisors and an association of industry representatives should speak with 'one strong voice', it serves to illustrate the hegemonic effect of power. There is no independent voice in this field, because virtually all the experts are in the pay of the industry. This is not just the case with ground-breaking science, but across all sectors of the economy. The strength of business is such that only those employed in an area really understand the area. Further, these industry associations are an important way for the large enterprises to maintain a sense of community with smaller enterprises, even while preying on them.

In 1992, SAGB held an 'employment roundtable' with industrialists, trade unionists and civil servants, sponsored by the Belgian Presidency of the EU. It concluded that "The key to employment lies in . . . access to modern technologies. . . . Biotechnology is particularly important." Shortly after, the European Commission embarked on active promotion of biotechnology. Internationally, the same process was underway through Transatlantic Business Dialogue: "Unilever for Europe and Monsanto on the US side will seek to identify potential causes for trade difficulties in the agro-food sector and propose ways to eliminate them." The breakthrough came in a paper from Commission President Jacques Delors where he extolled biotech as the brightest prospect for European competitiveness. It was not until two years later that NGOs realized the scale of the dangers and began to campaign in earnest, with the result that individual states within the EU began to break ranks and introduce their own controls. The European Roundtable of Industrialists swiftly backed up EuropaBio's demands that the Commission 'find a solution'. As I write, Austria and Luxembourg are likely to have their controls overturned at a European level. The legal powers in Europe are not equally accessible from above and below. They have been designed to be compatible with the power-over of business and international bureaucracy.

As for the millions of long term jobs that were forecast . . . according to German government figures, the German biotech sector was only good for 2,000 jobs a year, half of them financed by public money. Meanwhile, the continuing move from labour-intensive to capital-intensive agriculture means a steady loss of jobs on farms.

As the trading nations of Europe became more and more driven by the accumulation and growth of their wealth by mass production for trade, it became clear that the growth simply could not continue at such a rate within a limited market. The mainly subsistence agriculture of the South did not generate sufficient demand for the manufactured goods of the North. Local artisans and craftsmen were able to meet their needs perfectly adequately. Trade flourished with cultures with similar cultural outlooks, such as the monarchies of East Africa or the Empires of the Middle East. But when cultures clashed, and trading requirements proved incompatible, 'no' could not be taken for an answer.

Colonialism was the solution. First, of the supposedly 'uninhabited' lands, then of lands inhabited by 'primitive' or 'savage' people, and finally of recognizable civilizations; brute force enabled the expansion of trade to continue. In India the process was gradual—first setting up trading posts, then extending control over more and more of the production process; the East India Company became more powerful than the local state and eventually took it over. This process from trading mission to full administrative structure was made possible by the culture of enlightenment and civilization: it was seen as the 'white man's burden' to bring modernity to these backward people.

Colonialism brought access to land, and by doing so it also brought landlessness for the indigenous peoples. This generated a labour force, obliged to work for money to buy back that which they could once provide for themselves. And above all, the slave trade was the most openly brutal of the colonial practices. In the end, the contradiction between the ostensible mission of civilizing and developing the natives, and the harsh reality of slavery, meant it could not endure. That it continued as long as it did illustrated the importance of its economic function. It is possible that it would have continued further were it not for the liberation of the 'energy slaves' of fossil fuels.

Our understanding of the process of colonization has been radically expanded recently—in particular by Maria Mies and Vandana Shiva, who have identified the 'internal colonies' that are less visible, as they have no political/legal status, but are equally important. Subsistence farmers seem to be disconnected from the global economy; but they are a reserve army of labour, and absorb the cost of childrearing and social maintenance while releasing low cost labour to the colonial economy. Women are colonized within countries, within communities and within households. The sex industry and the electronics industry of South East Asia have used the weak bargaining position of unmarried women to make them into a pool of extremely cheap labour. The 'housewifeization' of women in Africa is another form of colonization of women. By geographically separating male migrant workers from their families, women are left to feed and bring up their families by themselves—a 'free' benefit for the colonial economy.[3] Superficially different, the process is the same: the use of force to create markets and labour, the exploitation of the household economy to support the commodity economy, and the establishment of a global discourse of consumerism. In fact the same processes had been carried out in Europe. The political structures of centralized states date from the Roman Empire and beyond, and the disruption of rural communities took place more recently, for example with the enclosures in the UK.

Colonialism, in the traditional sense of empire-building, never needed to be more than a temporary phase. There may have been those who genuinely expected the British Empire to rule directly from Hong Kong to the United States, but it was surely not necessary. Once the indigenous population had lost touch with their own culture and a new Western hegemony had been put in its place, or a new population of colonists introduced, the logic of power-over could be counted on to provide the conditions of production locally. Neo-colonialism simply proved more efficient, and side-stepped inconsistencies of having different forms of rule within an empire. The great anti-colonial struggles were principled and important acts of resistance. But they only succeeded in severing a link with the ruling élite, and as I have argued throughout this book, power relations do not come from above: they are reproduced locally, in our everyday lives. Colonization continued without the involvement of the colonizing powers. The dynamic of power-over was well enough established to thrive and prosper on the new soil, and would in time recreate seemingly bilateral but equally exploitative relations with the colonizing powers. Those, like Gandhi, who argued for a deeper struggle against the values, technology and power relations of the colonists, found it a far harder cause for which to build support. Imperial power is not a part of the dynamic of power-over, but rather a hangover from power-from, the system of gods and kings. Power-over builds hierarchies, but not pyramids: there is no top. The empire builders gave up because of resistance, and because of the moral disquiet felt at home; but they would have resisted longer and harder if there had not been a growing awareness that effective, competitive survival strategies required a more indirect form of control.

The Persistence of Colonial Strategies

The phrase 'neo-colonialism' implies that the appearance of independence is not a reality, and that these countries occupy a subordinate position in the world system, and I need to explain why I think this is so. Firstly, the influence of transnational companies is important—mainly those concerned with mining, agriculture and oil (though biotechnology and information are growing to rival them). They operate with great freedom, since they are the main providers of employment and 'hard currency', and they can set the terms on which they work in a way that they cannot in their 'home' countries. Transfer pricing, depressed commodity prices and repatriation of profits mean that the colonized country fails to build its own local wealth. As a result, we see a depressed economy with a very poor urbanized or migrant workforce drawn from a huge pool of landless or effectively landless peasantry.

Secondly, the pseudo-representative state is even less representative than in Western countries. A surprising number of countries still face autocratic rule from rulers installed by Western powers, supported by Western powers or subject to strong diplomatic influence from Western powers. It is worth noting, however, how many unelected leaders use precisely the same methods of building support and winning over the population as elected leaders; we are surprised, perhaps, to hear of public support for men such as Chile's Pinochet or Iraq's Saddam Hussein, but in fact both men used media, public appearances and issues to build a constituency just as candidates for election do. Consent is still necessary, even when elections have been dispensed with.

The political and legal frameworks were designed with Western values in mind, often cutting across indigenous, tribal patterns to the great detriment of both. The state totally lacks the economic base with which to deliver effective public services, leaving the population with a double burden of maintaining social care at the same time as commodity production. Many consider these countries to be the weak links in the global system, because their hobbled systems cannot deliver the benefits and the total domination that Western versions have. Power-to exists in much more active forms because so many people depend on it for survival. This is borne out by the strength of movements like the Brazilian homeless or the Indian small farmers. Set against that, the military and economic might of the Western powers is able to intervene more bluntly than it can on home ground, even though it is absent most of the time. As ever, power lies not in one place but in relationships: liberation movements in developing countries are strengthened when they have strong connections with radicals in the West.

The introduction and imposition of Western technologies is another important component of neo-colonialism. The acceptance of new technologies when existing indigenous techniques were often providing a good standard of living had a number of causes. The geographical transformation involved in creating plantations, cities, railways and roads gave the Western technology an edge, and disrupted traditional cultures. The health effects of poverty, and diseases introduced by colonists, invited technical fixes, and with them an experience of Western methods of easing suffering—despite the role of Western values in causing them.

Finally, there was violence on an epic scale. It is particularly noticeable how the composition of casualties of war was transformed from the nineteenth to the twentieth century. Previously, bodycounts were dominated by military personnel, with civilian casualties being in the minority. As the twentieth century progressed, civilian deaths formed a larger and larger part of death through conflict. Though this may have been partly to do with the massive bombing campaigns of the second world war, it has continued as a trend in neocolonial conflict, with genocides in East Timor, Rwanda and Central America. War is no longer being fought in order to control territory, but rather to establish lifestyles and behaviour among its inhabitants. Returning to the question of how power-over establishes itself, this suggests that progress has to commence with the destruction of the indigenous power relations, or their corruption. Power-from can be subverted into power-over by showering local community leaders with gifts; preventing self-reliant power-to requires a comprehensive dispossession, breaking the tie between people and the land. It is no coincidence that the crisis at the turn of the millennium is one of a growing army of refugees, homeless and without livelihood.

The role of the Eastern bloc during this period is important. This constituted an attempt to build the same relations of technology, government and defence as the Western powers without accepting congruent economic relations. The result was a kind of 'state capitalism' which rapidly accepted the rules of capital accumulation and commodification, and eventually had to concede competition as well. The countries which attempted to avoid neocolonialism by becoming Soviet client states fared little better, and often worse.

The force of Western hegemony, and the resources at its disposal, ensured that resistance was overwhelmed, and pliant ruling élites could always be recruited. One recent attempt to retain local control over resources, and develop an independent industrial base, was in Iraq. As an industrial power, Iraq was annihilated in a war which killed 300,000 Iraqis and less than 100 Westerners. The bombing campaign targeted water treatment plants, factories and power stations and reduced the country to dependency on imports in a matter of days. Public support for what is practically a fascist regime is guaranteed; however bad the government is in Iraq, their experience of the West is that it is more vicious still.

The international institutions established over this period demonstrate the way in which states were beginning to negotiate the structures of an international system so as to expand markets. The World Bank and the International

Monetary Fund linked flows of capital to the Western discourse of development. Those states which professed the strongest attachment to the goal of civilization were rewarded with credits and aid. Most of this aid failed in even its professed goal—factories were built which had no customers, austerity measures imposed when there was no entrepreneurial class to take advantage, nor mass of consumers seeking incentives. Even in its own terms it was a success only in a few countries where the dynamic of 'otherness' was able to gain some local autonomy and generate positive feedback. These Newly Industrialized Countries were held up as the model of development, and proof that the values of power-over were accessible to all. The local reality was environmental devastation, massive exploitation, rampant abuse of state power and an explosion of violence. With the recent Pacific rim recession, even the justification of wealth creation failed.

There are a few places left in the world where advanced indigenous cultures hang on. Helena Norberg-Hodge was able to study Ladakh, in India, shortly before and after transport links brought it into the world system. She found a happy society, free from crime, well nourished and with long lifespans, supporting a diverse ecosystem in a difficult niche, with a highly developed culture and arts in abundant leisure time. As she watched the ingredients of development introduced, she saw the collapse of care, of local production, of peace and of sustainable technology. The culture that existed there is giving way under a bombardment of Western media which promises prosperity and leisure, and delivers the opposite.[4]

The New World Order
There are now signs that neocolonialism itself is being superseded. Firstly, there is a growing layer of international organizations with more and more authority over states. The World Bank and the IMF have been in existence now for over 50 years, but they have been joined now by GATT and the World Trade Organization. These bodies take the process a step further. Where the former two used the levers of debt and commodity prices to draw neocolonized countries into the global trading community, GATT uses the force of law. This has become a powerful tool for two reasons; firstly, modern technologies and commodities are becoming harder and harder to produce at a national level. If your country tries to withdraw from the global culture of power-over, the population will experience a relative deprivation compared to the affluent, high-tech lifestyles that other countries appear to deliver. Secondly, international capital has gained a level of freedom from national controls that makes capital flight an effective punishment for transgression of the international community's codes. What these codes are is clear from practice; Nigeria can execute Ken SaroWiwa and the markets will not see any threat to stability, whereas a programme of nationalizing major industries (not in itself a radical move) will bring heavy punishment.

THE EUROPEAN BENCHMARK

The European Roundtable of Industrialists (ERT), founded in 1983, consists of 45 'captains of industry' from TNCs based in Europe. Oil companies are represented (Shell, BP), the motor industry (Fiat, Renault, Pirelli, Daimler Benz), chemicals (ICI, Bayer, Rhône Poulenc) and food (Nestlé, Unilever). What are not represented are small or medium-sized companies, co-operatives or trade unions. Although it undoubtedly gains influence through research and expert knowledge, close personal connections with European politicians are critical. Its interests are unexpectedly wide-ranging: it played a crucial role in pushing for the internal market in the 1980s ("Bearing in mind that when it was first launched governments were not very keen, we helped a lot to push it through"), as well as the huge trans-European road building plans. They also take credit for the successful completion of the Global Trade negotiations—at a two hour lunch, fourteen ERT members encouraged the French Prime Minister to proceed with signing GATT. Considering they must have represented a significant portion of his country's economy, and his government's revenue, it is not wholly surprising he agreed.

When Jacques Delors, EU Commission President, launched his White Paper on 'Growth, Competitiveness and Employment', it bore uncanny similarities to a paper launched a week earlier by the ERT. The same themes of deregulation, flexible labour markets and transport infrastructure recurred—and Delors was present at the ERT's launch and thanked them for their help at his own.

The current focus of the ERT is what they call 'benchmarking'—comparing countries' 'competitiveness' and grading their success in providing a good home for capital. "This is a footloose world. Companies make products wherever it is best for them to do so." The criteria for membership in the European Monetary Union are seen as part of this process, cutting public services to meet standards of fiscal respectability. The effect of this on social wealth and biological order is not a concern of theirs.

In 1993, the ERT published a survey of benchmarks for developing countries. It concludes, "Countries in the developing world have realized to what extent the impediments to private foreign and local investment were hurting their own competitiveness. Policy changes providing better market access for foreign investors . . . are now transforming earlier weaknesses into a formidable competitive challenge. The competitive challenge becomes even more powerful through the fact that in more and more cases these countries move ahead of Europe." The race for the bottom is underway.[5]

Where the World Bank and IMF operate in such a way as to establish a discourse of power-over in national economies, and discourage attempts to create fiefdoms of power-from, the language of free trade concerns the relations between those states and seeks to deny the right of states to control or regulate trade. Lang and Hines, in their book *The New Protectionism*,[6] describe powerfully the consequences of this shift. Where previously people have been able to use the powers available to them in their countries to compel governments to use tariffs and trading barriers to protect communities, industries, technologies and the global environment, now the states have a new argument to oppose them: 'We cannot protect you, because we will be punished by the global community—and in the short term, you will find that punishment worse than the absence of protection. The only hope we can offer is for you to embrace the values and practices of power-over, and use them more effectively than any other country'. For a particularly powerful example, look at the collapse of the trading agreement on bananas between the EU and various Caribbean nations. A long-standing agreement guaranteed the producers of the Caribbean favourable terms, and allowed the survival of small farms and organic farming methods. When the World Trade Organization ruled the agreement illegal, the consequence was destitution; the farmers were outcompeted by the corporate plantations of Latin America, where more intensive farming practices dominate. I have outlined the pure logic of the system: it should also be stressed that the system is far from even-handed. The case was brought to the WTO by the US, as one of a limited number of cases they are allowed to bring each year, shortly after the head of Chiquita (a large banana producer) made a large donation to the ruling Democratic Party. It is interesting to compare the two bodies of international law, the World Court and the World Trade Organization, and note how governments and businesses respond to the pronouncements of each. The World Court has recently issued a ruling saying that the use of nuclear weapons would be a breach of international law, and reaction has been virtually nil. What is more, it is noticeable that the World Court case on nuclear weapons was brought following pressure from citizen's movements in the nuclear powers, and in the teeth of opposition from their governments. The WTO case was referred to it by the President of the United States.[7] In short, violence is beyond regulation; protection of indigenous economies is effectively and internationally illegal.

Further layers of international government are set to follow. The Multilateral Agreement on Investment is presently being negotiated by the G8 nations, and whatever the outcome of those negotiations, it provides an interesting example of the direction of national agreement. The MAI exists to 'harmonize' the rules various nations have on investment. Principally, it calls for 'non-discrimination'; international capital investments should receive equal treatment to local investment. Let's be clear what that means: it could mean buying up land, or local businesses, or even an advertising campaign. It is saying that any effort to favour local economic activity over global should be subject to the force of law. This is worrying enough, but the text goes further. Some clauses seem to suggest that all regulation of investment should be illegal, and that an attempt to impose performance conditions (for example, requiring that a certain level of local employment be provided) should be subject to legal challenge. Elsewhere, the protection of investment is treated as so important that any law that threatens it (for example, a new law for environmental protection) should require compensation, and that even a company's reputation constitutes an investment that requires protection. Similar clauses in the North American Free Trade Agreement led to the Canadian government being sued when it outlawed a harmful chemical on environmental grounds. Nowhere is there any suggestion that multinational companies, or international agencies, should be subject to any legal challenge. This bodes ill for the future.

Beyond the Nation State

It is for this reason—the clear emergence of unaccountable international powers—that I was sceptical (see Chapter 8) of Alan Carter's claim that the nation state is the main explanatory factor in politics. At least from the point of view of the study of power, it does not appear to me that strong nation states are a key component of the dynamic of power-over. If they were, we surely would not see the rise of this international network of powers capable of setting limits on their activities. That isn't to say that I see the World Trade Organization as part of the dynamic either. I agree with Foucault that power is principally about real exchanges between real people, at the level of bodies and discourses. The particular institutions or legal frameworks are a second-order phenomenon. The organizations, their posts, the codified rules and the various patterns of words and numbers that purport to describe them are the effects that arise out of those real interactions, and which then serve or facilitate them. It would be a mistake to believe that someone holding a position of power in, say, the IMF, has any power to change the basic dynamic of global power. The best they could hope for is to prevent it supporting power-over so effectively. At the end of the day, power can get by very well without it.

One possible reason why the nation state is not putting up more resistance to the growth of international power is that civil servants are seeing instead new paths of career development opening, and more opportunities to climb the greasy pole. That few if any will gain posts in these international bodies is not the point. They all share the aspiration, and so they do not resist the shift. Another is that international capital has proved so essential to the political structures, delivering the economic and technological resources the state requires, that its demands cannot be resisted. The Faustian bargain between state and capital has led to the nation being emptied of content, and the state becoming a shell administering laws ensuring market access and security of property, and extracting finance for colonial relations of care. The nation state has not proved to be greatly needed in terms of power and survival under the hegemony of power-over. So it will be superseded. Institutions and organizations do not in themselves have any power; only the people in them and the strategies they pursue have a real impact on the shape of the future.

This kind of thinking has led many to focus on conspiracies of rich and 'powerful' individuals. The Bilderberg group—a private club of politicians, businessmen and financiers—is a favourite target, with its meetings and membership closely scrutinized. These kinds of conspiracy theories are missing the point. Such prominent individuals are functional to the power processes—not necessarily creating or driving them. An anonymous entrepreneur, bureaucrat or accountant is as likely to be building the links in power-over—and it is the millions of local interactions between 'ordinary' people that give such actions their force.

In fact, I would argue that conspiracy theories are positively dangerous. The more we say these people are powerful, the more we build them up; and a discourse of resistance to conspiracies has consistently led to fascist and neo-fascist political movements. If there is a conspiracy, we are all part of it.

The result is a race to the bottom in terms of the corporate environment (the 'conditions of production' mentioned in Chapter 8) that governments provide. A pattern is emerging of falling corporation tax everywhere—something which took commentators in Britain by surprise when it appeared as part of the New Labour government's first budget. The convergence criteria for European Monetary Union also fit this pattern. It is said that labour is cheaper in South Wales than in South Korea.

In summary, the local practice of accumulation and competition has generated concentrations of capital—symbolic power—on a global scale. The sustained use of violence to disrupt self-reliant economies has opened up virtually the entire planet to these currencies of power, enabling further accumulation, and the introduction of technologies which operate globally to colonize the living world.

The culmination of this process can be seen in the 1996 Kyoto summit on global warming. Here, the consequences of global colonization were writ large with apocalyptic warnings by the world's scientific community of flood, disease, extreme weather conditions and mass extinctions. An extended network of community activists was represented in the NGOs' parallel summit, but the most influential group present was surely the Global Climate Coalition—a body funded by hundreds of the world's largest corporations to discredit scientific evidence and remind world leaders of their obligation to provide a regulatory environment suitable for economic growth.

PEOPLE'S GLOBAL ACTION

Green and radical activists are increasingly organizing on an international level—particularly the youth groups. In Europe, ASEED, EYFA and the Young European Greens are all networking action and information with increasing effectiveness. The highly organized Green Group in the European Parliament, and the Federation of European Green Parties, provide a lot of support. Email is the preferred mode of communication, and they are not averse to seeking funding from the European Union through their programmes for increasing European cultural 'integration'.

With growing awareness of the likely impact of the MAI, the next phase of international organization is beginning. People's Global Action is the name of a new network linking astonishingly disparate groups—and for the first time creating a genuine alliance between 'developed' and 'developing' countries on issues of common concern. From Latin America, the Sandinista Party in Nicaragua and the Zapatista rebels of Mexico; from India and the Philippines, peasants' associations representing millions; from Brazil, the Movemento Sem Terra, which mobilized thousands of the landless poor in highly disciplined and successful land occupations. Now their members in the shanty towns are marketing the produce from their land to support more protest and action.

The PGA stresses its participatory ethic: "Direct action is about changing things through our own self-organization and ultimately taking control of our own lives and communities. The role of the PGA is simply to help such action to be communicated and co-ordinated across the world."

Already there have been a series of protests in which the complaints of the communities in the South (such as the Ogoni people, threatened by oil exploration) have been taken to the boardrooms and offices in the North (Earth First! protests at offices and filling stations belonging to Shell). Multinational companies are facing increasingly multinational resistance.

On the eve of the Millennium, the international activists' networks focussed their attention on the crucial World Trade Organization meeting, and turned out in huge numbers to attend and protest. The result became known as the 'Battle in Seattle' and it demonstrated beyond doubt that resistance is as international as power.

The thousands of protesters on the streets prevented the motorcades of the UN Secretary General and the US Secretary of State from getting to the WTO Conference venue, leading to the cancellation of the opening session. By the end of the negotiations, there was no agreement, with many developing countries in open revolt against the process, and no agenda for the next round.

Martial law was declared in Seattle for the first time since 1919. One eyewitness reported: "The solidarity here has been amazing, steelworkers supporting ecology activists supporting anarchists . . . The space being used by direct action networks is an amazing hub. The few days before this civil war erupted, they held workshops on legal rights, direct action training etc. . . . The organizing is incredible, medical and communication teams, daily meals, jail solidarity." [8]

The US delegation was not greatly affected by the environmental concerns of Vice-President Al Gore, but rather by the common sense of power-over as practiced in the daily lives of millions of their citizens. However much concern for the environment might be evidenced in the US, survival hinges on processes of extraction, manufacture and control that lead inevitably to global warming. It is this fear of a weakened position in an economy that is the only reality they know, that drives the resistance to environmental reform.

The power of the environmental backlash is that it tells people what they want to hear. The impact of stories of overseas exploitation and destruction is so great precisely because it is a challenge to a way of life that cannot easily be abandoned. Repeatedly, studies of television viewing habits say the same thing: international news is highly unpopular.

Change on a Global Scale

How can our resistance ever hope to challenge these global structures? The very thought induces despair. I talked to a German Green Member of the European Parliament, Frieder Otto Wolf, about the prospects for resistance to globalization. His view was that national regulation of capital was now impossible—transnational flows were simply too important to the basic functioning of the state. He argued that it might yet be possible to exercise some democratic control at the European level, since the dependence on outside capital was still relatively low—over 80% of transactions took place with the EU. For this reason he advised supporting moves toward closer Union, and the single currency. At such a higher level, it might be possible to steal a march.

I was, and still am, deeply sceptical about such a strategy. It sounds like another Faustian bargain; if we accept the undemocratic nature of EU institutions, and the further colonization of the European periphery, we will be granted the power we crave—we will get our hands on the levers of power. It is a grim logic, practised by desperate men and women. If we can run toward globalization ourselves, and join the climb up to the international level, we might just get ahead. It is the argument we have heard so many times before—play them at their own game because it is the only game in town. Don't rock the boat, because if we're good we might get a cut of the power they have.

I remain certain that it is not the only game in town—unless we all choose to join in. There is an alternative, of identifying the local rules that give rise to empowering structures, and building international networks of our own—countervailing sources of power, a practice that is in the mainstream but not of the mainstream. We do not have to match the scale of the multinationals. In a system on the edge of chaos, a small, even a symbolic movement can be effective in catalysing change. After all, the billions of units circulating in the stock exchange computers are themselves only symbols. It is not their sheer size which makes them effective, but the willingness of people to worship them—even while claiming to oppose them. Resistance to globalization does not stop because the nation state is no longer able to control capital—the nation state was never part of our alternative in any case. In fact it may be an opportunity to bring radical strategies into local government and community organizations.

The role of an international network of empowerment is the networking of information, the spread of hope and of tales of resistance. Co-operation can link producer and consumer, as in the growing fair trade sector. It can unify and inspire movements, as in the six international co-operative principles. It can share technical knowledge—my own UpStart Workers Co-operative has taken some of its ideas for starting new co-op businesses from the Vakgroep in Holland and from Mondragon in Spain. And the power of co-ordinated international action has yet to be tested, but the growing NGO and radical presence at international summits is causing increasing anxiety for the powers that be. Through international networks, the Green alternative can be more than the sum of its parts.

Chapter 12

We are more Possible than you can Powerfully Imagine

Social change does happen, but it is in the nature of complex systems that it is more often adaptive than truly revolutionary—notwithstanding appearances to the contrary. Acts of resistance, carried out by masses as well as by individuals, are more often symbolic than actual; they cannot touch our everyday lives.

Money is an example of a more substantial change—from barter to symbolic power. We can see the potential here for another, equally dramatic shift, as LETS establishes an alternative way of recording credit and value without scarcity or accumulation.

LETS and other innovations are typically the work of social entrepreneurs, making connections at the most local level often without recognition. However, they need to work with others who can make their radical ideas viable in the mainstream. When people actually have a chance to take part in an alternative dynamic of power, it is a very effective learning process.

The spread of ideas like this can resemble an infection, triggered by factors in the environment making change possible or necessary. Change is possible at any time, but innovation flourishes in high pressure situations. That does not mean that fear of environmental catastrophe will drive us to change; it may even reduce the opportunity for new ideas to spread.

The main interconnections in systems of power suggest certain key points on which social change activists could usefully focus, to strengthen the dynamic of power-to. A movement for social change will stand or fall not because of future rewards or pure altruism, but on the immediate benefits it delivers to its supporters.

> "Planning refers to the attempt to produce the outcome by actively managing the process, whereas design refers to the attempt to produce the outcome by establishing criteria to govern the process so that the desired result will occur more or less automatically . . . "—W. Ophuls, *Ecology and the Politics of Scarcity*

Our Experience of Change

Over my lifetime, my experience of the world around me—and that of many others—has been one of change and upheaval. I have seen the Berlin Wall fall, LPs succumb to CDs, home computers change from the ZX81 to the Pentium, a monarchy move from rulers to puppets, Fordism give way to Post-Fordism, disco become rave. . . . There is no end to the innovation and chaos that seems to rage around—and within—me. And yet, when the froth on the surface is cleared away, monolithic trends and unvarying uniformity are revealed beneath. Ownership of land has continued a process of concentration that has developed over a thousand years. Transnational corporations have inexorably overtaken national governments as the dominant powers. Languages and cultures have been eroded steadily to a homogeneous global culture. And the extinction of species has gone on and on, through the 19th century romantics, through the seventies eco-awareness, though the Earth Summits, and through all the rhetoric of repentance and justification. Some of these trends operate over millennia, some over decades; none of them has any sudden impact, as they unfold gradually and inexorably. But none of them has been present for the whole hundred thousand year span of human history—they are all contingent, historical, and subject to change.

Change is a reality, and it is present in those dynamic systems from the outset. A system may be described as stable in its outputs, but in its metabolism it is driven by change and discontinuity. The point is that those swings and tremors tend to balance and correct one another. This is the meaning of the seeming contradiction 'dynamic equilibrium': constant change in which every action leads to balancing reaction.

The self-stabilizing activity of the present dynamic equilibrium may look like change or progress, but it is insufficient for anyone seeking a sustainable society, or a release from the tyranny of power-over. There are far more significant changes that we can look to as examples: relatively short periods of history in which the equilibrium broke down, to be replaced by a completely different power system. I have in mind the dramatic switch from religious to scientific epistemology, led by Copernicus and Galileo. Or, for another (not unrelated) example, the industrial revolution, which mobilized millions from rural serfdom to production line urbanity. Alongside this chapter, I consider another such transformation, which took place alongside those two: the take-off of money from bartered gold to quantified power.

Revolting and Revolving

Why do I choose these rather dull technicalities rather than the revolutionary ideal of the masses in the streets, besieging public buildings? My point is that however spectacular the fall of established rulers, no matter how thorough the change of personnel, there will always be a deeper structure left behind. I consider the triumph of the ANC in South Africa to be a mighty political achievement, but we have to be clear that much of the old order remains—from the arms trade to the poverty of the black majority, from the killings and violence to the technology used on nature. A true social change must dig deeper, chang-

MAKING MONEY

On the face of it, the origins of money are straightforward enough. After all, barter has its limitations: what if you need to trade your potatoes now before they rot, but do not need anything in return at once? And what if the person you want to trade with has nothing you particularly need? And how do you assess which of two possible exchanges would be better for you? Surely you need some universal medium of exchange, something that holds its value. Shells were used in the past, and in some places today cigarettes are a widely accepted currency. But in the emerging city states, metals became an ideal currency: gold and silver.

However, the growth of the cities into empires was accompanied by a new development; metals were minted into coins, such as the Roman *denarii*. This is clearly connected to the creation of the professional army, employed by the state and paid to fight. Perhaps we might consider this money the first venture capital. By investing some effort and resources in minting a currency, an army of conquest could be raised to overwhelm neighbouring territories. The taxes raised there, both in the form of agricultural produce and money, would ensure that the money was respected. Recruitment of the Roman soldiers meant fewer people available to work the land. Without endless conquest and expansion, scarcity of food and surplus of money would lead to inflation.

In fact, the Romans did suffer from inflation—largely caused by the immense sums that had to be minted to pay off the landless poor. So from the outset, all the essential characteristics of the industrial system—concentrated land ownership, professional violence, poverty, fixed hierarchies and a hard currency—were present, and linked one to another. The same pattern can be seen in the paper currency issued by the Mongols in the 13th century. Marco Polo found it extraordinary: "All these pieces of paper are issued with as much solemnity and authority as if they were pure gold and silver . . . and the Khan causes every year to be made such a vast quantity of this money, which costs him nothing, that it must be equal in amount to all the treasures of the world." [1] Again, the Khan was issuing money in promise of the riches that would be gained from their conquests. Is this so different from the way banks today create credit to finance entrepreneurs?

We may never know who 'invented' money. Clearly, as the army and the city developed, it was a logical step towards giving their currencies of power material form. And yet there must have been a time when it would be an alien concept, and someone had to insist that yes, it could be done, it would work, and it would release a potential power that could not exist without it. Within a few years, thousands were spreading the idea in every single trade and exchange. And when the empires overreached themselves—as both the Romans and Mongols eventually did—their currencies were back to being just pieces of metal and paper again.

ing the less visible but more substantial facts of people's everyday lives. It must involve everyone, not just young men with time on their hands.

This is not to say that we should never take to the barricades. Uprising and resistance are important for a number of reasons. They are symbolic, announcing the possibility and the legitimacy of change. They are physical blockages of the flows of power-over, and they can deny or recapture important resources. They are a celebration of resistance and a collective experience that sharpens identity. Arendt argues that such crises for power stem from widespread disenchantment in society. "Textbook instructions on 'how to make a revolution' . . . are all based on the mistaken notion that revolutions are 'made'. . . . The superiority of the government has always been absolute; but this superiority lasts only as long as the power structure of the society is intact—that is, as long as commands are obeyed and the army and police forces are prepared to use their weapons . . . The question of this obedience is not decided by the command-obedience relation but by opinion, and, of course, by the number of those who share it."[2]

It is a consequence of this view that the actions of a few on an issue of principle are of no importance, except insofar as they are part of a collective force. But it is important to realize that an action involving a single individual or a handful of people can, when tightly focused and highly effective, be as powerful as that of a mob numbering tens of thousands. The action will have wider resonance if the onlooker can identify with it, and its underlying values—the Ploughshares action on British Aerospace fighter planes is a classic example of this.[3] Protest and civil disobedience will be a crucial part of social change, up to and including storming the citadels of power. But they are not the change itself.

There is another meaning to the old saying, 'The revolution will not be televised.' Not only is revolution not a spectacle, but something we participate in—and it is neither fast nor sudden. It is not one event, nor is the widest screen TV wide enough to capture its breadth. It is slow, it is piecemeal and it is mundane. Just like the destruction of the earth itself, it is in the cumulative day-to-day actions of millions. Andy Goldsworthy, the landscape artist, captured pockets of land inside walls and watched how they grew and changed when the sheep that usually grazed them could not get access to them. He concluded, "Sheep are powerful things. With their teeth they shape the land." We normally regard sheep as an icon of powerlessness—and yet it is the sheep in all of us that will ultimately settle the fate of the world. Every age will have its tiny minority of nonconformists and visionaries; but only when their vision becomes part of the daily experience of millions will it have any power.

The Role of the Individual
The awareness that social change requires action throughout society can make any individual feel small—and if it flattens fantasies of 'if I ruled the world',

BANKING ON IT: MAKING THE LINKS

It is remarkable how long it took interest to become a significant feature of economies. When you consider the limited nature of money, and its scarcity, it should surely be inevitable that those possessing it should see the advantage in charging to lend it to others. Indeed, this has probably always happened on a small scale. But the use of money as capital seems to be a modern invention.

There are a number of possible reasons for this. The close link between the military and money may well have meant that the repeated issues of coin to finance campaigns invariably caused inflation, which outstripped any return that interest might bring. It may also have been the case that the dynamics of power-from (from the monarch, from the emperor or from the deity) involved too tight a hand on the economy. There simply was not enough room for innovation or autonomous action. With such a singular source for social power, money could not develop a life of its own. Finally, there is the force of religious opposition to interest. Christianity and Islam both maintained a very effective ban on usury for centuries. This is very well illustrated in *The Merchant of Venice*. Shakespeare has Shylock say of Antonio:

> "I hate him for he is a Christian
> But more than that in low simplicity
> He lends out money gratis, and brings down
> The rate of usance here with us in Venice.
> If I can catch him once upon the hip,
> I will feed fat the ancient grudge I bear him.
> He hates our sacred nation, and he rails,
> Even there where merchants most do congregate,
> On me, my bargains, and my well-won thrift,
> Which he calls interest. Cursed be my tribe,
> If I forgive him!"

We may hazard a guess at Shakespeare's bias, and that of his audience, but this does illustrate that in the early modern era, the rise in mercantilism aided by seafaring technology was pushing to their limits the traditional taboos around the use of money. Although mighty empires were in existence all over the world, from Central America to Africa, it seems to have been in Western Europe where a combination of population pressures, short growing seasons, military competition and a protestant work ethic combined to make increasing demands on money. As they did, the bastions of power-from increasingly felt the heat.

In the sixteenth and seventeenth centuries, independent bases of financial power were rising in the cities. They were lending at higher and higher rates of interest to governments desperately in need of money to finance their armies.

In England, the crisis over taxation went unresolved for so long that it was a factor in the civil war.[4] Military competition was becoming technological competition, and this was extremely expensive. The cycles of power with which we are familiar today were starting to come together; the missing link was the systematic investment of finance in technological development, leading to further investment and further accumulation.

Christopher Hill describes the contradiction between banking and feudalism. "Banks had been viewed with suspicion by the governments of Charles II and James II. 'Where there is a bank', Harrington had said, 'ten to one there is a commonwealth'. Sweden was indeed the only monarchy in which a bank existed, and this was small and insignificant. . . . The only chance for a bank was a revolution,' Thorold Rogers put it."[5]

And a revolution was indeed what led to the formation of the Bank of England—though other European countries managed a similar process with less upheaval. The feudal age could be said to have come to an end when money was freed from all restriction and started to do what it did best; growing and concentrating, growing and concentrating, turning the Earth into commodities and people into workers. The growth of money in this way looked like prosperity, and yet it was a restless prosperity. Leisure time could only diminish as more and more of life become commodified, since any slackening in the pace of work would mean someone more tireless was moving ahead. Power-over had arrived, and could not rest until every corner of the world and every aspect of our lives had been colonized.

then that is no bad thing. But I don't believe that individuals have been the pawns of massive historical forces, nor that the inspiration that makes someone an innovator is pure luck or coincidence. There is still room for the social activist—someone who, by skill and persistence, makes a difference.

Equally, I don't want to suggest that any individual can make the world dance to their tune by sheer talent. What I want to stress is the need for connections—and the dramatic, synergistic effect of making a crucial linkage. The person who completes a circuit unlocks the potential of the nascent system, and can see exponential growth as that potential is realized. That is not to say they held or controlled all that power. They simply allowed the potential energy to discharge. But they can justly claim credit for the skill and perception that told them the connection was there to be made—as well as taking responsibility for the consequences. After all, you may see that there is an untapped reserve, or a niche in the market—but are you really certain you know what form the resulting system will take?

The social entrepreneur is a recurring figure in history, but not always a prominent one. Often, they do not wind up heading the organizations they founded, nor fronting the movements they brought together. And even more often they feel betrayed by those who do seem to take their creations down unexpected paths. But this is rarely the betrayal they take it for—only an unanticipated but logical development.

The 'Innovation Diffusion Game' developed by Alan AtKisson and the Context Institute in the US is a useful way to learn about the roles that individuals play in social change. It is a learning tool that takes the form of a role-playing game, with participants given a character and goals to act out. A 'problem issue' is given as the subject matter, and the game area represents somewhere relevant to that—for example, if the issue is consumerism, the players might be asked to pretend they are in a shopping mall. Out of twenty players, roles might be allocated as follows:

Innovator: the innovator is the one who is driven to experiment and come up with new ideas. Having come up with an idea, innovators then have to make contact with change agents and see if they can sell it to them. They can approach more mainstream characters—but they will probably only alarm them.

2 x Change agents: they are frustrated with the way things are, and open to alternatives. They've done the mainstream lifestyle, but they're very dissatisfied with it. If the innovator comes up with an idea that their experience suggests would be workable, they find the transformers in the mainstream and see if they can sell it to them.

2 x Mainstream transformers: they are basically happy to go along with the way things are; their main concern is just getting by. But they do have some nagging doubts about the set-up, and they'll listen to new ideas and maybe even try them—as long as it doesn't feel weird, or get in the way of meeting their needs.

3 x Mainstream laggards: they don't like change, and they like to know where they stand. For this reason they'll resist and avoid any new idea. But if it feels like everyone else is getting into it, they'll have to join in—and then they won't want to change back.

2 x Reactionary: they are actively benefiting from the way things are, and will work with other reactionaries to oppose change by (nearly) all means necessary. Having said that, they may be tempted to switch sides if it is clear that they've lost touch with the mainstream, because they need it so badly.

Iconoclast: they aren't very practical, but can see that the status quo is a good target for mockery. They will be a useless and unreliable partners for innovators and change agents, but could be a thorn in the side of the reactionaries.

Curmudgeon: they grumble about the way things are, but that's all. They've no real interest in talking about alternatives.

Spiritual recluse: they circulate widely, offering anyone who'll listen general truths and spiritual insights.

Of course, it's only a game. But it illustrates the way that bearers of new ideas tend to be outsiders, out of touch with the mainstream. It is the alliance between these creative thinkers and those more embedded in day-to-day reali-

THE POVERTY OF RICHES

Adopting a critical position to money seems to many to be a step too far. For many, money is surely too fundamental to our lives to be rejected. Shouldn't power be about taking the money from those who are misusing it, and putting it to better uses? Earlier, I argued for the need to build viable co-operative businesses, and adopt all the tactics of market research, business planning and investment that would bring capital under community control. Why then do I now say that as individuals we should seek to reduce our involvement with it? This view smacks of 'poverty consciousness'—a determination to remain pure by making sure you suffer. This kind of asceticism is accused of driving people with perfectly reasonable and harmless aspirations away from radical politics. Someone who works hard is entitled to a fair reward. Who will join a movement that opposes money as such?

Although it is certainly true that many radical co-ops struggle to pay decent wages, I am not advocating that we plan for that. I do believe in minimum hourly wages, and I have found by experience that any co-op unable to give a decent reward for the work put into it will surely fail. I'm not suggesting that we tolerate self-exploitation or persevere with ailing businesses, but rather that we look at what rewards we can gain other than money—time, peace, other forms of credit and recognition.

But this doesn't really answer the question. It may be very saintly to live one's whole life at a very basic level, living in the same shoebox room and eating the same lentils day in and day out, but most of us aren't saints. We want our lives to develop and improve; we want to work to support a family, gain space for leisure and recreation, broaden our minds with travel, and live in an increasingly comfortable and uplifting environment.

At least, I certainly do. So how do I expect to do that on a fraction of the average income? When I moved into Cornerstone Housing Co-op, my income remained unchanged. But I no longer had to go to the laundrette, because Cornerstone owned two washing machines. I didn't have to pay a lot for my internet access, faxes or photocopying: we shared these facilities. I was saved from catastrophes in numerous burglaries by the insurance paid for by the co-op. My fuel bills went down, because the co-op invested in insulation.

By building the assets of the community, we see solid benefits in our own lives. We don't have to have private, personal ownership of something to benefit. A common good can be just as good—better, even. Our incentive to work hard and provide professional services is our share of the community's wealth. This is sustainable because it is more efficient, it does not reward greed and it is not competitive. But this, too, is insufficient. Most of us also need something in our lives that is ours alone, independent and personal.

For that, I would suggest that Local Exchange Trading Schemes provide a qualitatively different way of rewarding work. I actually hope that my income in pounds sterling (or worse still, Euros) will in time be replaced by LETS. Money does not necessarily give you power over your own life. All that you can be certain of is that it gives you power over others. And although we may in the short term escape the power-over of others by getting some for ourselves, in the long term it digs us all deeper into trouble. Our aspirations should be to empowering solutions—no less tangible and satisfying, but focussed on building supportive relations with others rather than trying to scramble up on to their shoulders.

ties that brings about real change. For the most part, we like to drift—to find our place in the labyrinthine mechanisms of social order. Even those of us who believe we live independent lives must admit that without some shared experience and common aspiration to relate to, we are far from powerful. Of course, although the innovator might start the process of change, the final outcome will often be a surprise or a disappointment to him or her. A mainstream settlement will invariably look very different to the ideal conception.

The six Rochdale pioneers could not have known that their small retail co-operative would become one of the largest retail outlets in the country, and inspire other co-operators all over the world. Nor could the early co-operators in Mondragon have known that their co-operatives would be a significant part of Spain's industry in years to come. The man who inspired those first steps, Robert Owen, did harbour such dreams—but only when his ideas were connected to their determination was the potential realized, and it wasn't in his lifetime. An effective social change movement has to tolerate both the creativity and frustration of the innovators and the compromises and hesitancy of the change agents.

Learning Well

The key is to understand how learning takes place. Many political activists see their work in terms of education and communication, and speak of providing society with the information that will liberate it. And yet, perhaps surprisingly, very little politics deals with how people learn—how they gain the skills of power and gain the ability to use it in different ways. Learning is a key capacity that humans have, and it lies behind much of our ability to support complex, differentiated social systems. If we want to change those systems, we need to understand how people learn different ways of living and working.

Firstly, people always move from the known to the unknown. The learning process begins when a step presents itself that links established knowledge, something familiar and understood, with the new, difficult or radical concept. Motivation is also important—without the sense of a need that will be met, even an easy move from known to unknown will be difficult. The first shift towards gaining and practising a social change skill, then, is seeing a step from the familiar to the unfamiliar that is consistent with the learner's motivation. Maybe for some, the social goal will be sufficient inducement—this may apply to those who have developed a strong identification of their own aspirations with a political objective—but for most the motivation must come from a tangible, immediate gain.[6]

Even with motivation, the learning experience must be one that builds up a solid pathway in the memory. 'Dale's Cone of Experience' shows how different types of experience are more or less likely to be remembered. Dale found that when the cues are merely verbal, the learning experience is not very effective. For instance, only 10% of what people read, and 20% of what they hear, is likely to be remembered. Considering that most political propaganda begins and ends with words, it is staggering that so much has been achieved through it; the motivations of the audience may actually be greater than we think.

When the experience is more comprehensive, the remembering is superior. A moving picture can achieve 30-40% recall—when we actually see the thing to be learned, and the level of abstraction is much lower, the information is much easier to recall. However, to achieve higher levels of recall, something more is needed. The learner must actually be a participant. We remember 70% of what we say and write. You may ask, how can we possibly be learning anything if we can say it ourselves? The key is the idea of moving from known to unknown. If the step is small, it is possible to pose a question in such a way that the answer comes back easily—and is learned reliably.

It is feedback that ensures that the memory is repeatedly accessed and acted upon—when we can actually see the outcome of our actions and modify those actions to improve it. Repeated, sustained practice is the only form of political education worthy of the name. However, when a plateau is reached in the learning curve, it is crucial to have someone who asks the question, or prompts the action, that triggers a new phase of learning. That is the role of the social activist—not to lecture, but to stimulate and reward learning.

Finally, we remember 90% of what we say as we do something. When we do not just describe it, but actually do it, we learn rapidly and effectively. For this reason, people who have joined a credit union or a Local Exchange Trading Scheme have learned more about the nature of money than an entire library on economics could have taught them.[7] They have actually practised two different ways of measuring worth, contribution and wealth, and are able to assess the pros and cons of both.

The Hundredth Monkey

There are social activists working everywhere, and a great many are needed. Some are creating connections at a local level, and others trying to mobilize millions of dollars into social change. It is simply not possible to say that those

LETS—A CURRENCY BEYOND POWER

My relationship with money is one of mutual suspicion. Money is wary of me; as a low level consumer, money is reluctant to approach me, and my costs are higher than for most (a survey of utilities in the UK found that poor consumers were paying up to 30% more for each unit than rich consumers, because they could not pre-pay, or use direct debits or buy in bulk). I, in turn, am wary of money. Survival would be impossible without it, but I mistrust the claims it makes on my time, the divisions it opens between me and other people, and the responsibilities that its accoutrements place on me.

For me, then, there is a great deal of satisfaction in trading in a different way. If I want help redecorating my room, or I need a dental checkup, I can use my LETS directory to put me in touch with someone locally who will accept a cheque from my LETS account for the work. Meanwhile, if I put in a day of phoning advertisers for a local freesheet, 'Green Events', I will get paid in LETS for my time. Green Events, in turn, receives part payment for some of its adverts in LETS.

So what's the difference? The short answer is this. When we use cheques for a transaction in our bank account, it refers to the real, tangible, physical money we put in there. The LETS cheques refer to nothing but themselves. The transaction is recorded on our account with no real object to guarantee it. We have drawn on the collective goodwill of the community, and nothing else. If it seems like a cop-out to suggest that LETS is different to money, consider this: some well established LETS schemes have stopped recording transactions and continued as 'gift economies'. When the bond of trust is this well established, and your community sufficiently secure, you can get what you need for free.

This has a number of consequences. Firstly, when you are paid, you are really paid. The cheque cannot bounce, the bank cannot fail, and the person paying you cannot run out of money. Secondly, you can make a purchase regardless of how much or how little is in your account—unless people begin to think you are taking from the community without putting anything back, in which case they may refuse to trade with you. And if you are overdrawn, there is no interest; you create the credit just by writing the cheque. There is no cause or reason for accumulation, and no advantage in concentration. This is a currency shorn of power—or to put it more accurately, it is a medium of empowerment. There is no rich, no poor—just community.

LETS is a new idea. Developed in Canada in the 1980s by Michael Linton, it came to Britain in the 1990s and grew exponentially with the backing of the Green Party and other Green movement activists. They saw it as a radical anti-poverty initiative, a community-building device and a form of trade which could respect environmental limits. So if there was such a ready audience for it, why did it not happen sooner? Part of the answer is undoubtedly that it benefited from the inspiration of Michael Linton, who not only pioneered it but also pack-aged it in a very accessible way and spread the idea far and wide.

But this is not totally sufficient. We must also note that several other people had independently developed very similar ideas, which might equally have succeeded. The conditions seemed to be right for this breakthrough—so what had changed? Firstly, the cultural conditions—money is gaining an aura of ugliness and evil, and behaving in ways which no longer seem sane or desir-able. Whether it is currency speculators, yuppies or consumerism, it is not a pretty sight. There is an openness to alternatives.

Secondly, the LETS chequebook seems important. It is a simple copy of what everyone is doing with their personal chequing accounts, and yet if you think about it, it is fundamental to the system in a way that it is not to the money system. If you couldn't train people to write cheques, you would have had to issue notes—and the problems of scarcity would return. Of course, the pioneers could have introduced the idea of the chequebook themselves, but it would have made the task much harder.

So it was the widespread introduction of personal chequebooks—a rela-tively recent development—that laid the foundations for LETS. And cheques would not have been possible without the rise of the information economy. In short, I am trying to suggest that large scale, structural developments do make radical change possible—but not inevitable. There is a key role to be played by the social change activists—just as there had to be someone who would fight for banks in the seventeenth century. Could they have fought for LETS instead then? Actually, I think they could—and history might have been very different Of course, they would probably have failed—but then it is too early to say that we have succeeded today.

working with larger resources are playing a more significant role. After all, the 'hundredth monkey' syndrome comes into play: it may only be one more com-munity credit union, but if it is the one that completes the critical mass of accu-mulation that allows all the credit unions to federate and pool their resources, or establish a community bank, then the effect seems far greater. Every small achievement is laying the groundwork on which larger ones will be erected. Every little helps—provided there is an awareness of the potential of a critical mass.

In trying to visualize the dynamic of a social change, the dominant model is one of decision-making—we imagine society as a collective consciousness considering different courses of action and taking a decision. I don't believe this is a useful way to regard it, because social organisms simply do not behave like this. There is no 'seat of consciousness' where the decision is taken, nor is a course of action pursued consistently before or after the 'moment of deci-sion'. Instead of social psychology, I would suggest that the epidemiology of ideas is the appropriate discipline for research into social change.

In the language of epidemiology, the agent of infection spreads through 'vectors', endlessly reproducing and reinfecting. I would suggest that ideas, practices, modes of behaviour, model relationships and dynamics of power are the infective agents, capable of growing, reproducing and transmitting themselves through the vectors. An epidemic is said to occur at surprisingly low levels of infection—as few as 400 per 100,000 new cases a day, for an infection lasting only a few days. The point is that even such low levels provide the possibility of exponential growth—a longer lasting 'infection' would need even less than this. The vectors for social change are people, as with the study of disease, but also structures and organizations. Radical ideas can sometimes be seen to run riot through a community of organizations, leaving them changed and better adapted to their environment. Like disease, the nature of social change is such that the infective agent may well overwhelm the organization it infects, finding fertile ground for growth and reinfection until its base camp collapses under internal contradictions. Unlike disease, the infectious material of ideas is not wholly destructive, but can also generate new social structures to replace those it has paralysed, and can cause rapid expansion as well as attrition. Some organizations may not be affected one way or the other; they may simply be carriers for the new forms of power.

Malcolm Gladwell is one writer who believes that societies change in this dynamic way: he refers to the small level of disturbance that can trigger exponential change as 'the tipping point'.[8] He says that the level of the tipping point is determined by three main factors: the 'stickiness' of the infection (How attractive, compelling or infectious the new phenomenon is), the connectedness of the vectors (Are the carriers highly mobile, able to cross boundaries and link together different communities? Such people will have disproportionate influence in social change) and the context (Is the environment open to the infection? Do mechanisms and processes exist that will facilitate the spread?).

However, the spread of change is no automatic process. There has to be an opening, or a weakness, before even the most viable alternative vision can succeed. Just as the spread of an illness may begin with a depressed immune system, we have to ask what conditions make it possible for a message of change to be communicable.

In strategic terms, this suggests that the two initial factors of greatest importance are the heightening of 'felt' deprivation, and a clear contrast, or 'cleavage', between the movement for change and the establishment. In other words, our experiences have to be shown to be the result of systematic, rather than isolated causes, and as such can only be addressed by an organization that opposes the whole system and not just part of it. Having established this basic message, the problem is a tactical one of making the most of the available opportunities to promote it. Wolfgang Rudig's study of new party emergence, particularly European Green Parties, is also instructive. He finds that political science and social science models of social movements largely agree. The process begins with a stimulus, a problem that presents a challenge. The deprivation that this has caused may be experienced more strongly by some social groups or under some circumstances; and the solutions advocated may open up cleavages that polarize opinion. Whether this will lead to the emergence of a viable movement depends on the opportunities. There are social facilitators, like education, political awareness, shifting values and occupations. There are institutional facilitators, like electoral systems, bureaucracies and laws. And there are political facilitators, such as alliances, the behaviour of established forces and the strength of adversaries. I think the model lacks an economic and technological dimension, but it illustrates the way a new idea is driven by problems and its progress hastened by social opportunities. In the light of this, we can start to pin down more clearly what we mean by strategy. I think this is best done by making a distinction between strategy, tactics and survival. Survival is the prerequisite for everything else, but it is a very simple mode of thinking. It is simply the repetition of basic patterns of behaviour that have proved functional in the past. It is barely conscious of the environment within which one exists. Tactical thinking is more aware, and is the standard mode of most activists. It involves adaptation to the environment—seeing what opportunities are there and making the most of them. It is alert to trends and anticipates events. Strategic thinking goes one step further. Rather than responding to the environment, it seeks to change it. It is a long-term process of deploying resources not to directly achieve an end, but to establish a situation in which those ends are more likely to be achieved. Consequently, it frequently seems to make sacrifices, much like a gambit in chess. It, too, is alert to trends, but seeks to hijack, subvert or defuse them. Strategic action is at its most effective when it is making connections in an actual or potential circuit of power; when it is action in the fourth dimension of power.

Good in a Crisis

The most obvious trend that is relevant to our present strategies is the actual process of ecological degradation. From climate change to falling per capita harvests, the attrition of ecosystems is the principal 'push' to social change. Will it create an environment in which a sustainable dynamic of power-to can spread and replace consumerism and greed?

Those pursuing this line approach it in two different ways. Firstly, there is Sandy Irvine's grim conclusion that Greens will come to power not in order to forestall disaster, but because the disaster they predicted has come about: their task will not be to save the earth but to pick up the pieces.[9] Less grim is this comment from Andy Dobson: "Greens might argue that what is new to our particular time is that the external limits imposed by the earth circumscribe

DYNAMICS OF ECONOMIC CHANGE

So can LETS catalyse a major shift in economic power? The diagram opposite is a BOTMS (bordering on the misleadingly simple) depiction which contrasts the power-over economy and the empowering economy—both of which should be seen in the context of their roles in the wider social systems (see Chapter 8). Both economies have certain functions of trade, credit and ownership that need to be facilitated. These are the basic agreed relationships and processes between people and commodities that have to exist in order to routinely allocate resources—the essential function of an economy.

However, the type of economy which meets these functions through LETS is significantly different to one using hard currency. It has a dynamic of sufficiency rather than growth; it has no role for shareholders or moneylenders; it builds supportive links in a community, rather than a competitive struggle to gain control of capital. This alternative economy exists only in a sparse, skeletal form at present. It is being sustained more through the effects of social change activists than through its own dynamic.

However, there are a number of powerful inputs working in its favour. Radical Routes has already shown the effectiveness of highly focussed ethical investment. The danger here is that the use of hard currency to invest and reinvest can draw co-operatives into a cycle of personal acquisition. In Mondragon, the investment each member has to make in the co-op to join has risen to incredible levels due to the success of the businesses. The radical potential of co-ops has to be combined with LETS to make an effective community economy.

Ethical consumerism is another useful source of support—but it is offset by 'leakage' where radical businesses cannot find ethical sources for their materials, and have to trade on unequal terms with the grey economy. Anti-consumerism limits the ability of the grey economy to expand, and protects the environmental base on which both old and new economies depend.

Finally, the changes in social processes of aspiration and belonging play an important role. Depending on whether they reinforce the dominant culture (hegemonic) or undermine it (counter-hegemonic) they can create forms of behaviour and organization which build either capital or community. It is the balances between these various forces that determine which economy will rise and which will fail.

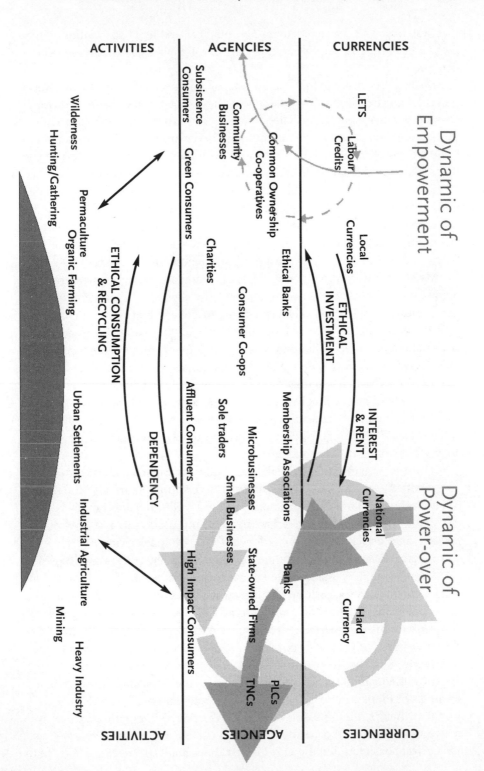

that system's room for manoeuvre. There is less and less space within which both to produce and to fulfil the expectations of consumption that the system generates."[10]

Dealing first with Irvine's point, one of the great difficulties that radical movements have faced in the past is that they come to power during times of total desperation, and immediately have to cope with starvation (the French Revolution), war (the Russian Revolution) or environmental collapse (as the Ethiopian government faced in the 1990s). All too often, the harshness of the times have caused ideals to be abandoned, risky stop-gap measures to be adopted, and compromises to be made. Certainly, this is a possibility that Greens need to be prepared for, but to plan for it risks firstly an interminable wait for the end of the world; secondly, a situation in which liberation and empowerment are all but impossible; and thirdly, hardening ourselves against destruction and suffering in the belief that things must get worse before they get better.

My objections to the other strategy, of taking advantage of the shrinking possibilities as the resource base is depleted, are slightly different. Firstly, it too has attendant risks; there is every reason to believe that rather than going steadily downhill, the decay will be characterized by prolonged periods of relative stability followed by sudden crises. This follows from systems and chaos theory; an integrated system will be able to regulate itself, up to a point which cannot be predicted; it will then flip into a new stable state without any further warning. This kind of progress allows proponents of technical fixes to gain credibility; a renewed period of stability looks like a success. Additionally, there is the possibility we might slip from 'too early to take advantage' to 'too late to do anything about it' very suddenly.

It further assumes that people are really experiencing these problems. Those with the most devastating patterns of consumption are also those who receive information via industrial mass media; a medium that is rapidly becoming a better way of obscuring reality than communicating it. The level of distraction and detachment from reality offered by a television set today is sufficient to distance oneself from or blot out totally the suffering of those on the receiving end of environmental collapse. The technological means of enhancing this vast spectacle are increasing continually; possibly, developments in 'virtual reality' (a sort of all round interactive television) will herald a qualitative jump in this vast spectacle. We should not underestimate the ability of our elected representatives and favourite performers to tell us what we want to hear. Is it the case that the Greens will be seen as the only ones able to rescue the situation? It is equally likely that people will turn to the rationalist technocrats and scientists or to the irrationalist strong leaders and faith healers.

Nevertheless, the meaning of threats like the disintegrating ozone layer and the growing greenhouse effect is to suggest that a Green society is not only a historical possibility, but the only historical possibility. If there is any truth to the 'ecological cleavage' theory of Green political mobilization, it suggests that environmental crisis will always be a spur to action for Green partisans, and a cause of the emergence of new parties and groupings. However, this does not mean it will determine their progress: other factors become relevant here.

One useful categorization of the different stages of successful social movements is the 'Movement Action Plan' developed by Bill Moyer out of experiences in the US anti-nuclear movement.[11] There are two features of MAP that make it particularly useful for us. Firstly, it has no end point, but rather consists of simultaneous struggles towards a series of progressively more radical goals on several different fronts—reflecting the diverse and continual progress of a Green strategy. A goal is adopted that we believe will build empowerment, and we begin to begin to build a campaign to achieve it. At the beginning, we will appear to be cranks; but as Schumacher points out, cranks make revolutions. The goal must be big enough to make a difference and to motivate the activists that will struggle to win it; but it must be small enough to be within reach, and not a tantalizing dream.

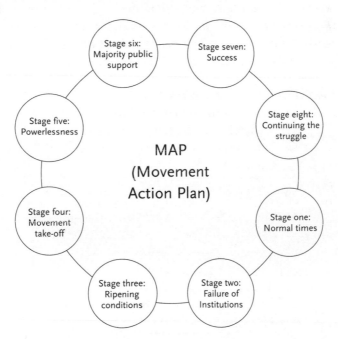

Secondly, he deals with the phenomenon of takeoff, and the seemingly contradictory stage of powerlessness that follows it. "After a year or two, the high hopes of movement take-off seems inevitably to turn into despair. Most activists lose their faith that success is just around the corner and come to believe that it is never going to happen. . . . Most surprising is the fact that this identity crisis of powerlessness and failure happens when the movement is outrageously successful."[12] The Euro election result of 1989 illustrates this for Greens; the phenomenal result was followed by a sense of anticlimax and directionlessness. Moyer identifies the causes of this as unreal expectations; the failure of powerholders to simply capitulate in the face of such success; disappointment that the take-off stage—a time of unsustainable activity—is short lived; and failure of the mass media to recognize the movement or credit it with concrete achievements. Burnout, organizational crisis, and directionless action are all likely in this stage. However, Moyer argues, if groups consolidate and provide personal and political support, retain a commitment to non-violence, adopt models of organization and leadership based on empowerment, move from protesters to long life social change agents, and develop a wider strategic understanding, then the movement can recognize success when it is being presented as failure, and move on to Stage 6: majority support.[13]

Each of these cycles represents the creation or breaking of a new linkage in the networks of power. It will never be possible to say, 'This is the end; we will have arrived in utopia when we win this campaign.' Each little victory will have shifted the balance a little, and strengthened the dynamic of empowerment at the expense of power-over. There is no end to the continual succession of tactical goals within the overall strategy of social change. Each one creates the opportunities for the next; but every time we are starting from square one.

Focuses of Activity for the Next Ten Years

At this stage I want to use the rough map of the emerging dynamic of power-to that developed in Chapter 8 to identify what targets we should set for the next few years. The overall social system we are trying to build looks something like this:

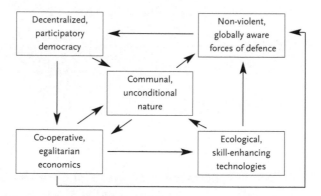

We would be missing the point if we interpreted this to mean that social change will result if we build a co-operative economy, or develop soft technology, or any of the other subsystems. In a systems model it is the processes and the connections that make the difference, rather than the nodes and subsystems. We are trying to create hegemony for sustainable thinking, and that is an emergent property of the system as a whole, rather than any one part of the system. Rather than taking it as a whole, however, we can see more clearly where to start if we just look at each of the main processes in turn.

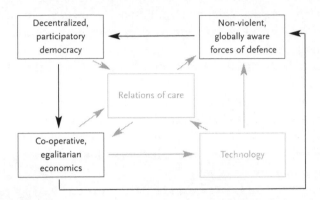

This is the cycle in which globally aware NVDA builds support for policies adopted through participatory, decentralized and democratic forms of governance, which in turn establish the conditions for the growth of co-operative and egalitarian enterprises, which provide a base of support for further NVDA. It is potentially a very powerful system, at least as much as its power-over equivalent.

Green campaigners have scored some spectacular successes in the last quarter of the last century. In Britain, a massive road building programme collapsed in the face of determined opposition. Significant reforms were made by Green-minded politicians, in response to the growing pressure from below. Green parties emerged all over Europe, in many cases evolving out of protest groups. The link between protest and politics has been made and has delivered results; but it is a linear cause-and-effect, with no positive feedback, and this is starting to show. Campaigners are dropping out, exhausted and unsupported; protest is seen as a youthful indulgence that cannot be sustained alongside adult responsibilities. Politicians are getting wise to the game; Green issues are neatly parcelled up and kept separate from the mainstream of policy. More radical policies are blocked by fears that they will 'harm the economy'. All these are classic symptoms of a political movement that lacks an economic base.

There are some encouraging examples. The Energy Conservation Act, largely the work of the UK Green Party, creates significant openings for new Green businesses, and support by local government for LETS has helped it to grow. But the alternative economy is tiny (for many, it is a hobby rather than a serious livelihood), and fragmented (most co-ops don't trade in LETS, most LETS members aren't in credit unions, and no credit unions are lending to help start co-operatives).

Meanwhile, the lack of a mainstream economic base is weakening Green campaigns. The activists who stick with it in the face of sustained poverty and marginalization include many that are somewhat obsessive, puritan characters, who find it hard to connect with the mainstream. Despite their undoubted courage and commitment, if they become a sort of sect or fundamentalist religion, they will never have deep roots in the community. Recent investigations into the animal rights movement in the UK found ALF activists turning to violence against people, and lying to their supporters about it. Without a clear commitment to non-violence, direct action will become the preserve of an irrelevant and persecuted minority—or worse still, reproduce coercive governance in a kind of 'eco-fascism'. I believe that connections with a Green economic base would bring a more diverse and mainstream character to the direct movement, and would build closer links between protesters and the wider community.

So what kind of initiatives would fill these 'missing links' between politics, economics and NVDA? Firstly, co-operatives that conduct a profitable trade, at the same time as employing and otherwise supporting activists, are needed. Ethical consumers are now numerous enough to buy eco-products like organic produce, renewable energy and recycled goods. What this brings in resources and security will more than make up for the time activists will have to put in. Secondly, Green political activists need to work hard to gain reforms benefiting co-operatives and the alternative economy. Preventing LETS earnings from being taxed in hard currency; getting more support for recycling and renewable energy; relieving co-operatives and community businesses from taxation and red tape. Those same activists then need to make sure that it is their members and supporters that take advantage of the opportunities arising.

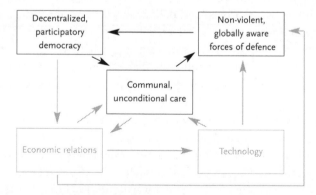

This second cycle also addresses the limited support available for activists, and the need for political agents to create indirect support. I can offer two examples of how this takes place. The UK housing co-operative sector is a significant support for protest. An increasing number of NVDA activists, unable to buy a home and unwelcome with most landlords, have joined communes, where relations of care are not specialized and patriarchal but collective and convivial. This is the kind of emotional and physical support which activists badly need to have available, as a counterweight to the extreme vulnerability of protest. Housing Co-ops have over the years benefited from campaigns for social housing and in support of the homeless; but today this pressure for social housing is increasingly being diverted into paternalistic housing associations and hostels. The difficulty here is a weak political voice for participation in social policy, and it does seem to be the case that grassroots campaigners have not actively supported those politicians that do support it. As a result, sanctuary and respite for those campaigners is rare and under-resourced.

Another example of radical community is in local groups fighting unwanted developments. It is worth noting that the most successful and sustained direct action campaigns have been those where local support has been so strong that the local community has effectively been providing welfare and social services to the protesters. In many of the UK roads protests, local people made their homes available to activists in need of warmth, a soft bed or a bath; donated food and medical supplies; and offered emotional support and solidarity. Much of this was organized through participatory, democratic residents' groups. Future protest needs to build on the parallel political structures emerging in 'communities in resistance', and their ability to support people independently of the welfare state.

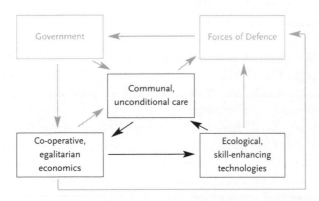

The third cycle is that of reproducing the alternative economy. Here, co-operative economic relations select 'soft' technologies and convivial lifestyles which enable local, participatory and empowering relations of care. These in turn provide the conditions of production for a co-operative economy—an empowered workforce, healthcare and social security.

Alternative technology and permaculture design are only just beginning to deliver benefits to the people who live with them—but their potential has hardly begun to be tapped. Sustainable building design could transform the home and work environment of those in the movement—many of whom are presently experiencing fuel poverty, damp, overcrowding and 'sick building syndrome'. Demand among 'Green consumers' for alternative therapies (natural, gentle, dealing with the 'whole person') may well begin to feed back into the economy more stable, relaxed and healthy workers. The growing range of training courses that the alternative technologists and permaculturists are running are developing into a programme of lifelong learning for Greens—building the skills that will be needed by the Green economy. By its very nature, this process will take longer to deliver tangible benefits, and will be harder to assess than the first two. Nevertheless, it is just as important a part of the jigsaw.

The more extended processes described in Chapter 8 can also be examined for guides to action. The link between alternative technology and NVDA, for instance, will be a key factor in building a dynamic of 'radical technology'. Protest camps powered by wind generators, diesel vans transporting activists powered by biofuels, low impact housing for occupying sites—alternative technology is not only lighter on the earth, but in its low cost and simplicity it empowers grassroots activism.

In all these dynamics, social change activists have to think of politics in a radically different way. It is not the acts of strong leaders, the laws passed by parliaments or the number of votes cast. It is much broader, and it demands political organizations that are embedded in the rising culture they seek to build. There is a model of 'total politics' practised by some radical parties in Latin America, or Sinn Fein in Northern Ireland (not that I am endorsing the other tactics they have employed). It is based on deep roots in a community, with the party seen not as representatives but as a mutual aid organization solving a range of local problems. If we remain wedded to the idea of politics as a specialized activity, then the only base of support for political activity will be the military industrial complex.

To sum up: social change arises not out of individual innovations and developments, but out of the dynamic relationship between all of them. By designing alternative social systems, we can set in train processes that have their own momentum. The sense that so many political activists have of trying to move a mountain arises largely from the fragmented nature of their work. With more interconnections, particularly those with critical functions in social systems, positive feedback can be liberated to give instead the sense of pushing at an opening door.

The Way and the Warrior [14]
Herbert Marcuse writes: "Social theory is concerned with the historical alternatives which haunt the established society as subversive tendencies and

MAKING CHANGES

Economic alternatives are insufficient if they do not link up with other forms of radical action. What kind of organization is capable of straddling these boundaries? We use all manner of legal structures—trusts, companies, membership organizations, unincorporated clubs and informal groups—all of which tend to do some things well and others not so well. I would argue that the following is a useful checklist: most organizations that are capable of linking up the different components of a social change movement will exhibit these characteristics.

• *Co-operative*. Generally speaking, an empowering organization will be mutual and democratic: the international co-operative principles are a good guide to what this means in practice.

• *Human scale*. Organizations that grow too large lose the element of participation and develop ossified élites at the top. Where large scale co-operation is required, federal rather than centralized structures will best preserve local affinity.

• *Autonomous*. Although radical organizations will work with other groups, and be active in multiple networks, they are accountable only to their own consciences.

• *Non-violent*. Conflicts are resolved peacefully, both internally and externally.

• *Goods and services*. They will not be dependent on state or charity, but will provide things that people really need and are willing to pay for. This would be a break from the tradition of radical organizations, which have always thought they have better things to do than get their hands dirty with commerce. But this is the point of connection with the unconverted; it is the source of self-reliance for political activists; and it opens the possibility of far greater growth for the movement. A society can only support a few radical philanthropic groups: it can support many thousands of trading businesses. Combining a trade with political action is not easy; it may in fact be that there are two separate organizations with largely overlapping membership. However it is achieved, the point is that the radical organization must be firmly based in an economy that meets people's needs.

• *Ecological*. Permaculture design principles are an excellent guide to designing organizations that are sustainable in every sense of the word.

• *Subversive*. Political education is given a high priority; such organizations are alert to processes of power and use them creatively. Their internal discourse is politicized and critical.

These seven characteristics form the mnemonic 'CHANGES'. I believe that this will prove to be an effective model for political activists in the future.

forces. The values attributed to them become facts when they are translated into reality by historical practice. . . . But here, industrial society confronts the critique with a situation which seems to deprive it of its very basis. Technical progress, extended to a whole system of domination and co-ordination, creates forms of life (and of power) which appear to . . . defeat or refute all protest." [15]

If I believed that this appearance was reality, I would despair. However, our hope is that the system of domination cannot exist without the survival of a similar system of organic, ecological power. The further development of the systems of domination are becoming increasingly restricted by the decaying resource base and the impact of this on communities. It is in this context that opportunities arise for change. There is no certainty how this will unfold—a progressive collapse of our species is just as possible as an ecological renaissance. It is the efforts of social change activists that will make the difference—their perception, their courage, their determination.

The great strength of this as a strategy is that it respects our needs. We cannot give up our lives for the revolution, and endure endless suffering in the hope that things must get better before they get worse. We can only keep to a moral path if it delivers our basic needs at the same time—community, liberty, sustenance. This is why it is so important to see social change in the co-operatives, the LETS schemes and the communes as well as in the political parties and the protests. They are the reservoirs of healing for the activists on the front line—a way of meeting needs without slipping into contradiction and co-option.

The idea that political involvement can—and should—be fun, is a relatively new one, and yet it should be self-evident that without a shared sense of exhilaration and adventure, of creativity and community, any political movement will founder and dissolve. There is an organization called the Association of Autonomous Astronauts, whose slogan is: "It is necessary to attempt the impossible in order to achieve the absurd." This leads them to ridiculous acts like playing a three-sided game of football on a hexagonal pitch in which the players can change sides at will. But their deeper message is that of the Situationists—that power structures exist only as long as we take them seriously and reproduce them willingly. Through that absurdity, we can find the community of resistance that we need.

It should not need to be restated: we are not engaged in the same power process as the industrial system in which power is accumulated through bitter, competitive struggle and effort. Our power arises out of the bonds between us and the shared experiences we have. Laughter and personal fulfilment are as central to our political endeavour as investment and the division of labour were in the industrial revolution.

Conclusion

I swear by the lake on the mountain
I swear by the blood that's red
I swear on the cool clear night air
And I swear on my child's head

That I will never rest
Until all oppression is ended
And I will never rest
Until all oppression is dead

I swear to the people in power
That I have a power too
Power to stand and to defend our land
With love, with compassion and truth

—Shannon Smy / Seize the Day

Clearly, there is no conclusion. In fact, what I have argued for is an opposition to conclusions, to simple answers and bottom lines. Too many political movements have built their ideologies on statements of the type, 'The root cause of our problems is . . . ', 'The source of all power is . . .' I have no wish to add to the competing grand narratives—to the extent that I would see attempts to explain things that I have described as issues of power in very different terms as perfectly valid and informative.

There is no root cause, there is no prime mover or first principle. Everything that we see is both cause and effect, in a historical chain stretching back beyond any possibility of re-creation. Even if something is clearly the outcome of something else, the complexity of social systems means that re-running the same process could lead to a different outcome.

Power is a social phenomenon, and that means it is a pattern in a complex system. All patterns in complex systems have some chain of positive feedback, a self-reinforcing cycle. That is how they endure and spread and act on the social system. The order arises not out of a single cause but out of its own potential for self-regulation. Equally, change is driven not from any point in the cycles and circuits but by the innate creative power of the system, and of the subsystems that make it up. Each time we act in a process of power (which we do all the time) we add something of ourselves to it, and in this process of reception, subtle mutation and reproduction we see innovation and originality emerging. Many or most of these 'unpatterned' acts of power will prove to be dead ends, and will not find the positive feedback that they need to endure. But others will, and they have immense transformative capability.

This means that traditional questions relating to power do not always receive simple answers. It is the efforts to find simple answers that lead to division and mutual incomprehension. But from this perspective it is possible to suggest some guidelines for political analysis and action.

What is power? It is the flow of matter and energy, and the influences that shape those flows. It is a social phenomenon, but it is also a physical one, and the distinction between these two aspects is not clearly defined. It makes possible all social action—indeed, seen in this wider sense it is the creative force behind all our experiences. For ourselves as individuals, the word encompasses our ability to make a life for ourselves. The power we have defines our identity and our sense of ourselves—this is the source of the 'will to power'. To be denied power over our lives is to be denied selfhood, and to struggle for that power places us under immense stress. Humans being as resourceful as they are, we invariably succeed in gaining power. But at what cost? Some forms of power strengthen the bonds between us, and the sense of community that is an equally fundamental need. But others destroy social solidarity by creating opportunities for themselves out of the divisions between people, and between humans and the ecosystem. It is these latter forms of power that are dominant in human society today, and together they form a strong and self-reinforcing network.

Who is powerful? There is no easy way to measure someone's power. The concept has to be broken down in two ways. Firstly, we have to ask what type of power it is that they are seeking to exercise. Is it power-over (in other words, are they controlling something outside of them) or power-to (affecting their own life)? This distinction is not always easy to make, but it is important. To even speak of an 'exercise' of power is misleading, since the processes and strategies of power extend far beyond the individual and his or her designs. Someone who has risen to the top of massive hierarchies may yet be unfulfilled in their own life, or unable to effectively conduct personal relationships or maintain their own health. If the distinction is obscure, one can only say it is in the nature of power to be obscure since it shapes even our perception and assumptions.

The second distinction is one of the site, or location, in which the person's power is to be assessed. We can begin with what Clegg calls the 'normal power' of social science: the contests between competing forces that take place according to social conventions. Here, the interests of the two sides are opposed, resources are deployed to best effect, and subject to skill, setting and luck, one may prevail. It is the visible, measurable and quantifiable aspect of power, and for this reason it has mesmerized social scientists. As Lukes points out, it is not simply a matter of winning or losing; it is also possible to keep an issue off the agenda and sideline or silence the opposition. These contests take place under rules and conditions that are taken as given. Laws may not be followed, and common social expectations may not be met; but they nevertheless provide the environment within which these exercises of power take place.

Lukes' third dimension of power goes deeper than these conscious battles, by questioning whether we are sometimes mistaken as to what our interests are. Do we fight battles against ourselves, buy products we do not want, elect our oppressors and buy the machines that enslave us? This is what is effectively happening when facts are distorted, information suppressed and experiences are selectively reported. We lose sight of what is really going on, and come to believe that our interests are being met when they are not. However, I do not believe that the story ends there. Not all of our self-destructive behaviour can be explained away as 'false consciousness' or deceit. More often, it is a series of Faustian bargains made on unequal terms in order to secure day-to-day survival. Faust at least chooses to make the deal, and has a modest but acceptable alternative. Our lives are full of difficult choices: between self and community, between truth and expediency, between prosperity and self-esteem, between integrity and social acceptability. If you choose to conform and abandon your principles, are you deluded about what is in your interests, or what is authentic for you? I would argue that such a decision is in fact based on a rational assessment of what is necessary to get by. It is a truism to say that modern life is stressful, and not even especially controversial to say that this stress comes from struggles with power. I argue that the nature of these struggles is between our authentic, inner desires, and our interest in security and comfort. I don't mean to imply that comfort is a luxury that people should do without: a life without it is precarious and soul-destroying, and a terrible thing to inflict on family or colleagues. No wonder most of us make choices every day that are at best uninspiring, at worst shameful.

The first level on which power structures these choices is in the source of the resources that we deploy in our episodic, 'normal' power games. These contests take place within certain arenas; social spaces that we can describe in broad terms. The areas I believe are key in most societies are economic relations, governance, forces maintaining consent (for instance, the army and police), technology and systems of knowledge, and relations of care (such as the public services of health and education). All of these arenas are structured and maintained by sustained support from elsewhere in the social system, and cannot survive without them. Any loss of legitimacy or strength in central government will leave actors in the economy insecure and anxious. Equally, if economic prosperity dries up, the technologists and manufacturers feel the pinch. So whatever they may feel instinctively, anyone dependent on economic relations for their wellbeing will stand up for strong government. Anyone who needs high energy technologies will respect the competitive economics that funds them.

And because the entire cycle is closed—all these social subsystems form a whole integrated system—there is no escape from it. There is a higher level of power created by the hegemony of this network, which limits us still further. You may excel at winning power contests; you may even be able to persuade people to trust you; let us say that you have even found some alternative source of support for your activities. But can you establish a whole alternative society? Because that is what you have to do to overcome the power of social conformity that shapes our lives.

By now this may seem a picture of stagnant, oppressive weight, limiting our every move. This would be to wildly overstate it. But if we want to raise questions of sustainability or social justice, then it is this most hidden and elusive form of power that we have to build. To be powerful in those terms is to innovate—to see the connections we can make that unleash positive feedback in a system. It is not particularly important to be adept at fighting for our interests—it may sometimes appear to everyone, including ourselves, that we are acting against our interests. But this may be necessary in order to gain some slight leverage over the social processes that form those interests in the first place. It has always been the case that revolutionaries deliberately choose the most precarious and insecure lives. They would appear to have given up wealth, high office and respectability, working instead to build solidarity and self-reliance in the most oppressed communities. It is not that they have renounced power altogether, but rather that they are in search of the most distant and elusive form that it takes.

When is power morally good? I have been at pains to stress that the choices concerned with power are real, are moral issues and (within the limits set by our context) are free choices. This means it should be possible to distinguish between good and evil in the exercise of power.

I take the view that the only viable and available ground for morality is nature, in the broadest sense. For all our veneer of civilization, we are essentially wild, animated by biological and pre-rational forces that we cannot cut ourselves free from. Those who draw moral guidance from faith, scripture and prophecy will have to disagree when I say that they are the outcomes of moral choices around power rather than the source for them. 'Nature' is of course a problematic concept, but I believe that the direction, or goal, of nature is a given, even though the many and varied forms it takes along the way are contingent on social action.

In this light, right livelihood is about sensing the purpose and flow in living things and seeking to work within that dynamic. I have argued that this means that the dynamic of power-to should be developed and defended; structures of power-over, which is inherently disruptive of self-organizing systems, should not be allowed to dominate our society. This is about compassion, about creativity, about connectedness and balance—in a community, in an ecosystem, and in one's self.

That's not to say these decisions are easy. Often we will be presented with a dilemma, where action or inaction may have different moral values analysed on different levels of power. When conservative journalists, for example, criticize protesters for 'provoking a violent, lawless situation', they are drawing on a widely shared sense of the morality of preserving a stable social order in which people can go about their lives safely and without fear. But if the paths that those lives follow are inextricably tied to a dynamic of power-over, then surely it is more moral to rock the boat than to leave things as they are. It is at the cutting edge of direct action where these dilemmas are played out most acutely. I argue, perhaps in a similar vein to Kant, that we should judge others on their intentions rather than the outcomes. The movement that I am part of, and that I feel solidarity with, includes all those struggling to preserve life and self-determination—even those who may unintentionally endanger life to achieve it. I do not feel the same bond to those who do good by accident, or for wealth or status, or in the pursuit of an essentially disempowering cause.

How can a movement for social change harness power? From the preceding chapters, I have derived some important conclusions for an effective political strategy. Firstly, everyone has access to power. There are no powerless people, only people connected to strategies of power that oppress them. Whether consciously or unconsciously, whether it is to our benefit or at our expense, we are all powerful. In a system of power-over, that means not only are we all oppressed, but we are all oppressors. For many, this will go too far in dissolving distinctions between classes, between ruler and ruled. I regret any offence I may cause with this, but I see the powerful/powerless dichotomy as morally hazardous. It excuses the 'ruled' from having to take any responsibility for their lives, and it scapegoats the 'rulers' and turns them into demon objects. Oppression does not automatically make heroes of us; in fact, it can damage us psychologically to the extent that we are more selfish and cruel than any overlord. Similarly, those who occupy senior positions in a hierarchy cannot simply be identified with that hierarchy; they are human beings, with all the subtleties and contradictions that implies.

Secondly, power is a process, not an object. We cannot change society by 'taking the reins of power'. We have rather to make connections, establish strategies of power where empowerment leads to further empowerment.

Means cannot justify ends, because the means become the ends; we cannot isolate the use of power in the means from the further uses of power they enable. So our model is that of the network, in which people with the will to challenge power-over connect with each other to circulate information, resources, inspiration and action that build resistance.

Thirdly, this process has to change us. We have to be aware that we too are the product of a lifetime of control and regulation, and that the habits and assumptions will continue to drive us. Revolution is a process of self-discovery, as we go deeper to discover the authentic values and culture that give us control over our lives.

Fourthly, we have a vital ally in our struggle; the biosphere and ecosystems of the earth. The flows of energy and matter through the Gaian system are themselves processes of power, different only in medium from those of social power. By coming to know intimately the species and cycles of your immediate environment, you can connect with processes of power that nurtured us through our evolution. That same biological productivity can now resource our lives independently of social institutions—provided those institutions do not destroy Gaian self-regulation first. This is why access to the land has historically been such a contested issue.

Fifth, a study of strategies of power shows that they form consistent patterns; that power used or applied in a certain way tends to lead to further flows of power in that style. Today, the dominant form that power takes is power-over; this contrasts with the more ecological power-to, and with the archaic and superstitious power-from. Consistency is crucial in our strategy—the success of empowerment/power-to will lead to further success, while the use of power-over will weaken and divide our movement. Wherever people have resisted specific instances of power-over, they have found structures of power-to the most effective tools. A movement emerges as these campaigns of individual resistance find strength in co-operation.

Power-over is a pervasive and effective process of objectification: it renders the world into an endless chain of active subject and passive object, of one way exchanges. Every time our movement employs power-over, it entrenches this pattern. Equally, every time we co-operate to resolve conflict, and enable people to take responsibility for their actions, the outline of an alternative society comes further into focus.

These connections come full circle to make self-sustaining cycles. It should come as no surprise that society has this systemic nature; it is a pattern found in complex phenomena of all types. The task of a movement for change is to complete these circuits, to create positive feedback for social change. This means two kinds of activity. Firstly, building social alternatives in five broad areas—the economy, government, care, technology and defence. Secondly, making the connections between social change activity in these different areas.

As the system of alternative practice becomes more integrated, it can become as hegemonic—as ubiquitous—as power-over is today. This can be seen happening at a very local level today, within social change communities. A new logic of thought and behaviour can begin to take on a life of its own. It is this that makes such communities 'in resistance' targets for repression. For the local initiatives to spread and link up, more radical change is needed.

This can only come from a careful engagement with the system of power-over—not by withdrawing from it. The resources under its control must be recolonized. At the same time, this has to be achieved without co-option into the system. The key lies in identifying points in the system which are vulnerable—where power can be diverted from power-over to power-to, or simply incapacitated. In politics, this means engaging with the electoral process, and making the most of whatever concessions to democracy have been secured. In the economy, it means bringing money—the ultimate currency of power—under the control of co-operative organizations, and reinvesting it in social change.

Although power is essentially a local phenomenon, the networks extend across the whole planet. Power-over is moving into a new phase—that of globalization. This means technologies, divisions of labour and economic regimes that can be applied over the whole planet. However, information technology is proving effective at enabling an equally global resistance. The unevenness of power-over's hegemony can be exploited to good effect, with the mental walls between colonist and colonized beginning to crumble.

Change is more than possible. I have experienced it, and you can too. You can see people, places and entire communities that are 'moving to the beat of a different drum'. There is nothing that cannot be achieved through co-operation, no need that cannot be met. We do not require power over others, nor have we ever required it. That it has taken over our lives and our world is a historical accident—the dark side of humanity run riot. We can't go back; indeed, if we did it might not be long before that dark side rose again. We can go forward, though, to a 21st century in which the products of our resistance—democracy, co-operative economics, egalitarian communities, non-violent conflict resolution and ecological technology—are the basis of our livelihoods.

References

Chapter 1
1. Bertrand Russell, *Power: A New Social Analysis* (Norton, New York 1938).
2. Dahl, 1957.
3. Steven Lukes, *Power: A Radical View* (Macmillan, New York 1974).
4. Thomas Hobbes, *Leviathan*.
5. If it's not clear why Nagel withdrew this, think of it this way: does Santa Claus have power over people?
6. In Olsen and Marger (eds.), *Power in Modern Societies* (Westview, Oxford 1993).
7. Weber, quoted in Mokken and Stokman, in Barry (ed.) op. cit.
8. Quoted in Mokken and Stokman, op. cit.
9. Quoted in Mokken and Stokman, op. cit.
10. Mokken and Stokman, op. cit.
11. In Barry (ed.) *Power and Political Theory* (Wiley and Sons, London 1976).
12. Quoted by Starhawk in *Truth or Dare*.
13. David West, *Authenticity and Empowerment*.
14. Alan Carter, 'A "Counterfactualist" Four Dimensional Theory of Power' in *Heythrop Journal* XXXIII (1992).
15. From 1982, quoted in Paternek, *Norms and Normalisation*.
16. In Roszak, Gomes and Kanner (eds.) *Ecopsychology* (Sierra Club, San Francisco 1995) p.257.
17. Quoted by Peter Stalker in *New Internationalist* 191 (January 1989)
18. This categorization comes from Ralph Grillo, 'Anthropology, language, politics' in *Social Anthropology and the Politics of Language* (Routledge, London 1989).
19. Fischer and Ury, *Getting to Yes*.
20. Kenneth Galbraith, *The Anatomy of Power* (Houghton Mifflin, Boston 1983). Kenneth Boulding has a similar categorization in *Three Faces of Power* (cited below).
21. See, for example, Brian Barry (ed.) *Power and Political Theory*.
22. If we assume that all communication must involve at least an acknowledgement.
23. Kenneth Boulding, *Three Faces of Power* (Sage, California 1989).
24. Cited in Edward Goldsmith, *The Way* (Rider, London 1992) p.310.
25. Ibid, p.344.
26. Lao Tse, *Tao Te Ching*.
27. Goldsmith, op. cit, p.344-347.
28. *Time* magazine, 17th June 1996.
29. Elizabeth Frazer and Deborah Cameron, 'Knowing what to say' in *Social Anthropology and the Politics of Language* (Routledge, London 1989) p.25
30. Ibid, p.32-33.
31. Steven Lukes, op. cit.
32. Alan Carter, op. cit.
33. David West, *Authenticity and Empowerment*, p.100.

Chapter 2
1. Aneurin Bevan, *In Place of Fear* (London, Heinemann, 1952) pp.20-21, quoted in Urry and Wakeford (eds.) *Power in Britain* (London, Heinemann 1973).
2. Maurice Mandelbaum, Societal Laws, in *Modes of Individualism and Collectivism* (London, Heinemann, 1973), p.168.

3. S.A. Rice, *Quantitative Methods in Politics*, New York, 1928.

4. Alan Carter, 'A "Counterfactualist" Four Dimensional Theory of Power' in *Heythrop Journal* XXXIII (1992), pp.192-203.

5. Michel Foucault, 'Truth and Power' in *Power/Knowledge*.

6. Alan Carter, 'On Individualism, Collectivism and Interrelationism' in *Heythrop Journal* XXXI (1990), pp.23-38.

7. J.A. Camilleri, *The State and Nuclear Power* (Wheatsheaf, UK 1984) pp.1-3.

8. *A Programme of Nuclear Power* (HMSO, 1955).

9. J.A. Camilleri, *The State and Nuclear Power* (Wheatsheaf, UK 1984) p.4.

10. H. Patricia Haynes, *Earthright*, quoted in Rowland Morgan, *Planetgauge* (4th Estate, London 1992).

11. Alan Carter, 'On Individualism, Collectivism and Interrelationism', op. cit.

12. Andrew Dobson, *Green Political Thought*, (Unwin Hyman, London 1990) p. 37.

13. Laura Sewall, 'The Skill of Ecological Perception', in Roszak, Gomes, Kamner (eds.) *Ecopsychology* (Sierra Club, San Francisco 1995) pp.207-209.

14. Ervin Laszlo, *Introduction to Systems Philosophy* (Gordon and Breach, London 1972) p.98; see also *Individualism, Collectivism and Political Power* (The Hague, 1963).

15. Alan Carter, 'On Individualism, Collectivism and Interrelationism', op. cit.

16. J. A. Camilleri, op. cit. Ch 1.

17. Oliver Stone, *JFK*.

18. POWE 14/869. N.J. Gibson to Clerk of the Parish Council, Bradwell, 6th March 1956.

19. Andrew Blowers and David Pepper, 'The Nuclear State—from Consensus to Conflict' in *Nuclear Power in Crisis*, Blowers and Pepper (eds.) (Croom Helm, London 1987) p.3.

20. See *The Verge* (European Youth for Action, Amsterdam) May 1996.

21. 'Nuclear Energy in France' in Blowers and Pepper, op. cit.

22. Jerry Mander, *In the Absence of the Sacred* (Sierra Club Books, San Francisco 1992) p.35.

23. Ivan Illich, op. cit, p.51.

24. Fritjof Capra, op. cit, p.290.

25. Simon Lewis, 'Biodiversity Loss and Fragmentation of the Wild', in *Do Or Die: Voices from Earth First!* 5 (Dead Trees Earth First!, UK, 1995).

26. See Fritjof Capra, *The Turning Point*.

27. Simon Lewis, op. cit.

28. Michels, *Political Parties*.

29. "What people are trying to do . . . is to save a party—no matter what kind of party, and no matter for what purpose. The main thing is for it to get reelected to parliament in 1987" Rudolf Bahro, *Building the Green Movement*, p.210, Heretic 1986.

30. Hubert Kleinert in Ebermann and Trampert in *Konkret* 7, 1988, cited by Sarkar in 'Accommodating Industrialism' in *The Ecologist*, Vol. 20, No. 4, 1990.

31. Die Grünen, *Umbau der Industriegesellschaft*, Bonn 1986, p.9, quoted in Sarkar, op.cit.

32. The issue over which Bahro left Die Grünen.

33. Derek Wall, *Weaving a Bower Against Endless Night*, The Green Party, Wales, 1994.

34. Jonathan Porritt, *The Coming of the Greens* (Fontana, London 1988) p.13.

35. Andrew Blowers and David Pepper, 'The Nuclear State—from Consensus to Conflict' in Blowers and Pepper (eds.) *Nuclear Power in Crisis* (Croom Helm, London 1987).

36. See Porritt in Goldsmith and Hildyard (eds.), *Green Britain or Industrial*

Wasteland?, (Polity Press, Oxford 1986).

37. Michel Foucault, 'Disciplinary Power and Subjection' from *Power/Knowledge: Selected Interviews and Other Writings 1972-1977* (Random House, London) and reproduced in Steven Lukes (ed.) *Power* (Basil Blackwell, Oxford 1986).

38. Ibid p.234.

39. Ibid p.233.

40. Ibid, p.234.

41. Bart de Ligt, *Conquest of Violence* (Pluto Press, London 1989) p.113.

42. Andrew Dobson, op. cit., p.30.

43. Ivan Illich, op. cit.

44. *The Guardian* (Society section, p.4) August 21st 1996.

45. Centre for Alternative Technology, *Memorandum to the Commons Select Committee on Energy* (CAT, Machynlleth 1991).

Chapter 3

1. Ken Jones, *Beyond Optimism* (Jon Carpenter, Oxford 1993) p.43.

2. Once again, see Foucault, who has written at length about 'constituted subjects'.

3. Quoted in Jones, op. cit, p.37.

4. As Chomsky has suggested. Recent research in a Nicaraguan school for deaf children, where pupils developed their own sign language, appears to bear this out.

5. Roy Morrison, *We Build the Road as we Travel* (New Society, Philadelphia 1991) p.56.

6. Quoted in Mike Cormack, *Ideology* (Batsford, London 1992).

7. Ibid.

8. Ibid.

9. Ibid.

10. Edelman, *Neural Darwinism* (Basic Books, New York 1988).

11. See Clive Ponting, *A Green History of the World*.

12. *New Scientist* Editorial, 4th April 1997.

13. Candice Pert, quoted in Morrision, op. cit.

14. Erich Fromm, *The Anatomy of Human Destructiveness* (Penguin, London 1977).

15. Rudolf Bahro, *Avoiding Social and Ecological Disaster* (Gateway, Bath 1994) p.216.

16. M. Scott Peck, *The Road Less Travelled*.

17. Rudolf Bahro, *Avoiding Social and Ecological Disaster* (Gateway, Bath 1994) p.178.

Chapter 4

1. James Lovelock, *Gaia: the practical science of planetary medicine* (Gaia Books, London 1991).

2. Ibid., p.12.

3. Howard T. Odum, *Environment, Power and Society* (Wiley, New York 1971) pp.38-39.

4. Ibid., p.142.

5. Lovelock, op. cit., pp.123-5, p.147.

6. See various publications from the Baby Milk Action Coalition.

7. Cited in *Caring for the Earth* (IUCN, UNEP, WWF 1991); data from Vitousek, P.M., P.R. Ehrlich, A.H. Ehrlich & P.A. Matson, 'Human Appropriation of the products of photosynthesis' (*Bioscience* 36 (6) pp.368-373).

8. Odum, op. cit., p.174.

9. Odum, op. cit., p.191.

10. Adherents of this theory range from Hobbes to Hardin (op. cit).

11. Irvine and Ponton, op. cit.

12. Dobson, op. cit.

13. "The first phase of the domination of the economy over social life brought the degradation of 'being' into 'having'. The total occupation of social life by the spectacle leads to 'having' becoming 'appearing'." Anon, possibly Raoul Vaneigem, in *Bete Noire* no.1 (Oxford University Anarchists, 1989).

Chapter 5

1. Paul Harrison, *Inside the Inner City* (Penguin Books, Middlesex 1983) pp.138-9.

2. Leeds Child Action Poverty Group, *Always Struggling* (quoted in the Yorkshire Evening Post 29/9/94 p.12).

3. International Labour Organization.

4. Mari Marcel-Thekaekara, *Poor Relations* in the Guardian 27th Feb 1999.

5. Quotes from *Less is More* by Goldian Vandenbroeck (Inner Traditions, Vermont 1991) pp.15 & 16.

6. From *Less is More*, ibid p.17.

7. Dahl, 1957.

8. Joanna Macy in *Ecopsychology*, op. cit.

9. Cited in *Empowerment and Estate Regeneration*, Murray Stewart and Marilyn Taylor (Policy Press, Bristol 1995) p.12.

10. Michel Foucault, *Power/Knowledge* (1980)

11. Quoted in Jonathan Porritt, *Seeing Green* (1984) p.8.

12. Sara Parkin in Felix Dodds (ed.) *Into the 21st Century* (Green Print, Basingstoke 1988) p.173.

13. Guy Dauncey, *After the Crash* (Green Print, London 1988) p.256.

14. *The Guardian*, 8th July 1995, p.26.

15. Barry Knight and Peter Stokes, 'Self-Help Citizenship' in *The Guardian* Society section, 30th October 1996, p.3.

16. *The Guardian*, 8th July 1995, p.4.

17. Quoted in Paul Harrison, *Inside the Inner City* (Penguin, 1985) p.330.

18. Ibid.

19. Ibid.

20. Paul Harrison, *Inside the Inner City* (Penguin, 1985) p.403.

21. Philip Priestley, 'Crime without Punishment' in *The Guardian* Society section, 24th Aug 1994.

22. Janet Alty in *The Saffron Walden Papers* (The Green Party, 1991) and *Towards a Green 2000: The Reasons Why* (Green 2000, 1991). Both are quoted by Nick Wilding, op. cit.

23. Andre Gorz, *Farewell to the Working Class* (Pluto Press, London 1980) ch 5.

24. Marilyn Ferguson, *The Aquarian Conspiracy*.

25. Erich Fromm, *The Anatomy of Human Destructiveness* (Penguin, London 1977) p.394.

26. Riane Eisler, *The Chalice and the Blade* (Harper, San Francisco 1987).

27. Starhawk, *Truth or Dare*, p.9.

28. In Warren (ed.) *Ecological Feminism* (London, Routledge 1994).

29. Warren, op. cit, p.182.

30. See The Ecologist, *Whose Common Future?* for more in this vein.

31. Alison Ravetz, quoted in *Tenants Take Over*, Colin Ward.

32. Paul Harrison, *Inside the Inner City* (Penguin 1983) p.212.

33. Stanley Alderson, quoted in *Tenants Take Over*, Colin Ward.

34. Nick Wilding, *The Green Party and Power* (University of Southampton, 1991) p.18.

35. Ken Jones, *Beyond Optimism* (Jon Carpenter, Oxford 1993).

36. Rudolf Bahro, op. cit., p.223.

37. Alex Begg, *From Dream to Transition* (Alex Begg, Leeds 1991) p.19.

38. Die Grünen, *Umbau der Industriegesellschaft* (Bonn 1986) quoted by Sarkar, 'Accommodating Industrialism' in *The Ecologist*, Vol. 20, No. 4, 1990.

39. Andrew Dobson, *Green Political Thought* (Unwin Hyman 1990) p.168.

40. James O'Connor, 'A Political Strategy for Ecology Movements' in *Society and Nature* 3 (Society and Nature Press, Athens 1993).

41. David West, *Authenticity and Empowerment* (Cambridge University Press) p.99.

42. John Hayes, and Gerry Williams, quoted in Colin Ward, *Tenants Take Over* p.60.

43. 'Estate Designers' in *Northern Star* 26th March 1992 (Leeds Alternative Publications).

44. Derek Fox, quoted in Colin Ward, op. cit., p.72.

45. Colin Ward, op. cit., p.81.

46. 'Estate puts its house in order . . .' in *The Yorkshire Evening Post*, 6th Dec 1995.

47. 'Community Control Spreads' in *Northern Star*, 17th Oct 1991 (Leeds Alternative Publications).

Chapter 6

1. John Elkington, *The Green Capitalists* (Gollancz, London 1989).

2. Rolf Osterberg, *Corporate Renaissance* (Nataraj, California 1993) p.39.

3. Letentiay, in *Sweeter than Honey*, Jenny Hammond (ed.) (Third World First, Oxford 1989) p.110.

4. Mahta, ibid, p.4.

5. Zafu, ibid, p.111.

6. Eysa Mohammed, ibid, p.105.

7. Besserat, ibid, p.116.

8. See Val Plumwood in Warren (ed.) *Ecological Feminism* (Routledge, London 1994).

9. Quoted in Plumwood, ibid, p.67.

10. See Bookchin and Foreman, *Defending the Earth*.

11. bell hooks, *Talking Back* (South End Press, Boston 1989) p.22.

12. The Ecologist editors with Anita Kerski, 'Who are the Realists?' in *The Ecologist* Vol. 25 No. 4 (Ecosystems Ltd, Dorset, England 1995) p.131.

13. *Ethical Consumer* #39 (ECRA, Manchester 1996).

14. Ron Arnold, quoted in K Goldburg, *More Wise Use Abuse* (Dimension Publishing, 1994) p.27.

15. Quoted in Brian Tokar, 'The Wise Use Backlash' in *The Ecologist* Vol. 25 No. 4.

16. Stauber and Rampton, 'Democracy for Hire' in *The Ecologist* Vol. 25 No. 5 p.177.

17. From Tony Gibson, *The Power in Their Hands* (Jon Carpenter, Oxford 1996) p.197.

18. Plumwood, op. cit, p.72.

19. Quoted in Stewart Clegg, *Frameworks of Power*, Sage Publications, p.206.

20. Plumwood, op. cit, pp.75-76.

21. Roderick Martin, *The Sociology of Power* (Routledge, London 1977) p.51.

22. Plumwood, op. cit.

23. Kidron and Segal, *Business, Money and Power* (Pan, London 1987).

24. Rolf Osterberg, *Corporate Renaissance* (Nataraj, California 1993).

25. Ibid, pp.39-40.

26. Elkington, *The Green Capitalists* (Gollancz, London 1989) p.232.

27. Derek Wall, *Getting There* (Green Print, London 1990) p.61.
28. Dick Morris, 'Behind the Oval Office', quoted in *The Guardian* supplement (13/1/97) p.3.
29. Horkheimer and Adorno, *Dialectic of Enlightenment* (Allen Lane, London 1973) p.4.
30. Horkheimer, *Eclipse of Reason* (OUP, New York 1946).
31. I am indebted to a paper by Andrew Dobson, 'Critical Theory and Green Politics', which he submitted to the ECPR Joint Session at Essex Univeristy in March 1991.
32. PR Watch, Vol. 1, No. 1 (Centre for Media and Democracy, Madison 1993) p.5, quoed in *The Ecologist* Vol. 25 No. 4.
33. Plumwood, op. cit, p.79.
34. Starhawk, *Truth or Dare*.
35. Kidron and Segal, op. cit, p.162.

Chapter 7

1. Starhawk, *Truth or Dare*.
2. See Croft and Beresford, *The Politics of Participation* (Critical Social Policy, 1992).
3. Stewart and Taylor, *Empowerment and Estate Regeneration* (Policy Press, Bristol 1995).
4. Croft and Beresford, *The Politics of Participation*, in Critical Social Policy 1992.
5. From Stewart and Taylor, *Empowerment and Estate Regeneration* (Policy Press, Bristol 1995) p.15. Adapted from Lowery, de Hoog and Lyons (1992).
6. Starhawk, *Truth or Dare*.
7. The final sentence of Arthur Miller's autobiography.
8. Friedman, *Empowerment: the politics of alternative development* (Blackwell, Oxford 1992) p.68.
9. See Tony Gibson, *The Power in our Hands* (Jon Carpenter, Oxford 1997).
10. Roy Morrison, *We build the road as we travel* (New Society, Philadelphia 1991) p.10.

Chapter 8

1. Michel Foucault, 'Disciplinary Power and Subjection', in Lukes (ed.) *Power* (Basil Blackwell, Oxford 1986) p.234.
2. Descartes, quoted in Fritjof Capra, 'Deep Ecology: a New Paradigm', in Sessions (ed.) *Deep Ecology for the 21st Century* (Shambhala, Boston 1995).
3. Derek Wall, *Getting There* (Green Print, Oxford 1990) pp.74-75.
4. Fritjof Capra, *The Turning Point*, (Fontana, London 1983) p.26.
5. Ibid p.305.
6. Ervin Laszlo, ibid.
7. Taken from Roderick Martin, *The Sociology of Power* (London, Routledge and Kegan Paul, 1977) p.4.
8. Quoted in Martin, op. cit, p.18.
9. Hannah Arendt, *On Violence* (Allen Lane, London 1970), p.56.
10. Gene Sharp, *The Politics of Nonviolent Action*, (Porter Sargent, Boston 1973) pp.12-16.
11. Arendt, op. cit, p.4.
12. W. J. M. Mackenzie, *Power, Violence, Decision* (Penguin, UK 1975) p.92
13. Quoted in Martin, op. cit, p.20.
14. Ibid., p.21.
15. Cynthia Enloe, *Does Khaki become you?* (Pluto Press, London 1983) p.208.
16. Korzybski, *Science and Sanity*, 1993.
17. Enloe, op.cit.

18. Morris Berman, 'The Cybernetic Dream of the 21st Century' in John Clark (ed.) *Renewing the Earth* (Green Print, London 1990), p.17.
19. Ibid. p.24.
20. Morris Berman, ibid p.28.
21. Capra and Spretnak, *Green Politics* (Paladin, London 1985) p.54.
22. Quoted in Kelly, op. cit, p.135.
23. Quoted in Petra Kelly, *Nonviolence speaks to power* (Centre for Global NonViolence Planning Project, Hawaii 1992) p.73.
24. Cynthia Enloe, *Does Khaki become you?* (Pluto Press, London 1983) p.18.
25. Enloe, op. cit, p.87.
26. Hannah Arendt, *On Violence* (Allen Lane, New York 1970) p.9.
27. On the subject of the ego, see M. Scott Peck, *The Path Less Travelled*.
28. James O'Connor, 'A Political Strategy for Ecology Movements', in *Society and Nature* No.3 (Society and Nature Press, Athens 1993).
29. Alan Carter, *Towards a Green Political Theory* (Heythrop College, unpublished 1991).
30. Ibid.
31. Alan Carter, *Marx: a Radical Critique*.
32. Guy Dauncey, *After the Crash* (Green Print, London 1988) pp.282-283.
33. Ivan Illich, *Tools for Conviviality* (Fontana, UK 1975) p.66.
34. Carter, op. cit.
35. Ibid.
36. Capra and Spretnak, *Green Politics* (Paladin, London 1985) p.64.
37. Ibid., p.34.
38. Kelly, op. cit, p.67.

Chapter 9
1. Quoted in Jonathan Freedland, *Memo to politicians: tell us a good tale*, in *The Guardian* newspaper.
2. See Plekhanov, and Lenin's *What is to be done?*.
3. Carroll (ed.), *Organising Dissent* (Garamond, Canada).
4. Bocock, *Hegemony* (Tavistock, London 1986).
5. David Edwards, *Free to be Human* (Green Books, Devon 1995) p.12.
6. Chomsky and Herman, *Manufacturing Consent* (Pantheon, New York 1988).
7. Guy Debord, *The Society of the Spectacle*.
8. Larry Law, *Cities of Illusion* (Spectacular Times, London 1987).
9. Guy Debord.
10. Spice Girls, *Wannabe*.
11. Michel Foucault, 'Theories et institutions penales' in *Annuaire du College de France 1971-1972* p.283, quoted in Alan Sheridan, *Michel Foucault: the Will to Truth* (Tavistock, London 1986) p.131.
12. Clegg, *Frameworks of Power* p.215.
13. Ibid, p.219.
14. C. Wright Mills, *The Power Elite* p.6.
15. See, for example, Russell, *Power: a new social analysis* p.35.
16. Theodore Roszak, *The Making of a Counterculture* (Faber and Faber, London 1970).
17. R. D. Laing, *The Politics of Experience* (Penguin, Middlesex 1969) p.109.
18. In Carroll (ed.) *Organising Dissent* (Garamond, London).
19. Quoted in Edwards, *Free to be Human* (Green Books, Devon 1995).

20. Roger Hallam, *Anarchist Economics* (Roger Hallam, Birmingham 1996).
21. Bocock, *Hegemony* (Tavistock, London 1986).

Chapter 10
1. *The Guardian* Society section, January 22nd 1997 p.15.
2. *The Guardian* Society section, January 15th 1997 p.7.
3. *The Guardian* Society section, April 16th 1997, p.11.
4. *The Guardian* Society section, June 11th 1997, p.19.
5. Derek Wall, *Getting There* (Green Print, 1990) p.75.
6. Roger Hallam, *Anarchist Economics* (self published, 1996).
7. 'Autonomy, Resistance and Mediation' in *Do or Die 6* (Do or Die collective, Brighton 1997).

Chapter 11
1. E. F. Schumacher, *Small is Beautiful*.
2. Clive Ponting, *A Green History of the World*.
3. See, for example, Maria Mies, *Patriarchy and Accumulation on a Global Scale*.
4. Helena Norberg-Hodge, *Ancient Futures*.
5. *Europe, Inc* (Corporate Europe Observatory/ASEED, Amsterdam).
6. Lang and Hines, *The New Protectionism*, (Pluto, London 1996).
7. There is an excellent article on the banana issue in *The Observer* newspaper, November 1997.
8. 'We are everywhere', *PGA bulletin 5*, UK edition.

Chapter 12
1. Kidron and Segal, *Business, Money and Power* (Pan, London 1987).
2. Arendt, op. cit.
3. Five women disarmed a warplane bound for East Timor, and willingly presented themselves for trial. They were acquitted of criminal damage by a jury who agreed that the planes would be used for repression.
4. Christopher Hill, *Reformation to Industrial Revolution*, Pt 2 Ch 6 (Penguin, London 1967).
5. Ibid, pp.183-184.
6. Peter Firkin, *Training Skills* (Directory for Social Change, London 1997).
7. Dale is quoted in Winman and Mierhensy, *Educational Media* (Merrill 1969).
8. Malcolm Glaswell, *The Tipping Point* (Little Brown, 2000).
9. Sandy Irvine, *Developing an Ecological Economics*, Green Party Discussion Paper 1990.
10. Andy Dobson, *Green Political Thought* (Unwin Hyman, London 1990).
11. Moyer, *The Movement Action Plan* (Movement for a New Society 1986) and (revised) Social Movement Empowerment Project, San Francisco 1987.
12. Moyer, op. cit, p.7.
13. Moyer op. cit, p.10.
14. Nathaniel Altman, in *The Nonviolent Revolution* (Element, 1988, p.53) reminds us that the word 'warrior' comes from the Tibetan *pawo*, meaning 'one who is brave'.
15. Marcuse, *One Dimensional Man* (Sphere, 1970), Introduction.

Index